in **DETAIL** Housing for People of All Ages

in **DETAIL**

Housing for People of All Ages

flexible · unrestricted · senior-friendly

Christian Schittich (Ed.)

with essays contributed by
Peter Ebner
Joachim Giessler
Lothar Marx
Eckhard Feddersen and Insa Lüdtke

Edition DETAIL – Institut für internationale
Architektur-Dokumentation GmbH
München

Birkhäuser
Basel · Boston · Berlin

Editor: Christian Schittich
Editorial services: Alexander Felix, Astrid Donnert, Michaela Linder,
Melanie Schmid, Cosima Strobl, Andrea Wiegelmann

Translation German/English:
Catherine Anderle-Neill (pp. 26–143, 166–176)
Susan Richter (pp. 9–23, 145–165)

Drawings: Nicola Kollmann, Marion Griese, Daniel Hajduk,
Martin Hemmel, Caroline Hörger, Claudia Hupfloher, Elisabeth Krammer,
Cathrin Peters-Rentschler, Andrea Saiko

DTP: Peter Gensmantel, Andrea Linke, Roswitha Siegler, Simone Soesters

A specialist publication from Redaktion DETAIL
This book is a cooperation between
DETAIL – Review of Architecture and
Birkhäuser – Publishers for Architecture

Library of Congress Control Number: 2007927593

Bibliographic information published by the German National Library
The German National Library lists this publication in the Deutsche
Nationalbibliografie; detailed bibliographic data is available on the Internet at
<http://dnb.d-nb.de>.

This book is also available in a German language edition
(ISBN: 978-3-7643-8118-9).

© 2007 Institut für internationale Architektur-Dokumentation GmbH & Co. KG,
P.O. Box 33 06 60, D-80066 Munich, Germany and
Birkhäuser Verlag AG, Basel · Boston · Berlin, P.O. Box 133, CH-4010 Basel,
Switzerland

This work is subject to copyright. All rights are reserved, whether the whole or
part of the material is concerned, specifically the rights of translation, reprinting,
re-use of illustrations, recitation, broadcasting, reproduction on microfilms or in
other ways, and storage in data banks. For any kind of use, permission of the
copyright owner must be obtained.

Printed on acid-free paper produced from chlorine-free pulp (TCF ∞)

Printed in Germany
Reproduction:
Martin Härtl OHG, München
Printing and binding:
Kösel GmbH & Co. KG, Altusried-Krugzell

ISBN: 978-3-7643-8119-6

9 8 7 6 5 4 3 2 1

Contents

Senior-friendly, integrated, flexible Christian Schittich	8
Integrated Living Peter Ebner	10
Project Summary	24
"Miss Sargfabrik" in Vienna BKK-3, Vienna	26
Multi-generational House in Stuttgart Kohlhoff & Kohlhoff, Stuttgart	32
Multi-generational Housing in Vienna Franziska Ullmann and Peter Ebner, Vienna	36
Apartment Building in Vienna PPAG Architects, Vienna	42
Renovation of a Department Store in Eschweiler BeL, Cologne	46
Community Centre in Stuttgart Lederer + Ragnarsdóttir + Oei, Stuttgart	52
Seniors' Residence in Zurich Miller & Maranta, Basle	58
Multengut Seniors' Residence near Bern Burkhalter Sumi Architects, Zurich	64
Housing Development and Aged Care Centre in Alicante Javier García-Solera Vera, Alicante	70
High-rise Apartment Building in Rotterdam Arons en Gelauff Architecten, Amsterdam	74
Senior Dwellings in Domat/Ems Dietrich Schwarz, Domat/Ems	78
Centre for Seniors in Lich Pfeifer Roser Kuhn Architects, Freiburg	84
Long House on Henza Island Kawai Architects/Toshiaki Kawai, Kyoto	90
Seniors' Centre in Magdeburg löhle neubauer architects, Augsburg	94
Residence for Seniors in Neumarkt am Wallersee Kada + Wittfeld, Aachen	100
Centre for Seniors in Steinfeld Dietger Wissounig, Graz	104
Ambulant Care Day Centre in Kamigyo Toshiaki Kawai, Kyoto	110
Residence in Gstadt Florian Höfer, Oberneuching	114
Multi-generational House in Waldzell Helga Flotzinger, Innsbruck	116
Multi-generational House in Darmstadt Kränzle + Fischer-Wasels Architects, Karlsruhe Klotz + Knecht Architects, Darmstadt	120
City House in Munich Fink + Jocher, Munich	124
Multi-generational Housing Development in Freiburg Pfeifer Roser Kuhn, Freiburg	130
Housing Development in Wiesbaden Dietz Joppien, Frankfurt am Main	134
Housing Development in Ypenburg van den Oever, Zaaijer & Partners with John Bosch, Amsterdam	138
Building in Accordance with the Needs of the Elderly by Joachim F. Giessler	144
Barrier-Free Design and Construction for New and Existing Buildings by Lothar Marx	150
Kitchen and Bathroom as Living Space by Eckhard Feddersen and Insa Lüdtke	158
Architects – Project details	166
Authors	172
Literature	173
Illustration Credits	176

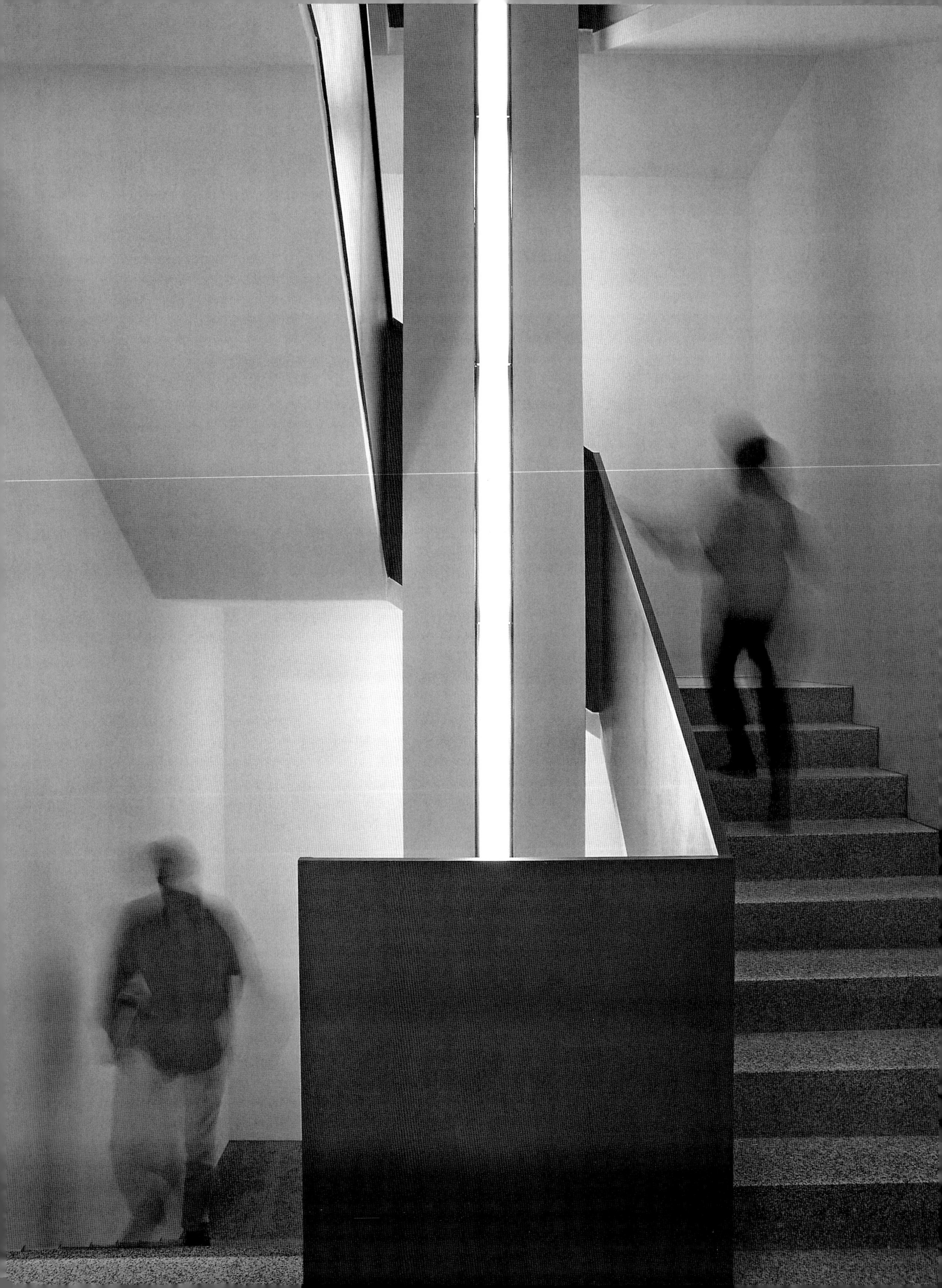

Senior-friendly, integrated, flexible

Christian Schittich

Our society is getting on in years. Increasing life expectancies accompanied by a drop in births are leading to a drastic shift in our age structure – a process that calls for new strategies and responses in a great variety of areas. Housing construction, too, must react with new and intelligent solutions. The concept of Integrated Living is one of the possible responses to this challenge.
Integrated housing facilities as multiple-generation homes are supposed to offer older people a social environment that encourages their integration into society, much more than specialized senior facilities ever could. At the same time they allow seniors to remain in their own homes longer, where they can continue to lead highly self-determined lives.

Yet Integrated Living does not remain restricted to the integration of the elderly. Other changes in our society require new residential concepts. As traditional family bonds dissolve before our eyes, the classic nuclear family as a communal household is being replaced ever more frequently by singles, childless pairs and single-parent families. At the same time it is important to integrate immigrants and the disabled.
Stripped to its principles, Integrated Living means different groups of the population living together under one roof, and, as such, different residential forms in the same building. The goal is mutual enrichment and support. Integrated Living means communal residences, housing for multiple generations, barrier-free housing, homes for families; in the extreme it can also allude to the spatial proximity of living and working or leisure activities.
In institutions exclusively for the elderly one speaks of Integrated Living when care and provision services are offered within a special facility with self-contained residential units.

Just as widely differentiated as the manifestations of Integrated Living are the examples presented in this book. From housing estates built for baby carriages and wheelchairs, to senior-friendly furnishings, all the way to the modernization of existing buildings, the selected projects offer a comprehensive overview. The emphasis here is placed on residences for the elderly, which deserve special attention for the reasons mentioned above.
Floor plans and concepts are in the foreground. But the details of construction also receive ample attention in the solutions introduced here. Especially for barrier-free building, the detailed solutions for level transitions to balcony or patio, for instance, take on an importance all their own. As in all volumes of the In Detail series, the specialized articles explain the background and offer valuable planning tips. In his introductory essay, Peter Ebner defines the concept of Integrated Living and works through its typology. Additional chapters analyse the structural requirements of building in accordance with the needs of the elderly, special demands on the kitchen and bathroom, and barrier-free design and construction in new and existing buildings.

1.1 Community Centre Pasing, 2002; Landau+Kindelbacher

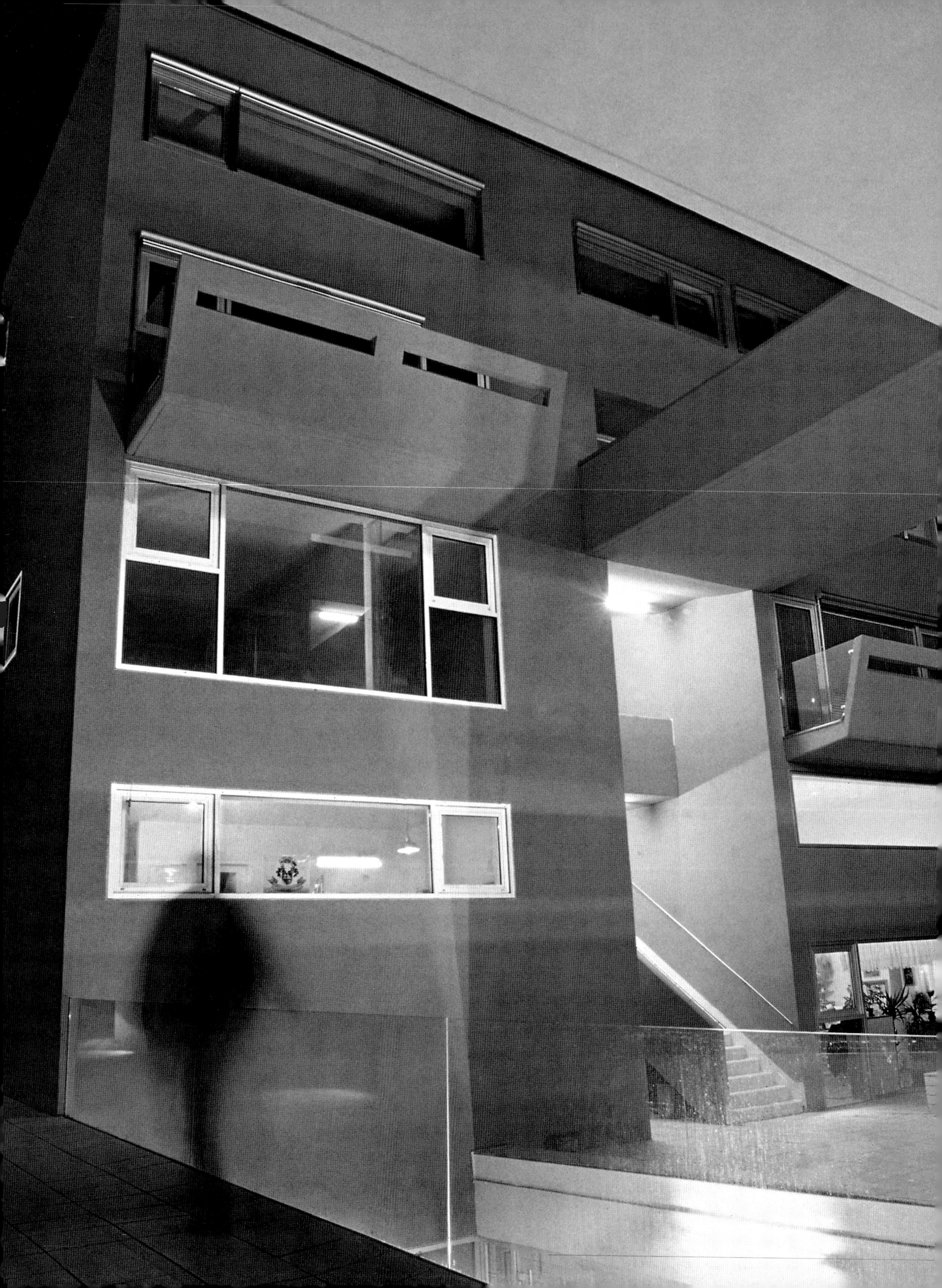

Integrated Living

by Peter Ebner

Roman Höllbacher
Markus Kuntscher

Thematically Oriented Residential Projects

In recent years new themes have become established in residential housing. Ecological, sustainable construction; housing suitable for the elderly, for women, children, the disabled; energy-conscious housing developments closed to automobile traffic (passive, low, or zero-energy buildings) are some – but by no means all – of the favorite approaches in this sector. In other words: Theme-specific residential developments are booming, and popular among real estate developers as well. Social scientists, trend researchers and prognosticators generally dictate the rhythm and the themes. But another type of tradition in innovation is taking place as well: Small groups identify a problem, often because they are personally affected, and make their voices heard with vehemence and perseverance. Remember when groups of activists began experimenting with heat pumps and improved thermal insulation, only to be derided as "eco radicals"? These achievements are among today's standards in housing construction. At the same time, thematically oriented planning of residential housing fits in very well with our post-industrial society. Here, too, heterogeneous lifestyles demand differentiated approaches that are clearly directed toward these target groups. As a result, the workers' apartments of "Red Vienna" and *Das Neue Frankfurt,* the *Neue Heimat* projects of the post-war reconstruction period and their offshoots in state-subsidized housing have been consigned to the past once and for all.
A clear additional function of thematically or project-oriented residential developments consists in trying out innovative solutions and introducing them to a broader social discourse. However, they are equally at risk of being used as a fig-leaf for much-needed, but neglected, structural adjustments. One could even say that theme-specific housing developments reflect the resistance to innovation in the construction industry (as the sum total of architects, developers, sponsors, financiers, politicians). Franz Sumnitsch of BKK-3, referring to the emergence of the *Sargfabrik* ("coffin factory") project, described it thus:
"The group of residents that came to us in the late eighties was looking for a form of living that offered more than the mere fulfillment of demands by the square foot. In order to realize this we had to open the system from the inside out. To be able to assert our interests in the face of an rigid construction industry, the first step was thus to found a real estate development association."[1]
The *Verein für integrative Lebensgestaltung,* which emerged from this initiative, acquired a property which once was the site – this is true Austrian sur-reality – of the monarchy's largest coffin factory, where coffins were produced for the emperor's subjects, with the vision of erecting upon it one of the most refreshing residential housing developments of the last decade. The resourceful association defined the entire area as a *Wohnheim* ("residential accommodation"), which not only made it eligible for additional subsidies, but also released it from the rigid directives on floor plans for normal state-subsidized housing. These days entities known as "alternative groups", "resident associations" or "residential groups" are as successful as professional developers; what's more, their creativity in interpreting norms, regulations and terms for subsidization has yet to meet its match (ills. 2.2, 2.3).

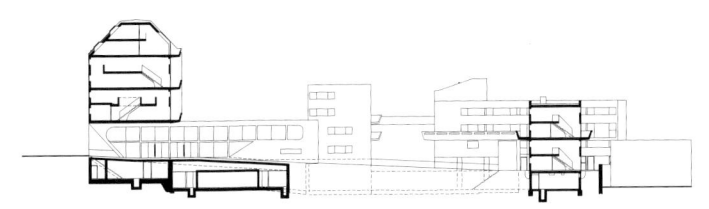

Integrated Living – Expanding the Concept

In the literature and on the relevant web pages, "integrated living" is frequently reduced to the perspective of different generations living together (multi-generation residences) or the integration of physically and/or mentally disabled persons into the living environment of a residential development. In integrative housing developments, "… different groups of residents live together, usually in larger residential complexes, which are initiated by special sponsors and do not originate with the residents themselves. Their objective is to improve neighbourly support between different generations (multi-generation living) and groups of residents with different needs. The exchange of mutual support measures is supposed to alleviate the handicaps given for each specific group and combat tendencies toward isolation. To encourage collective living there are meeting spaces and in some cases, assistance from trained staff."[2]
While this definition can be accepted in principle, in some aspects it is very strict. For instance, it is completely incomprehensible why only special sponsors should be the organizers of integrative living, and not the the residents themselves. Several of the most interesting examples in this area impart precisely the opposite experience.
Important is the indication that people with restricted mobility can be integrated into everyday life not only through appropriate construction measures in the housing development and in the residences, but rather by mixing various groups. The worksheets published by the Bavarian building authorities, entitled *Bauen und Wohnen für Behinderte* ("Building and

2.1 "Sargfabrik" in Vienna, 1996; BKK-2
2.2 "Sargfabrik" in Vienna, 1996; BKK-2

Housing for the Disabled") endeavour to expand the concept, emphasizing the model of urban sociology toward which integrated living aspires:

"The idea of "integrated living" is to encourage different groups of residents who can mutually support each other to live together. The long-acknowledged desire to live in a residential environment that allows in equal measure both independence without isolation, and informal community with safety and security, is shared by the elderly and the disabled with other groups of residents, for instance single parents or parents of large families. These ideas are oriented on the small town, the suburban community or the expanded residential quarter, on their variety of different groups of residents and social classes."[3]

The small town, suburban community, and expanded residential quarter as models for integrated living are not exactly free of idealizing projections, of course; nevertheless, this definition emphasizes the valuable principle of "small is beautiful" and thus surveyability, which is regarded as a prerequisite for mutual participation in the modern urban space, counteracting the tendency toward anonymity. As a social parameter, mutual support within a certain facility, housing development or quarter points beyond the architectural in and of itself. What is essential is that we conceive of building, literally as well as metaphorically, as a social act with its own intrinsic *integrative* power. In this we understand architecture to be the *background and space* of human interaction, which can be encouraged or prevented by what is built, but never has the automatic result of generating a social network per se. Believing in this would amount to regressing to a kind of determinism that we have long since abandoned. Many model buildings and settlements of integrated living proceed from a group of committed people, who never saw housing construction as the abstract product of a development agent. This is certainly the core of one of their secrets of success, one of the reasons why they can not be duplicated.

Today the integration of the elderly and disabled, of immigrants, and inter-cultural and inter-religious exchange are considered features of integrative housing developments. For this reason we advocate that "integrated living" be understood as encouraging different groups of residents to live together, whereby the special needs of the disabled, the elderly, immigrants, single parents, families with many children, teenagers and other sociologically categorized groups are the object of the special design and architectural efforts – with the goal of imparting to them the feeling of safety and security in an informal community.

In summary, the following residential forms are to be subsumed under the concept of integrative living:
- housing that caters to the elderly and (multi-)generation living
- barrier-free housing designed for the disabled and wheelchair-bound
- inter-ethnic and inter-cultural living (religion, culture)

In addition to these come the needs of groups whose needs still attract (too) little attention today:
- families with many children
- single parents and singles
- children and teenagers

In the process of realizing a residential construction project this means that the demands dictated by group-specific needs are summarized into a consistent model, on the basis of which the planning and financing of the project can be conceived. Since the above-mentioned groups are by no means mutually exclusive, what emerges is not only a new, expanded concept of "integrative living", but also a series of new problems rooted in the potential conflicts of objectives that arise from those contents of integration which can not be harmonized.

We should therefore conceive of "integrative living" as a dynamic model, which accentuates some or several of the forms of living and needs addressed, and which depend on location, formulated objectives, and those social parameters of the future users that are already known. Obviously, the weights will be different; sometimes the integration of the disabled will be in the foreground, in another case perhaps the integration of immigrants. But in principle "integrative living" means taking a stand against social exclusion and considering this in the conception of new residential projects. The subject matter addressed here is thus, of course, based on the sophisticated perception of sociological phenomena and, as a consequence, open to new developments in our society. Integrative living in its final consequence means reflecting on the complexity of our society, being on the lookout for new tendencies, and offering suitable structural solutions in housing. Integrative living is not a minority program – so to speak, the free skating after the obligatory figures – but rather entails penetration from the macro-level into the micro-organics of our society. Reducing its complexity and the barriers to "the other" where they constrain groups, and, inversely, drawing boundaries where they are required. Integrated living paints a cheerful picture of our society. It is the utopia in which the "other" and the "alien" are seen not as a threat, but rather as a benefit, and where monostructural concepts like race, class, or the dichotomies of sex are finally abandoned in favor of real diversity in our society.

New Lifestyles. Economic Transformation as the Trigger for Developing Integrative Forms of Living

The development of the past decades has led to a pluralization of lifestyles, which, in turn, are considered to be the consequence of post-industrial economic forms. What we have

2.3

recognized on the levels of social economy and political discourse has left barely a mark on the mechanisms of housing production. As a consequence, the established cooperative housing associations came under enormous pressure, especially from the 1990s on, experiencing much greater difficulty selling their products than before. In addition another problem arose:
"In the mid-1990s, the "moving house boom" confronted the cooperative societies most of all. They found it increasingly difficult to rent their existing real estate, because hardly any parties could be found for their flats in the high-priced segment, who were both interested and belonged to the group targeted by regulations and rental and occupation criteria."[4]
This assessment refers to the rental market in the city of Zurich, but in fact, the problems exist pretty much everywhere. In keeping with the economic transformation to a service society, the shift of industrial production to low-wage countries and the process of globalization, large industrial areas are becoming free in all central European cities at the same time. The developers' strategy of covering these fallows with service complexes led to an overheated market, which soon collapsed. In this phase committed groups were founded in Zurich, in Vienna and other cities, who took aspects of social reform into consideration in developing new housing projects that were integrative in today's sense of the word, and soon found support for these among local institutions. These groups are in large part responsible for the fact that this picture of cooperative residential construction is undergoing radical change. The new lifestyles propagated by these groups may also be regarded as a motor for integrative living.

Integrative Living and the Demographic Transformation of Society

The problem of ageing in our society will intensify in the future, because it has at its core a dual cause: Not only are more and more people becoming older, but there are ever fewer young people. In the future very many old people will be alone, without any younger family members to care for them, as many have today. Quality medical care not only allows people to become older, they also remain active longer. The elderly want to lead self-determined and independent lives for as long as possible. Sometimes a number of measures directed at their support suffice: simple services, care by mobile attendants, improved products for the household or, indeed, even accessible housing and an housing enivronment that allows integration. Today's only alternatives – independent living versus retirement home – can no longer serve as a model for the future. New lifestyles are thus less a phenomenon of the young, despite the impression imparted by the life-style-adoring media, so tailored to a young audience; on the contrary, they are a phenomenon of the elderly (ills. 2.4, 2,5).

In recent years a number of excellent examples of retirement homes have been realized. Rainer Köberl's retirement and nursing home in Nofels and the Spirgarten residence for

2.3 "Sargfabrik" in Vienna, 1996; BKK-2
2.4 Spirgarten residence for seniors, Zurich-Altstetten, site plan scale 1:4000, 2006; Architects: Miller & Maranta
2.5 Spirgarten residence for seniors, Zurich-Altstetten, 2006; Architects: Miller & Maranta

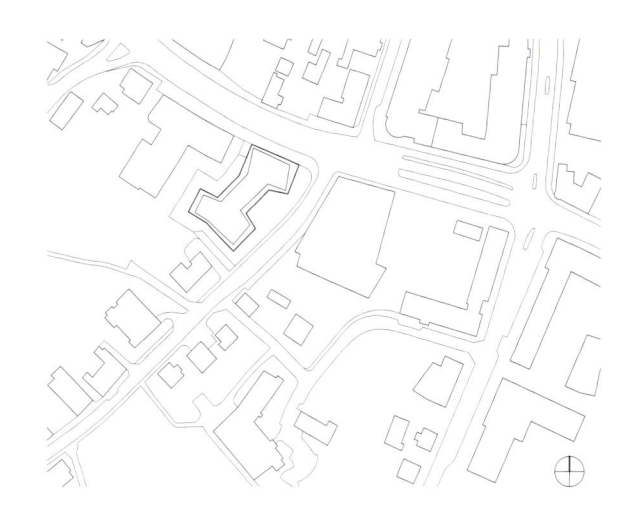

2.6

seniors in Zurich, designed by the Swiss architects Miller & Maranta, are worth mentioning here. Construction of the latter was completed in 2006 by the non-profit Atlas Foundation founded in 1972.[5] The project integrates many features of integrative living, although its basic approach, namely as a home for the elderly, does, in fact, contradict the principle of the projects introduced here: Each housing unit has a large loggia, with low wall soffits granting even bedridden residents a view to the outdoors. In terms of city planning the project was anchored so that the small forecourt, positioned through the configuration of the buildings to mark the entrance, takes reference to the development's most important traffic arteries. Many may regard such aspects as obvious in a project of this kind; yet, if that were the case, we would not need to emphasize such structures and their quality. A residence for seniors like that by Miller & Maranta, which intentionally alludes to the character of a hotel as a temporary residence facilitating an extravagant lifestyle, is the exact opposite of the traditional, time-honoured home for seniors, where our finite existence in this life often takes the form of an unbearable preview of the infinitude of the hereafter. Moreover, recent studies show that, under certain circumstances, the elderly – despite the assumption of their immobility – are indeed willing to change their place of residence. However, with increasing age people are increasingly less able to manage moving house on their own. The German Schader Stiftung, a foundation dedicated especially to the study of the needs of the elderly, submits the following remarks on this:

"Many communities and housing associations have recognized the hurdles the elderly must clear to move house, and now offer assistance. The initiatives extend from flat exchanges, to bonus programs, all the way to comprehensive relocation management. In general the trend has prevailed that those communities and housing associations which previously relied on bonus systems are giving way to a more complex relocation management system, in the framework of which bonus points primarily have the function of cushioning the cost of relocation. Comprehensive concepts by various communities rely on individual care and a package of bonus points, organizational and technical assistance."[6]

Singles and Single Parents
A further aspect of social differentiation is the rising number of single households and single parents. The factor "integration" is important for these groups, too, albeit in an entirely different way than in the cases discussed above. The high percentage of singles and the increasing number of single parents place new demands on the socio-cultural surroundings of a flat or a housing development. A housing development must be conceived and planned as part of a neighbourhood. What environment already exists there? What effect will/should a housing development have on an existing neighbourhood? These are questions that have been dealt with in the past only secondarily, if at all. Single parents have some needs that are similar, and some that are entirely different from those of singles without children. Neighbourly support – along the lines of "Who can babysit my little daughter this

2.6 Cafe Rigoletto, Rosa-Aschenbrenner-Bogen 9, Munich, 2004; A2 Architects
2.7 Multi-generation living "In der Wiesen-Nord", axonometric, floor plan mini-loft, 2005; Architects: Ebner + Ullmann

evening?" or "Could my teenage son stay overnight at the neighbours'?"– are the kinds of issues presented. Ideally new neighbourhoods could develop in integrative housing developments, in which the elderly could re-assume child-rearing duties (ill. 2.6).

The housing development on Rosa-Aschenbrenner-Bogen, by Wagnis e.V. in Munich, is such an example of a neighbourhood-oriented housing development, in which the managers have endeavoured since its founding to set up a residential community uniting people of all ages. Construction of the housing development with 92 dwellings in four buildings was completed in 2005. A long, five-storey block around 100 metres in length and smaller-scale individual buildings are grouped around a tree-lined courtyard. This courtyard accommodates community facilities, the Café Rigoletto and commercial units. The dwellings in the upper storeys of the main block are accessed via 1.30 m-wide covered walkways. In front of each covered walkway is anchored a scaffold 2.50 m deep, which residents can use to install a balcony platform at their own expense. Thus the residents have the opportunity to install a terrace with a view to the park and the activity on the neighbourhood courtyard, in addition to the western balcony standard in each dwelling. The impact of this generous supply of communicative spaces became clear shortly after the building was completed. The result was active zones, which have nothing more to do with green separation areas and the left-over spaces provided by housing construction of the past. In the study carried out by our department the residents' satisfaction with their living situation was expressed quite clearly. One female resident went on record with conviction, remarking: "Moving in here was the best decision I ever made."[7]

Multi-Generation Living

For the gigantic city expansion area in the south of Vienna called In der Wiesen-Nord, we, that is, Atelier Ebner/Ullmann, constructed not only the master plan, but also a multi-generation housing development. In this new district for a good 10,000 residents it was possible for the first time to realize a large housing development in Austria using an approach that spans the generations. Since the project is introduced in its own section of this publication, our main intent in this context is to depict the discursive environment (ill. 2.7).

The principle guiding the design of our multi-generational housing development was the motto *"We're taking our parents with us!"* With this model we wanted to create a type of building that makes it possible for younger families to accommodate their parents in the housing development, albeit intentionally not in the same unit. Closeness and distance between the generations were to be kept in a controllable relation. This building with a total of 92 units was also designed to house eleven mini-lofts for students (approx. 31 m^2) and 30 supervised-living units (48 to 55 m^2) for elderly residents. The ground floor of the western wing houses medical practices. While the barrier-free entrances, the low window soffits, the connection between living and sleeping areas, the communicative arrangement with covered walkways and a courtyard may all be elements we conceived with a view to the elderly residents, they are equally appreciated by the younger tenants.

2.7

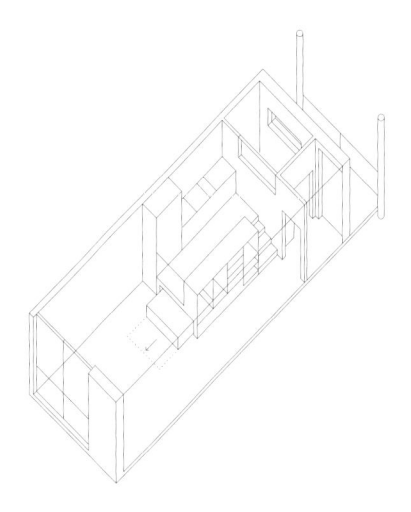

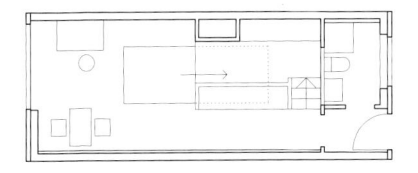

The student mini-lofts, positioned in the first upper storey of the east wing, exploit the full potential of the 3.20 m-high space while occupying as little area as possible. Thanks to the unusual height of the rooms, the bed can be pushed under the kitchen platform. An element familiar from Japanese living culture is that the bed is stowed during the day. From the raised kitchen platform one has a view of the activity in the open spaces in the courtyard. This solution was possible only because we were also able to design the interior of these dwellings, and because the users are only temporary tenants. Because the students do not need to buy any furniture, they can move in right away with nothing more than a suitcase. It is not possible in the context of this essay to go into all aspects of this large-scale housing development built in the tradition of Viennese housing. However, I can not emphasize too strongly the importance of conceiving a leap in scale. The bold design depends on the details; inversely, the most sophisticated solution, like the stow-away bed, is worth nothing if the surroundings, the mood in the newly created ambient, are not right.
When we were planning the multi-generation housing development In der Wiesen, there were a number of humble design programs and just a few residential projects in the periphery of the university, like the one for six families constructed in Brunn am Gebirge near Vienna in 1986. The difficulties in realizing a multi-generational project became apparent in the example of a project completed in Berlin in 1995. At that time the Stadtwerkstadt Berlin renovated a housing development from the 1950s that had been slated for demolition, expanding it and adding a unit for the elderly. Together with one of the existing structures, this new wing created a contemplative courtyard. Based on a type of object from Dutch architecture, the planners designated this a "Hofje". Without relating the details of the housing development, the following quote emphasizes how little understood and how underdeveloped the discussion regarding housing

2.8

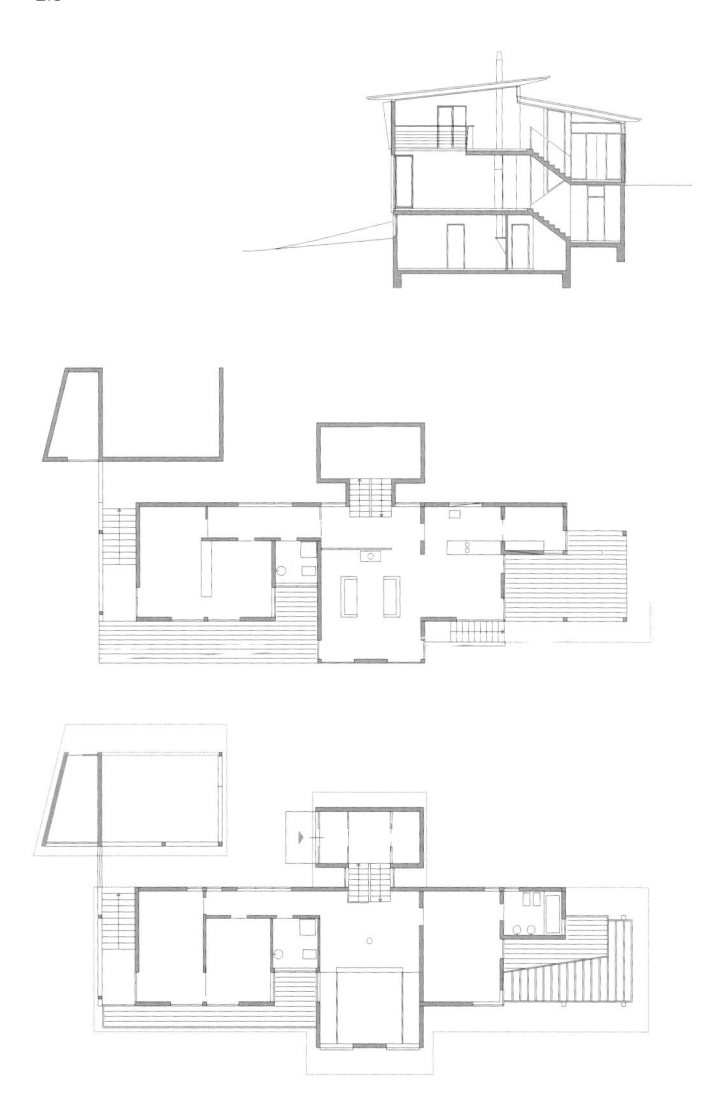

to integrate the elderly was just ten years ago:
"Living in an alliance of generations – actually completely natural, the most human way to live. Sad that an association has to be founded to enable it, that our everyday architecture is apparently largely unsuitable. Despite the humble scale of the project, much can be learned from the Hofje."[8]
Less humble in terms of its architecture is the multi-generation residential building built by architect Ernst Roth in Feldkirchen/Kärnten in 1994. While the two examples cited above were to some extent before their time in terms of the social subject matter, they remained traditional in terms of their architecture, not to mention humble. Yet this does not diminish the achievement of the planners and managers, which can hardly be underestimated for the intensity of their commitment and their success in "confronting the ideas" (ill. 2.8).

The building – a split-level type, as Otto Kapfinger establishes concisely – is significant because of its skill in combining aspects like one spatial system for the cohabitation of multiple generations, and openness for the shift in uses and life-cycles, with ecological precepts in the selection of materials and energy balance.[9] Innovative construction methods in terms of space and design are used to address an innovative social issue. Roth used industrially prefabricated wood elements with large, glazed openings, designed generous balconies and brought the topic of multi-generation living out of its socially marginal corner. Their added value can be measured against the fact that the sociological discourse becomes a social form through architecturally innovative means. Projects like the *Hängende Gärten* residential project in Vienna, realized by the architects Lautner and Kirisits[10], or the *Generationenwohnen Mainz* project, planned by 03 München, Büro für Städtebau und Architektur, which emerged from a competition, make clear how much breadth the topic has taken on, especially in urban space (ill. 2.9, 2.10).

Two projects in Switzerland that have long since attracted international attention and whose model character has been studied comparatively, are the *KraftWerk1* and the *Regina-Kägi-Hof* near Zurich.[11] The objectives of both projects were characterized by integrative aspects, as expressed in the following quote from a study about the two housing developments:
"The composition of the participants and the approach in realizing both housing developments are characterized by a wide variety of innovations. Unaccustomed are the plots, located in former industrial areas; the building volumes, which are rather large for co-operatives; their appearance; the concepts of space and use; the consideration of ecology and building biology – although to differing degrees; and the thematization of social aspects, which are certainly marked by the historical context of the co-operatives and took on particular value in the developments. Both housing developments also offer living space for groups that face disadvantages in the free housing market (the disabled, large families, single parents, foreigners and lower-income households)."[12]

2.9

It is problematic that the initiators of such projects want to do so much at once, and thus the high objectives of KraftWerk1 were not achieved in all aspects:
"The KW1 project aspired to a composition of residents that corresponds to the average population of the city of Zurich. For the first occupancy this goal was achieved only in part. Instead of the 30% foreigners living in Zurich, only 15% of

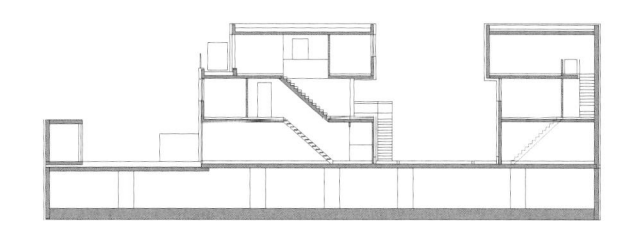

the KW1 residents are foreigners. The elderly population in KW1 is also strongly underrepresented. While the group of people over 64 years of age amounts to nearly 18 % in Zurich (2001), this group is not represented at all in KW1."[13] (ills. 2.11, 2.12)

According to the planners, in the years since the study these population ratios in *KraftWerk* have shifted toward the desired average parameters.[14] What I would like to point out in this context, however, is not whether or not the percentages correspond exactly to the desired goals. More important is that the integrative measures like the communal facilities and residential communities in *KraftWerk* are experiencing a renaissance.
Architects like Arno Lederer actually regard the "senior flat-share" as *the* model for the future. Lederer propagates senior flat-shares as shared-risk communities, in which the members offer mutual support, combine forces to manage the household and keep house, and where the large number of singles can lead a socially integrated life at an advanced age. Regardless of whether or not this 1960s-style model is actually established beyond isolated cases, in those cases where it is realized it will contribute to overcoming the disadvantages of demographic change.

Intercultural Living

Against the backdrop of immigration to Europe and the social deficits in the districts of the city and suburbs characterized by immigrants, the concept of integration is particularly topical. Integrating people from other cultural, ethnic and religious backgrounds is a challenge, which for the states and cities of the European Union has long since become a question that can not be left to chance. The tensions in German cities, the violent confrontations in the *banlieus* of Paris, which are also problems of social segration due to the form of city planning, again open up the question as to how architecture can be used to combat these developments.
In this it should be clear that "tolerance toward foreign cultures must also find its limits where the rules required for the smooth functioning of the division of labour in modern society are violated".[15]
On the other hand, segregation as a model of cohabitation should not be rejected per se, nor integration understood as a panacea. On the contrary: Segregation is actually a feature of urban agglomerations, as the sociologists of the Chicago School emphasized. For them "the segregation of the various ethnicities in a city is, so to speak, organic, because each individual group needs and seeks a special terrain corresponding to its needs and abilities".[16] Such areas have the advantage that immigrants erect their networks and neighbourhoods where they can live whilst preserving their identity, which, in turn, is a prerequisite for integration. People who are uprooted and robbed of their cultural identity can not integrate into society.
This view is opposed by advocates of the contact hypothesis.

2.8 Feldkirchen multi-generational residence, 1993; Architect: Ernst Roth, floor plan, sections
2.9 Multi-generational residence in Mainz, 2005; Architects: 03 München
2.10 Multi-generational residence in Mainz, 2005; Architects: 03 München

2.10

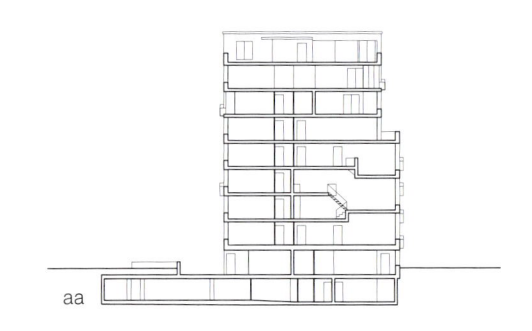

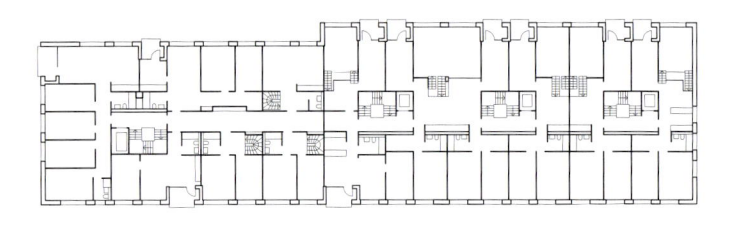

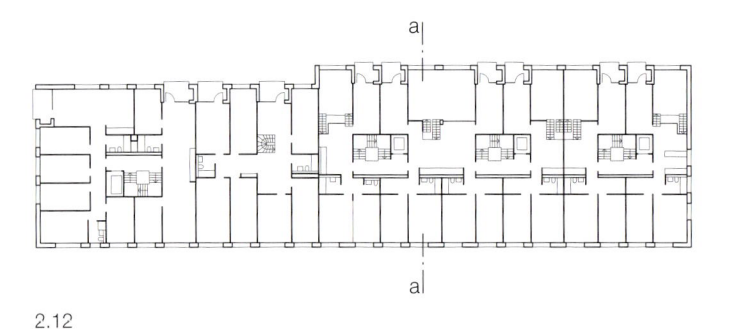

According to their view, the mixture of different ways of life encourages understanding and tolerance. However, we would like to advance the hypothesis that the model of integration actually rather approaches the scale, the understanding and the type of the European city.
In Vienna – whose share of 18% foreigners certainly qualifies it as a city of immigration – the topic is virulent, and the parties with the strongest anti-foreigner slogans are successful in local elections. The development of integrative approaches for residential housing is thus also the attempt to propagate the topic in the public. Although the *Interkulturelles Wohnen* project, planned by the architects Heidecker and Neuhauser and completed in 1996, certainly could be regarded skeptically, according to a statement by the developer, in 2006 it was able to look back on a successful decade of integration work: "A functioning house community evolved!", was the message imparted.

The *Interkulturelles Wohnen* housing development by Heidecker/Neuhauser accommodates residents from Hungary, Sri Lanka, Bosnia, Poland, Russia, Turkey, Iran and the Philippines in addition to Austrian-born tenants. A total of 20% of the primary tenants were born abroad. Around 12% of the residents live in mixed partnerships – the rest (68%) are native Austrians. A recent resident survey revealed a very high degree of satisfaction with the housing situation, which was also corroborated by the very low fluctuation of tenants in the residential facility's 51 subsidized rental dwellings.[17]
Worth emphasizing is that the formation of the neighbourhood was encouraged above all by an accompanying project by the Viennese housing research association, which organized tenant meetings to introduce residents to their possibilities for self-determination on issues concerning the facility. Architecturally, an intimate inner courtyard, a communicative system of covered walkways and attractive communal rooms encourage contact within the residential community.

»Neither melting-pot nor ghetto« was the motto for this interethnic living project by Peter Scheifinger, which offers gardens in spite of its high housing density. All of the dwellings in the two central wings have a private garden, and each of those on the ground floor has a private front garden of its own. The maisonettes in the first through third floors, accessed via a central walkway on the second floor, have private roof gardens of their own, each with its own entrance to the shared staircase. To break up the monotony of the central walkway this passage is extended by means of common loggias. The dwellings in the upper North wing and the lower South wing have private loggias and common gardens on the roof, the latter of which are tended by the property developer. Garden-plot idyll on the roof to encourage a sense of identification in immigrants from rural areas. The extent to which such ideas are more than the ornamentation of social realities has yet to be seen. In any case this project deserves praise for bringing the topic of integrating people with an immigrant background into the bastions of (Viennese) communal housing (ill. 2.13).

Norms for Barrier-Free Dwellings and Housing Developments
The requirements for barrier-free construction in Germany are governed by parts 1 and 2 of the DIN 18025 norm, whereby part 1 is conceived for the planning, execution and construc-

tion of wheelchair-accessible flats and part 2 concerns the accessibility of flats and housing developments more generally. The objective is supposed to be to build barrier-free state-subsidized housing, and to aspire to this standard for housing construction as a whole. In planning such projects it is imperative to consult this cited comprehensive body of legislation.[18] Because they are discussed extensively in a separate essay in this volume, here we would like to concentrate on aspects that extend beyond literal compliance with the norms. For it is by no means certain that a housing development can be called integrative just because the access areas and floor plans are designed according to the norms. We should not build housing and then painstakingly install doors according to the stipulated width, but rather from the outset design flats with open floor plans, which avoid the entire problem of passages and corridors that may be too narrow. The integration of the disabled and residents with limited mobility demands a departure from residential floor plans that are designed specifically for the functional segmentation of living space. With this even people who are disabled by illness in the short term or permanently weakened or bedridden can be integrated into a communal everyday residential situation.

The goal of barrier-free integrative housing developments is the mixture of different social groups and forms of households. Such projects thus demand a wide variety of changeable types of dwellings, communal rooms and free accessibility. In the study about barrier-free housing developments we asked the residents about these subjects and the answer was by and large clear (ill. 2.17).

The message is that dwellings should be conceived from the outset so that they can be adapted easily at a later point in time if necessary, leaving open the possibility of connecting or dividing rooms flexibly. Advantageous for this are concepts of usage-neutral floor plans, which allow retrofitting to increase accessibility with a minimum of expense and effort. For dwellings that can not become barrier-free per se, like townhouses, split-level flats or maisonettes, the demand is altered accordingly: to keep at least the most important spaces on the entry level accessible. Yet the inverse deduction, that such types of dwellings and houses should be disqualified as generally inaccessible, does not apply. It would be absolutely incorrect to demand that only one-floor dwellings in the classic sense be considered barrier-free.
To mention one example for a functioning and popular maisonette development, I would like to refer to a building in Günzburg, in which the accessibility of the dwellings is provided by the passage of covered walkways (ills. 2.14–2.16).

Barrier-Free Is Not the Same As Wheelchair-Accessible
The core issue of a barrier-free housing development is that all rooms belonging to the dwelling be accessible, as well as all communal rooms provided for the residents of the housing development, so that all communal rooms can be used by all of its residents, from the laundry to the subterranean garage,

2.11 KraftWerk1, Zurich, 2001;
 Architects: Bünzli Courvoisier Stücheli, 2001
2.12 Floor plans + sections of KraftWerk1, Zurich
 Architects Bünzli Courvoisier Stücheli
 section, floorplans, 2nd and 3rd floor
2.13 Interethnisches Wohnen in Vienna, 1991;
 Architect: Peter Scheifinger

2.13

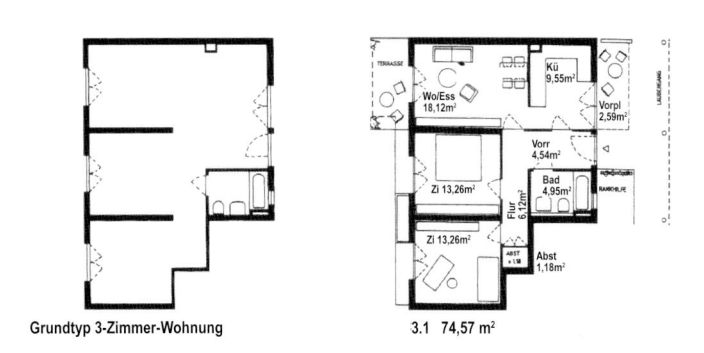

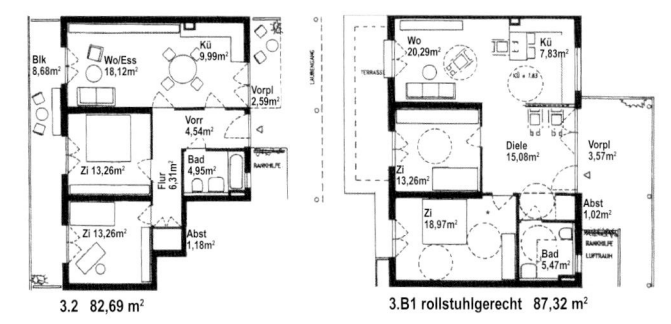

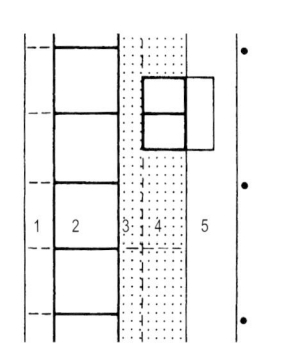

for the most part independently and without outside assistance. This demand sounds quite straightforward. Yet the study cited above revealed that in the housing developments we investigated, the greatest deficits with regard to accessibility were established for precisely these communal spaces; this becomes critical when wheelchair accessibility is also required. Points criticized by the residents included the lack of zoning in the entrance areas and the parking spaces. At least in the projects studied in the cited paper,[19] the majority of the wheelchair parking spaces were inconveniently located. The solution of combining the required spaces with the bicycle room was rejected roundly, as it results in unacceptable competition for space. The location of the parking spaces for cars is particularly important, and a veritable red flag for persons of restricted mobility. Subterranean parking spaces are designated as "spaces of fear": the fear of being locked in manifests itself even more strongly in the disabled. In general this circumstance should prompt treatment of subterranean garages as more than a mere engineering and technical problem.

Integration into the Residential Neighbourhood
With increasing immobility due to age, illness or physical disability, the question as to where the most important kitchen and infrastructure facilities are located takes on decisive relevance. What is the good of a residence designated as barrier-free or friendly to the disabled if no corresponding infrastructure is available in the immediate surroundings? We have to plan and co-ordinate the spatial relations in the residence, in the development, in the vicinity of the development, and in its context in the given town or village centre. The studies of integrative housing developments performed at the Department for Housing and Housing Economics[20] yielded that 64 % of the residents surveyed do their daily errands on foot (ill. 2.17).

In our opinion it would be ideal if all of the supply facilities needed in everyday life could be reached within 500 metres. Where possible, facilities for shopping, care and treatment should be combined with spaces offering leisure activities and opportunities for socializing. If these are not available within a neighbourhood, at least a regular connection to public transport is an imperative prerequisite, whereby then, again, accessibility must be guaranteed. Insular locations are to be avoided.

The Economic Framework

The study about barrier-free and integrated housing developments performed at the Department for Housing and Housing Economics of the Technical University of Munich concluded that these were constructed at a cost between 1,090 and 1,560 Euro/m² of living space.[21] This makes some of them slightly more expensive than the average conventional state-subsidized housing unit. Property developers and architects agree that compliance with every letter of the DIN 18025 norm entails high costs, and thus advocate the possibility of interpreting the regulations more liberally. In return, however, such developments show clear added value, which is expressed both in a higher architectural standard and in the constructional facilities that encourage communication.
Yet this poses the question of how to finance this added value.[22] After all, the survey of the housing associations revealed

that only the fewest of such housing developments can be run with a positive economic balance. This is not exactly encouraging, whereby this was due to a variety of causes: in one case there were significant defects in construction, the correction of which was very expensive; in another case the occupancy rate was too low.

In the long term such projects can be run only with great commitment by the housing associations, also in terms of financing. Potential for savings certainly lies in the consideration of accessibility at an early phase of the planning process, as retrofitting is expensive. Yet the more matter-of-fact barrier-free construction becomes, the more economical the price development will be. In future the state will have to see its obligation not only in supporting the facility, but also in the maintenance of communal facilities. With a view to the demographic shift – that is, the ageing of our society – barrier-free construction is urgently recommended, from the economic perspective as well. Our study also showed that all facilities can be erected only with significant public sponsorship, and that they were all created by cooperative housing associations or church-affiliated institutions. Private developers quite obviously give this field a wide berth, a circumstance that is exacerbated by the fact that the majority of the dwellings are slated for rental.

Communal Areas: Experiences and Recommendations
Even if, as emphasized above, the costs for barrier-free housing with timely preliminary planning do not, or only slightly, exceed those for conventional housing, the communal facilities, outdoor installations and other structural measures that offer space for what takes place between people, the interpersonal, can not be supplied for free. In the study so often cited above it was demonstrated that the communal spaces provided often were not used very intensively. The picture that results is quite ambivalent. Ultimately, it turns out here, too, that a purely structural measure is by no means sufficient to create the corresponding social utility. This is especially true for spaces created without any definite concept for use. Communal rooms are successful where various functional spaces and lounges are combined. That no clear conceptual formulation, definition and responsibilities are required is also clear from the responses to the residents of such developments (ill. 2.17).

More generous exterior installations, roof terraces and communal terraces or rooms cost money: in planning, construction, and above all in operation. Therefore they should have locations and designs that make residents embrace them. In general, very positive experiences have been made with facilities that are available not only to the residents of the specific development, but to the whole neighborhood, like Café Rigoletto in the housing development on Rosa-Aschenbrenner-Bogen, Cafe Etwas, the day-care station in the development in Kempten or the event rooms in the *Sargfabrik*, which have taken on even national importance.

The Network of Partners
Co-operation between the various actors in planning is required for an integrative housing project to be successful: planners, the building company or group, city planning authorities, state and local welfare organizations and other specialized authorities must work together during this phase. From the experiences of model projects in Bavaria it can be

How do you do your everyday errands? On foot?

yes	no
64%	36%

How important to you was the idea of integration when you moved in?

very important	important	less important	did not matter	not familiar with the idea
24%	18%	17%	25%	16%

Would you want your dwelling to be adaptable to different residential situations?

yes	no	somewhat
63%	32%	5%

Do you think that the project is successful in this regard?

absolutely	somewhat	hardly	not at all
63%	40%	18%	12%

Do you have more or less contact to your fellow residents than you did in your previous dwellings?

more	less	don't know
53%	32%	15%

How would you characterize the house community?

village	many friends	recognize everyone	casual contacts	few acquaintances	quite anonymous
21%	25%	39%	9%	4%	2%

Do you use the communal areas?

intensively	occasionally	seldom	never
21%	26%	19%	34%

Are there communally organized events, parties or the like?

yes	no	don't know
63%	31%	6%

Is there neighbourly support in the housing estate?

always	occasionally	seldom	never	don't know
31%	41%	12%	11%	5%

2.17

2.14 Integriertes Wohnen in Günzburg, 1996; Architect Georg Sahner;
Floor-plan variations in this housing development
Basic 1-bedroom dwelling
Basic 2-bedroom dwelling
Basic 3-bedroom dwelling
Basic 3-bedroom maisonette
Basic 4-bedroom maisonette
The open construction grid offers the possibility of a wide variety of floor-plan layouts in the various types of dwellings
2.15 Integriertes Wohnen in Günzburg, 1996;
Architect Georg Sahner;
Basic 3-bedroom dwelling floor plan
2.16 Integriertes Wohnen in Günzburg, 1996;
Architect Georg Sahner;
Floor plan schema: 1 private area; 2 individual rooms; 3 transition zone; 4 communal area; 5 access walkway with niches
2.17 Excerpt from a study "Barrierefreies und integriertes Wohnen", qualitative and quantitative survey of residents to evaluate Bavarian models of experimental housing construction; Oberste Baubehörde im Bayerischen Staatsministerium des Innern (Ed.), LWW Prof. P. Ebner, Dachau 2006

2.18

deduced that higher costs are accrued on the planners' part, primarily resulting from the increased expense of moderating among the above-mentioned groups and institutions. This higher expense in the development, control, and co-ordination of the project is above all a problem for the architect, because it generally cannot be billed over the Fee Structure for Architects and Engineers. Should integrative projects become the standard case, a greater portion of the additional costs originating from more expensive planning must become billable and eligible for subsidy. While commitment is always a requirement in architecture, it alone should not have to carry the system in the long term. Localities should assist developers on all possible levels, both instrumentally and institutionally, in building integrative housing developments. Under some circumstances an accelerated construction process can save far more money than could be contributed through direct financial support.

The Future of Integration

We undertook the attempt to depict all facets of integrative housing construction, and in so doing were forced to differentiate: multi-generation living, barrier-free housing, inter-ethnic living; today each of these appear to lead a parallel existence. The sometimes confusing plethora of concepts should not deceive us, however, for in essence all integrative housing construction is about a modern, humane and open city. The variety merely shows that we have to create the possibility to choose.
Yet we will also continue to need types of buildings tailored to certain groups, like nursing homes and facilities for the disabled. For a certain, more solvent clientele, senior residences will become the optimum solution. Professor Welsing of the Royal Danish Academy, at a recent symposium in Milan entitled "New Housing Concepts", propagated housing developments for the senile, whose unbiased avowal to creating a

2.18 Day-Care Centre in Japan, 2006;
Architect: Toshi Kawai

residential situation segregated from the surroundings make them worth closer attention. The circular development in the model is surrounded by a fence, and allows the mentally disabled and senile residents to move freely, but enjoy protection throughout the facility.

For its part, Japan is pushing "Day-Care Centres". Seniors are brought to such facilities once a week. Here they cook together, receive sanitary and medical attention, and enjoy the opportunity for social exchange. The care staff reports that the visits, preparation and follow-up generally occupy the seniors for around three days per week. This model from the Far East could perhaps replace the standard, weekly visit by a care worker on a tight time budget, which is perceived more as an intervention into the seniors' private sphere than as a relaxing visit. The senior flat-shares favoured by Arno Lederer, for instance, could be another model with a future. Yet what is certain is that we must consider how we can make ageing with dignity possible at a low cost for many seniors (ill. 2.18).

In this integrative housing developments will play an important role, but they are not institutions for the disabled or seniors. Rather, expressed with all caution, they could weave a bit more closely the social network that has shown signs of wear. Our study revealed that the human virtue of solidarity has by no means disappeared, as many of our pessimistic contemporaries would have us believe (ill. 2.17).

In contrast to the egotistical image of humanity, a considerable number of people in such integrative housing developments emphasized their willingness to get involved within this community, whereby the most frequent activities were helping with errands and shopping, standing in during vacation, and assistance in the household, followed by babysitting. The fact that we can achieve something by shaping house communities in integrative residential developments was shown by our study, even in cases where the idea of integration had not yet been recognized as significant at the time the residents moved in. For the question, "How important to you was the idea of integration when you moved in?" yielded the following spectrum of reactions (ill. 2.17):

That a special consciousness must not necessarily be developed in order to later appreciate a living situation that encourages contact was revealed by the following question, "Do you have more or less contact to your fellow residents than you did in your previous dwellings?" (ill. 2.17)

The success of increased endeavours toward integration is ultimately difficult to depict quantitatively. Even for those 69% of the residents of integrative residential developments surveyed who responded that they had contact to disabled persons in their neighbourhood, we know nothing about the quality of this relationship. We presume that it is an open, mutually respectful relationship and thus constitutes an essential step toward integrating disabled individuals. This or something like it, our conclusion, will be the result for other contents and aspects of integration. It is no coincidence that the most important integrative residential projects in the middle of historical cities frequently originated on industrial fallows. Their urban identity also confirms the insight that the social one-dimensionality of the suburb can become very lonely, especially in old age. These buildings are not only integrated into their immediate surroundings in the city, but achieve the integration of different concepts of life, as they emerge along the rupture between industrial and service society.

Notes:
1. Partizipation als Chance für die Architektur. Ein Vortrag von Franz Sumnitsch, in: LWW, Prof. Ebner, Housing is back, Vienna 2006, p. 44
2. In addition to describing the attempts at conceptual definition cited above, the web site www.Neue-Wohnformen.de also discusses other attempts like residential groups, multi-generation living, etc.
3. Cf. "Bauen und Wohnen für Behinderte" working papers No. 5, cited in: Oberste Baubehörde im Bayerischen Staatsministerium des Inneren. Abteilung Wohnungswesen und Städtebauförderung (ed.), Barrierefreies und integriertes Wohnen. Forschungsbericht zur Nachuntersuchung ausgewählter Modellvorhaben und Landeswettbewerb. Konzept, Untersuchung und Forschungsbericht: Department for Housing and Housing Economics, Professor Peter Ebner, Technical University of Munich, Munich 2006, p. 6
4. Andreas Huber, Susanne Rock, Margrit Hugentobler, Gewohnte Utopien. Die innovativen Siedlungen KraftWerk1 und Regina-Kägi-Hof in Zürich. Bericht zur Erstevaluation, p. 33
5. Cf. Hubertus Adam, Urban und öffentlich. Miller & Maranta: Seniorenresidenz Spirgarten, Zürich-Altstetten, in: archithese, 1, 2007, pp. 14–17
6. Cited in: Rolf G. Heinze, Volker Eichener, Gerhard Naegele, Mathias Bucksteeg, Martin Schauerte, Neue Wohnung auch im Alter. Folgerungen aus dem demographischen Wandel für Wohnungspolitik und Wohnungswirtschaft. For further literature and references, see the web site of the Schader-Stiftung (www.schader-stiftung.de).
7. Lehrstuhl für Wohnungsbau und Wohnungswirtschaft, TUM/Oberste Baubehörde im Bayerischen Staatsministerium, Abteilung Wohnungswesen und Städtebauförderung, Living Streets – Laubengänge, Munich 2006, pp. 38ff.
8. Falk Jaeger, Integriertes Wohnen in Berlin-Neukölln. In: Bauwelt, Nr. 7, 1996, pp. 38–41
9. Otto Kapfinger, Neue Architektur in Kärnten, Salzburg 2006, Mehrgenerationen-Wohnhaus R. Feldkirchen, Object No. 3/5
10. This project which was completed in 2003, although not strictly multi-generational housing, demonstrates how the concept merges with other innovative sectors of social housing construction. This housing development combining living and working functions, also offers interconnecting dwellings appropriate for multi-generational living. Apartments located in the lower storey can be directly connected to adjacent apartments.
11. Andreas Huber, Susanne Rock, Margrit Hugentobler, Gewohnte Utopien. Die innovativen Siedlungen KraftWerk1 und Regina-Kägi-Hof in Zürich. Bericht zur Erstevaluation
12. ibid. p. 12
13. ibid. p. 168
14. The author was assured of this by the managers during a visit to KW1 in early 2007.
15. Herbert Ludl (ed.), Das Wohnmodell interethnische Nachbarschaft. Vienna, 2003, p. 33
16. ibid. p. 34
17. Cited according to a press release by GEWOG, Gemeinnützige Wohnungsbau Ges.m.b.H, OTS original text, of 2/5/2006
18. Bayerische Architektenkammer und Oberste Baubehörde im Bayerischen Staatsministerium des Inneren, Barrierefreies Bauen 1, Barrierefreie Wohnungen, Planungsgrundlagen, Leitfaden für Architekten, Fachingenieure, Bauherren zur DIN 18 025 Teil 1 und 2, Ausgabe 1992 Additional norms on the subject of accessible construction: Bayerische Architektenkammer, Oberste Baubehörde im Bayerischen Staatsministerium des Inneren und Bayerisches Staatsministerium für Arbeit und Sozialordnung, Familie und Frauen, Barrierefreies Bauen 3, Straßen, Plätze, Wege, Öffentliche Verkehrs- und Grünanlagen sowie Spielplätze, Leitfaden für Architekten, Landschaftsarchitekten, Fachingenieure, Bauherren und Gemeinden zur DIN 18 024 Teil 1, Ausgabe 1998, Munich, 2001
19. op. cit, note 3, cf. especially pp. 104f.
20. ibid. pp. 108f.
21. From these statistics it is apparent that barrier-free living space according to part 2 of the DIN 18025 norm can be constructed at approximately the same cost as conventional residential housing. This was also proved in various studies by the Oberste Bayerische Wohnbaubehörde. Cf. on this especially the working papers "Bauen und Wohnen für Behinderte", No. 5, "Wohnen ohne Barrieren", Oberste Baubehörde im Bayerischen Staatsministerium des Inneren. Further: IFB Forschungsbericht 1995, Barrierefreies Bauen und kostengünstiges Bauen für alle Bewohner – Analyse ausgeführter Projekte nach DIN 18025-2, Fraunhofer Institut, 1998; Oberste Baubehörde im Bayerischen Staatsministerium des Inneren. Abteilung Wohnungswesen und Städtebauförderung (ed.), Barrierefreies und integriertes Wohnen, op. cit. This study looked at housing developments in the following localities: Bad Babach, Hans-Moser-Straße; Dorfen, Kloster Algasing; Günzburg, Ludwig-Heilmayr-Straße; Ingolstadt, Hollerstauden; Kempten, Brennergasse; Manching, Schulstraße; Munich, Volpinistraße; Regensburg, Rote-Löwen-Straße
22. In Bayern, for instance, the creation of barrier-free residential space has been subsidized more intensively since 2003. Prerequisite for subsidization is that in buildings with more than six dwellings, the dwellings on one floor and the access to these dwellings is designed in accordance with part 2 of the DIN 18025 norm, and that this is possible under the conditions existing in the object at economically acceptable costs. According to part 1 of the norm, the subsidy for the construction of housing can be increased to up to 10 %. Moreover, adaptations to the dwellings and improvements to the surroundings as well as the creation and construction of communal spaces can be subsidized in accordance with DIN 18025.

Bibliography:
1. Arch+ Nr. 176/177, May 2006
2. Archithese No. 5/2006
3. Ludl, Herbert (ed.), Das Wohnmodell interethnische Nachbarschaft, Vienna 2003
4. LWW, Housing is Back, Vienna 2006
5. Oberste Baubehörde im Bayerischen Staatsministerium des Inneren, Abteilung Wohnungswesen und Städtebauförderung, Barrierefreies und integriertes Wohnen, Dachau 2006
6. Oberste Baubehörde im Bayerischen Staatsministerium des Inneren, Abteilung Wohnungswesen und Städtebauförderung, Living Streets – Laubengänge, Munich 2006
7. Oberste Baubehörde im Bayerischen Staatsministerium des Inneren, Abteilung Wohnungswesen und Städtebauförderung, Wohnen in allen Lebensphasen, Munich 2006
8. Oberste Baubehörde im Bayerischen Staatsministerium des Inneren, Abteilung Wohnungswesen und Städtebauförderung, Alternative Wohnformen, Wohnmodelle Bayern Vol.1, Stuttgart Zurich 1997
9. Weeber & Partner, Gemeinschaftliches Wohnen im Alter. Bauforschung für die Praxis, Stuttgart 2001
10. Wehrli-Schindler, Birgit, Wohnen im Alter – zwischen Zuhause und Heim. Braucht es neue Wohnformen für Betagte? Zurich 1997
11. Wohnbund-Informationen (2/2004), Schwerpunktthema: Selbstbestimmt wohnen im Alter, Munich 2004

Project Summary

page		area	seniors	care facilities
26	"Miss Sargfabrik" in Vienna BKK-3	residential floor area 2,820 m²		
32	Multi-generational House in Stuttgart Kohlhoff & Kohlhoff	usable floor area 4,200 m²	10 shared living units for 2 seniors each (90 m²)	
36	Multi-generational Housing in Vienna Franziska Ullmann and Peter Ebner	residential floor area 4,905 m²	30 assisted living apartments (51.5 m²)	
42	Apartment Building in Vienna PPAG Architects	residential floor area 2,655 m²		
46	Renovation of a Department Store in Eschweiler, BeL	usable floor area 1,465 m²	4 barrier-free apartments (58–78 m²) shared accommodation for 6 seniors (210 m²)	
52	Community Centre in Stuttgart Lederer + Ragnarsdóttir + Oei	usable floor area 1,177 m²	8 1-room barrier-free apartments (43 m²) 2 2-room barrier-free apartments (52 m²)	
58	Seniors' Residence in Zurich Miller & Maranta	total floor area 9,289 m²	8 1-room apartments (26 m²) 56 2-room apartments (47–51 m²) 4 3-room apartments (59 m²)	18 single care accommodation rooms (19–25.5 m²)
64	Multengut Seniors' Residence near Bern Burkhalter Sumi Architects	usable floor area 10,851 m²	98 apartments	26 care accommodation rooms
70	Housing Development and Aged Care Centre in Alicante, Javier García-Solera Vera	total floor area 2,674 m²	36 2-room apartments (40 m²)	aged care centre
74	High-rise Apartment Building in Rotterdam Arons en Gelauff architecten	residential floor area 11,924 m²	104 apartments	
78	Senior Dwellings in Domat/Ems Dietrich Schwarz	usable floor area 1,680 m²	20 2-room apartments (57 m²)	
84	Centre for Seniors in Lich Pfeifer Roser Kuhn	usable floor area 3,199 m²	27 2-room apartments (51 m²)	56 care accommodation rooms (24 m²)
90	Long House on Henza Island Kawai Architects/Toshiaki Kawai	usable floor area 1,244 m²		18 care accommodation rooms, aged care centre
94	Seniors' Centre in Magdeburg löhle neubauer architects	total floor area 8,470 m²	93 single rooms (16.2–21.5 m²) 25 double rooms (24.4–27.2 m²)	6 care accommodation rooms (16.3–24.5 m²)
100	Residence for Seniors in Neumarkt am Wallersee, Kada + Wittfeld	usable floor area 3,900 m²	50 single rooms (25 m²) 5 double rooms (31 m²)	
104	Centre for Seniors in Steinfeld Dietger Wissounig	total floor area 3,658 m²		8 double care rooms 34 single care rooms (19–28 m²)
110	Ambulant Care Day Centre in Kamigyo Toshiaki Kawai	total floor area 187.55 m²		aged care centre
114	Residence in Gstadt Florian Höfer	usable floor area 432 m²		
116	Multi-generational House in Waldzell Helga Flotzinger	residential floor area 366.8 m²	1× apartment (46.9 m²)	1× apartment (59.6 m²)
120	Multi-generational House in Darmstadt Kränzle + Fischer-Wasels Architects Klotz + Knecht Architects	residential floor area 1,061 m²		
124	City House in Munich Fink + Jocher	residential floor area 2,066 m²	15 barrier-free apartments	
130	Multi-generational Housing Development in Freiburg, Pfeifer Roser Kuhn	residential floor area 1,929 m²	6 1-room apartments (47 m²) 3 2-room apartments (56 m²)	
134	Housing Development in Wiesbaden Dietz Joppien Architects	usable floor area 4,715 m²		
138	Housing Development in Ypenburg van den Oever, Zaaijer & Partners John Bosch	usable floor area 19,850 m²		

wheelchair facilities	families	young people	additional facilities	structural system/facade
3 wheelchair-friendly apartments	32 apartments (1–3 storey) 5 home offices (3 storey)	1 shared accommodation for 8 young people	communal kitchen, library, club room	reinforced concrete comp. therm. insul. system
all apartments wheelchair-friendly		child care centre for 120 children in 9 groups	café, service offices	reinforced concrete face brickwork, timber frame
	6 maisonettes (98.6 m²) 26 2-room apartments (54.7 m²) 13 3-room apartments (78.8 m²)	12 mini-lofts (31.4 m²)	care station, shops, café, medical practices, offices	reinforced concrete comp. therm. insul. system laminated timber panels
	32 apartments (61–103 m²)	temp. shared acc. for teenagers 4 1-room (11–21 m²)	comp. therm. insul. system	reinforced concrete
1 wheelchair-friendly apartment (67 m²)			shops (320 m²) function room (330 m²)	reinforced concrete skeleton comp. therm. insul. system
2 1-room apartments (48 m²)	1 caretaker apartment (95 m²)		1 apartment for carer (32 m²)	reinforced concrete, face brickwork comp. therm. insul. system
all apartments wheelchair-friendly			public café, inglenook, library	reinforced concrete, glass, concrete with Jurassic lime
			inglenook, lecture room, library, wellness area	reinforced concrete
3 2-room apartments (40 m²)			community facilities	reinforced concrete glass facades
all apartments wheelchair-friendly			community facilities ground floor	reinforced concrete glass facades
all apartments wheelchair-friendly				reinforced concrete, latent heat storage modules, comp. therm. insul. system
all apartments wheelchair-friendly			café, chapel	reinforced concrete, brickwork, timber frame
			café, dining room, relaxation room	reinforced concrete, cedar cladding
9 wheelchair-friendly rooms (18.2 m²)			dining room, terrace	reinforced concrete glass facade, perforated aluminium sheeting
all rooms wheelchair-friendly			chapel, dining room	reinforced concrete, larch cladding
all rooms wheelchair-friendly			dining and event hall, chapel, library	reinforced concrete stacked-board construction timber frame
			tea ceremony room, tatami room	reinforced concrete
entire house wheelchair-friendly				timber-frame with three-ply larch panels
entire house wheelchair-friendly	1× apartment (197.8 m²)		therapy pool	reinforced concrete metal facade
	3 maisonettes for multi-generational living		communal terraces and recreational areas	reinforced concrete face brickwork
2× 3 room apartment	6 maisonettes		7 shops, communal room with kitchen, playground	reinforced concrete comp. therm. insul. system
3 2-room apartments (56 m²)	18 apartments (54–117 m²)			sand-lime masonry with reinforced concrete slabs
wheelchair-friendly ground floor apartments	70 apartments (55–100.5 m²)			reinforced concrete lightweight masonry
2 residential groups (3,000 m²) with 48 rooms (14 m²)	120 terrace houses (90–170 m²)			reinforced concrete face brickwork, timber construction panels

"Miss Sargfabrik" in Vienna

Architects: BKK-3, Vienna

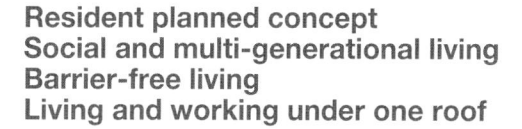

Resident planned concept
Social and multi-generational living
Barrier-free living
Living and working under one roof

The "Miss Sargfabrik" confidently dominates a corner block in the 14th district in Vienna; the elongated window bands repeatedly bend and stretch within the glowing orange facade, creating significant areas of glass and revealing the abundant variety of functions behind. A generously glazed entrance leads towards the private sunken courtyard. Five additional, smaller entrances provide access to the "home offices"; which combine living and working functions within various levels.

A large range of people come together in this socially integrated community; traditional family units, single parents, singles, young people, retirees, refugees and people with various disabilities.

Self-determined living

All residents are members of an association which is simultaneously owner, builder and landlord of the complex. Rather than paying rent, the residents pay off the building loan and cover maintenance fees. When a resident leaves the complex, his apartment reverts to the ownership of the association. There are, however, some apartments which are available for rental for a pre-determined period of time without the tenants being required to become members of the association.

The members were actively involved in the planning process of the complex. Particular points of interest of the small but economical apartments result from the irregular party walls, the sloping ceilings and the variations in ceiling heights – from 2.26 to 3.12 metres. There are single storey apartments, three of which are wheelchair-friendly, maisonettes and larger dwellings which stretch over three storeys. Internal ramps and stairs connect the various floors thereby allowing even the smallest of apartments to benefit from interesting spatial sequences.

Focus on community

Although the apartments do not have private balconies they are interconnected by the communal access balconies which can also function as outdoor seating areas where they widen. Extensive glazing to the balconies ensures the openness of the individual apartments and indicates the willingness of the residents to be a part of the communal project.

Communal facilities further assist in enhancing communication; a kitchen, library, media room, laundry, and for the younger generation a club room have been incorporated. Shared accommodation on the first floor for up to eight young people has also been provided.

Even the vehicles on the three parking spaces within the "Miss Sargfabrik" are available to all residents.

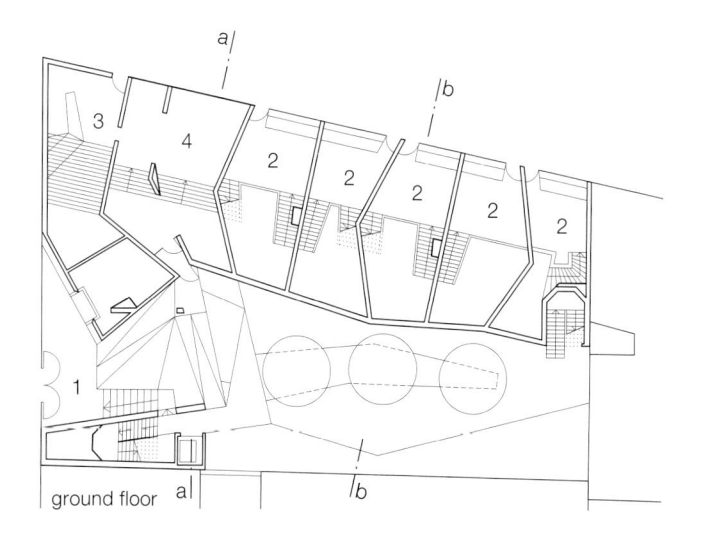

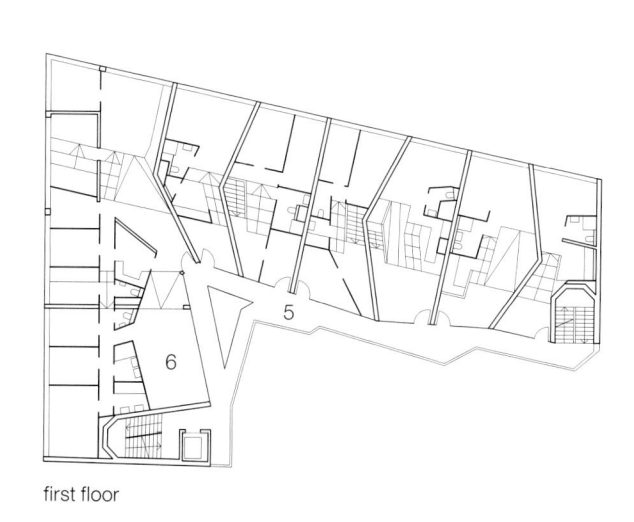

aa bb

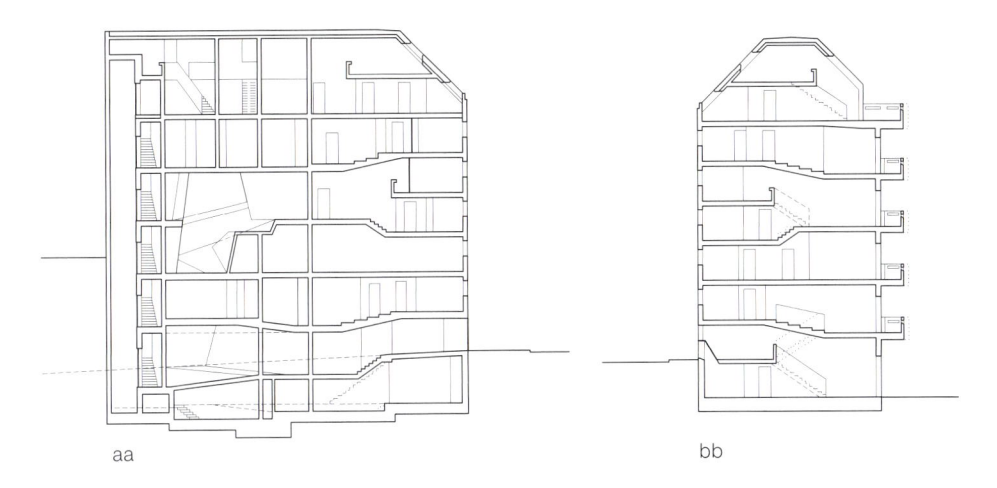

Project Details
Usage: socially integrated living and working places
Units: 35 apartments
(3 wheelchair-friendly)
1 shared accommodation for young people
5 home offices
Access: access balconies
Internal room height: up to 4.1 m ground floor
2.26–3.12 m upper floors
Construction type: reinforced concrete
Total internal volume: 11,166.06 m³
Total floor area: 4,371 m²
Residential area: 2,820 m²
Communal area: 220 m²
Total site area: 850 m²
Covered site area: 607.6 m²
Construction cost: 3.8 million Euros
Funding: Verein für integrative Lebensgestaltung
Heating consumption: 32.84 kWh/m²a
Construction time: 1999–2000

site plan
scale 1:4000
floor plans · sections
scale 1:500

1 entrance
2 home office
3 club room
4 garage
5 access balcony
6 shared accommodation for 8
7 communal kitchen
8 laundry
9 wheelchair-friendly apartment

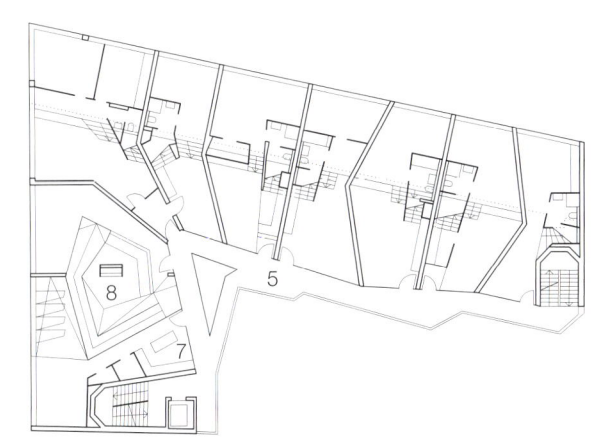

third floor

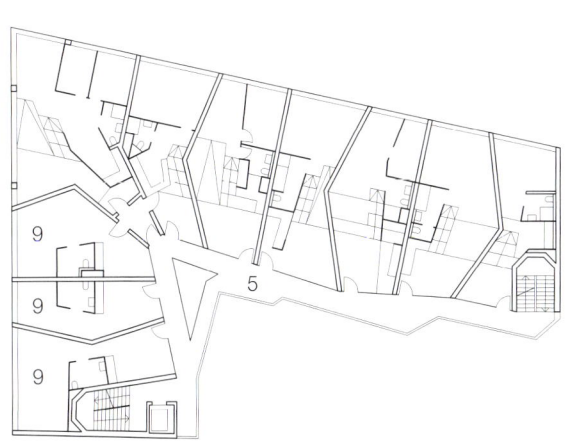

fourth floor

27

vertical section   scale 1:20

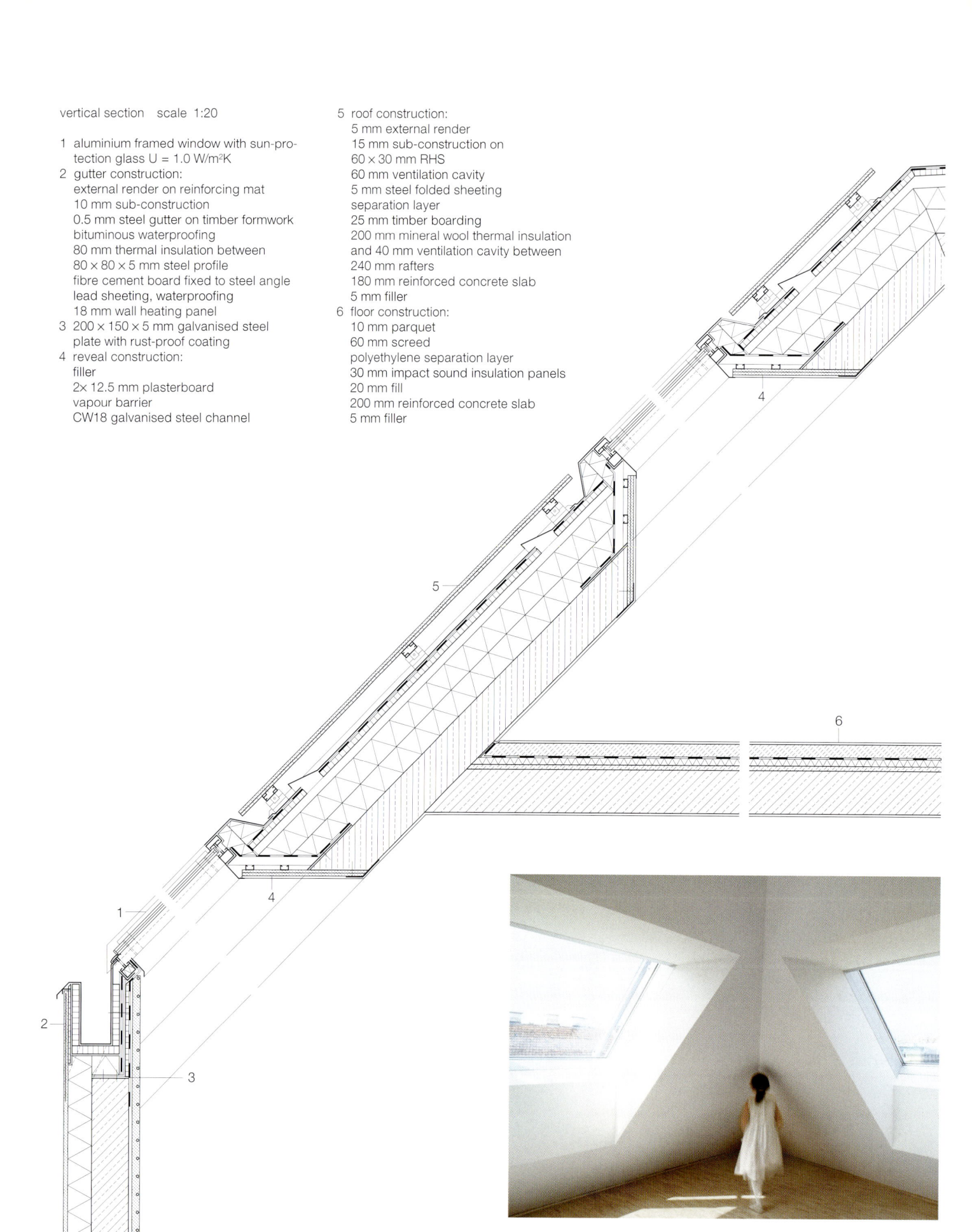

1 aluminium framed window with sun-protection glass U = 1.0 W/m²K
2 gutter construction:
   external render on reinforcing mat
   10 mm sub-construction
   0.5 mm steel gutter on timber formwork
   bituminous waterproofing
   80 mm thermal insulation between
   80 × 80 × 5 mm steel profile
   fibre cement board fixed to steel angle
   lead sheeting, waterproofing
   18 mm wall heating panel
3 200 × 150 × 5 mm galvanised steel plate with rust-proof coating
4 reveal construction:
   filler
   2× 12.5 mm plasterboard
   vapour barrier
   CW18 galvanised steel channel
5 roof construction:
   5 mm external render
   15 mm sub-construction on
   60 × 30 mm RHS
   60 mm ventilation cavity
   5 mm steel folded sheeting
   separation layer
   25 mm timber boarding
   200 mm mineral wool thermal insulation
   and 40 mm ventilation cavity between
   240 mm rafters
   180 mm reinforced concrete slab
   5 mm filler
6 floor construction:
   10 mm parquet
   60 mm screed
   polyethylene separation layer
   30 mm impact sound insulation panels
   20 mm fill
   200 mm reinforced concrete slab
   5 mm filler

4

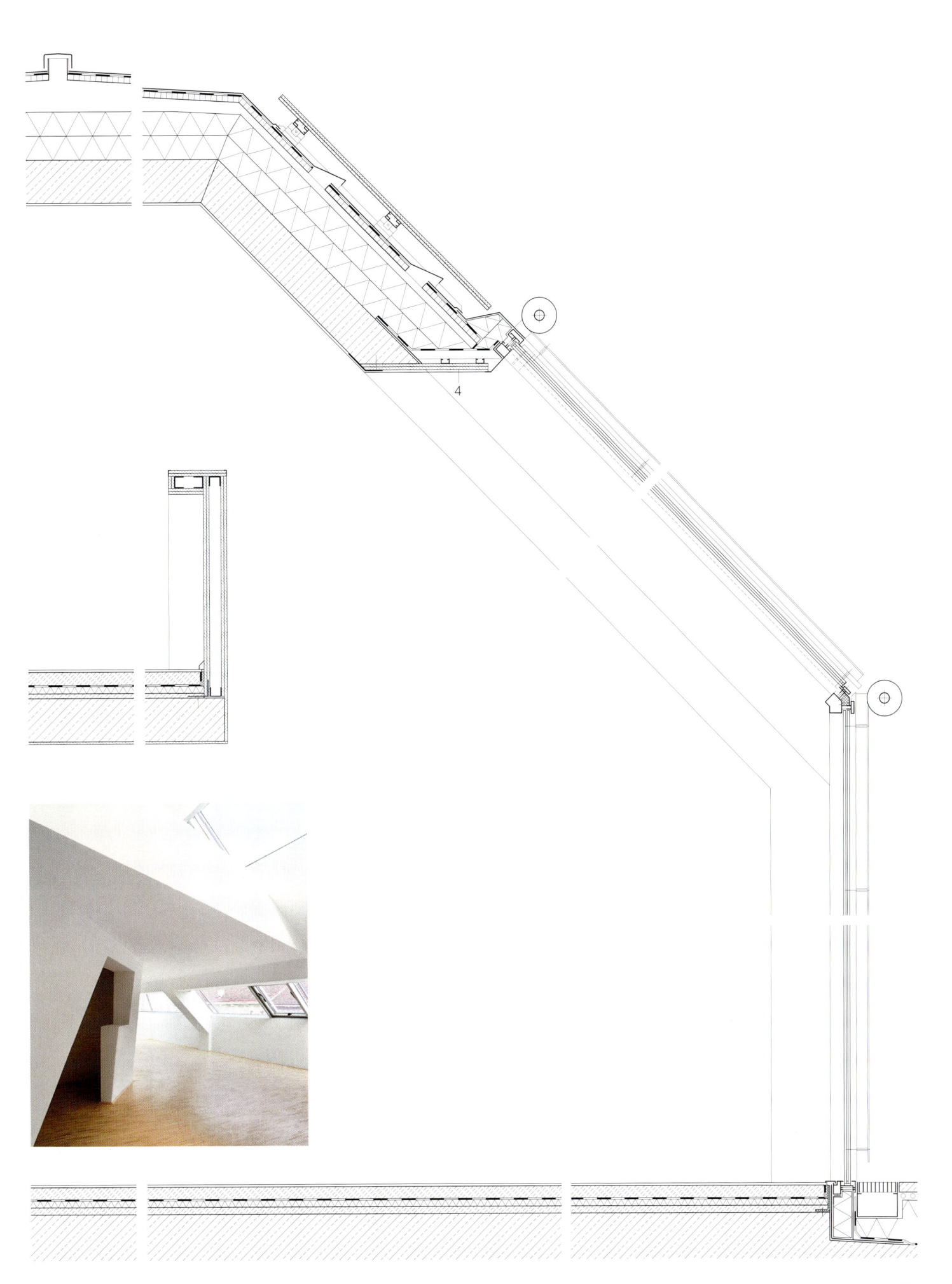

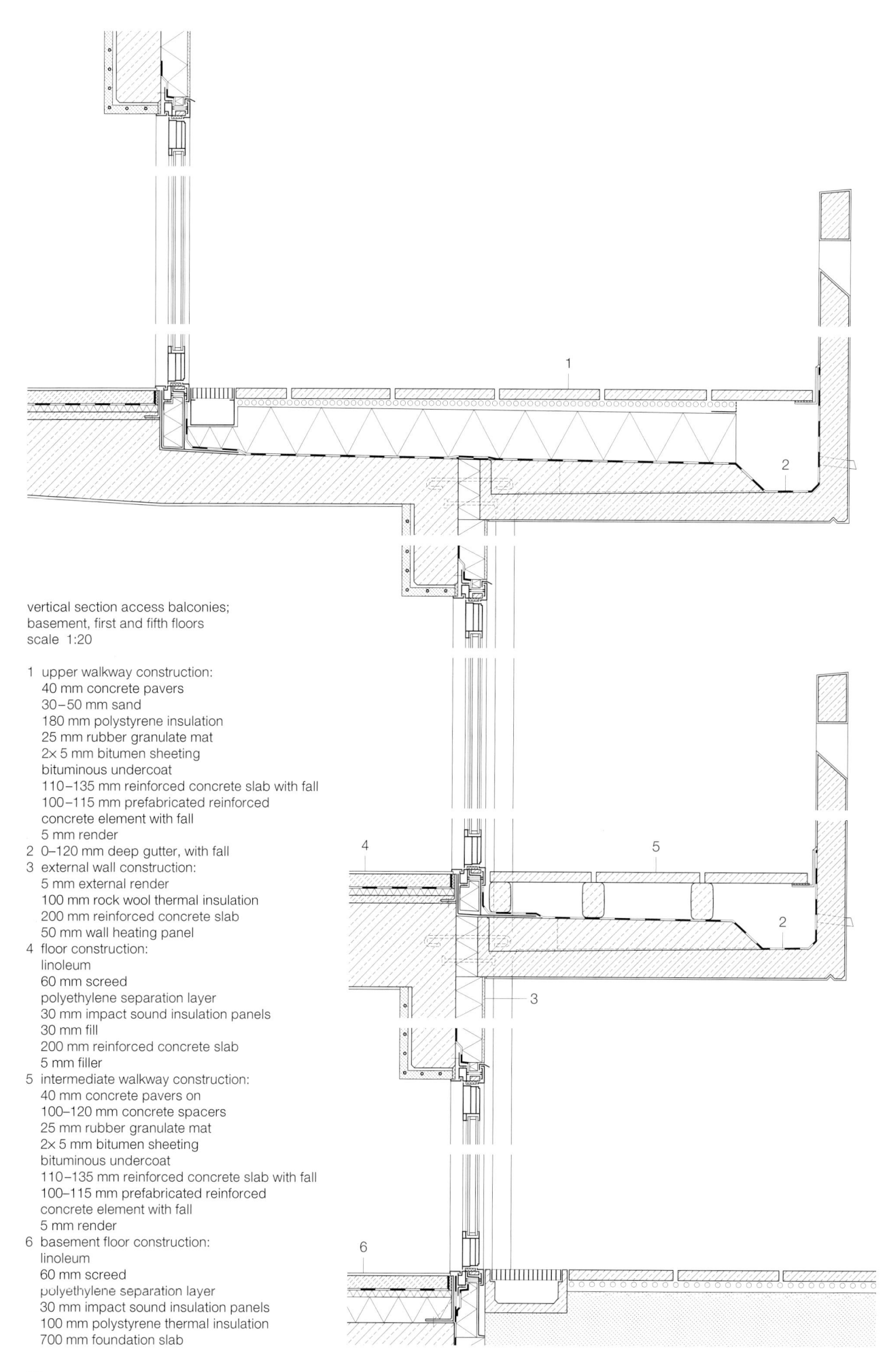

vertical section access balconies;
basement, first and fifth floors
scale 1:20

1 upper walkway construction:
 40 mm concrete pavers
 30–50 mm sand
 180 mm polystyrene insulation
 25 mm rubber granulate mat
 2× 5 mm bitumen sheeting
 bituminous undercoat
 110–135 mm reinforced concrete slab with fall
 100–115 mm prefabricated reinforced
 concrete element with fall
 5 mm render
2 0–120 mm deep gutter, with fall
3 external wall construction:
 5 mm external render
 100 mm rock wool thermal insulation
 200 mm reinforced concrete slab
 50 mm wall heating panel
4 floor construction:
 linoleum
 60 mm screed
 polyethylene separation layer
 30 mm impact sound insulation panels
 30 mm fill
 200 mm reinforced concrete slab
 5 mm filler
5 intermediate walkway construction:
 40 mm concrete pavers on
 100–120 mm concrete spacers
 25 mm rubber granulate mat
 2× 5 mm bitumen sheeting
 bituminous undercoat
 110–135 mm reinforced concrete slab with fall
 100–115 mm prefabricated reinforced
 concrete element with fall
 5 mm render
6 basement floor construction:
 linoleum
 60 mm screed
 polyethylene separation layer
 30 mm impact sound insulation panels
 100 mm polystyrene thermal insulation
 700 mm foundation slab

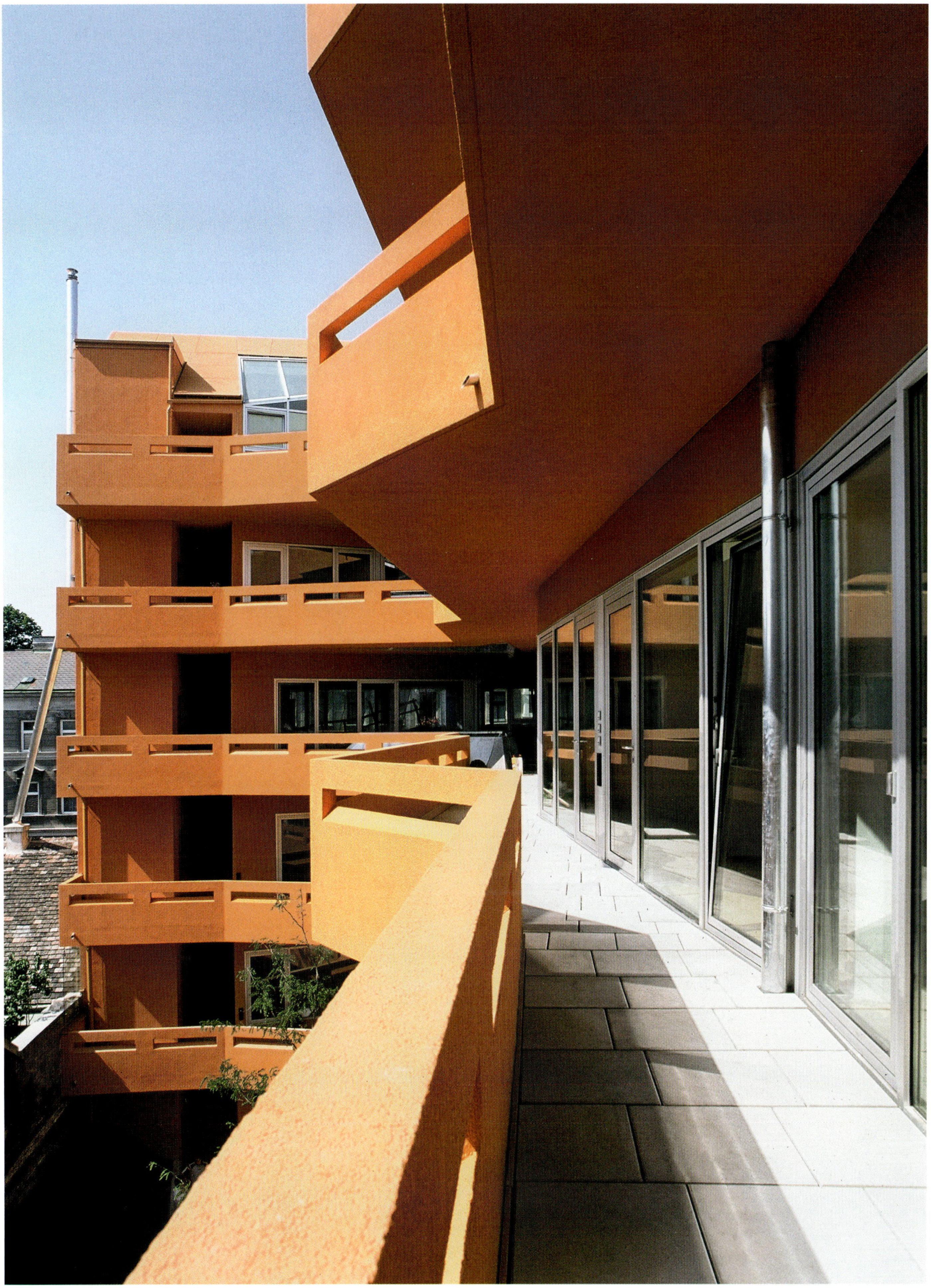

Multi-generational House in Stuttgart

Architects: Kohlhoff & Kohlhoff, Stuttgart

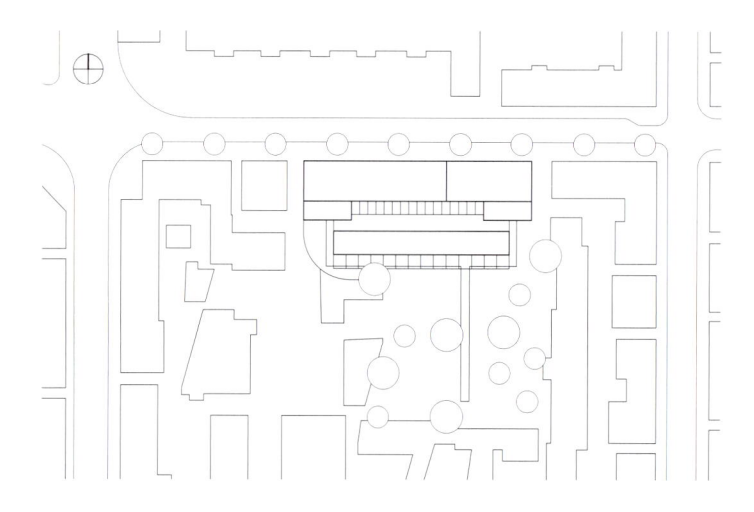

Increasing residential urban density
District and communication centre
Child care centre for 120 children
Assisted accommodation for seniors

This elongated five storey construction can be found in one of Stuttgart's most densely populated western districts. A publicly accessible green zone is concealed within this peripheral development in the midst of the urban environment. Apart from an advisory centre and a public café, a child care centre and apartments for seniors have been incorporated into this scheme, with the goal of enhancing interaction between the various user groups and counteracting social isolation. Thus a new district centre was created combining a multitude of different uses.

Social communication centre

Marking the entrance to the multi-generational house is a so called "city loggia", while a glazed portico leads into the open foyer. From the foyer there are visual connections with both the upper levels and the garden; thus revealing the transparency and complexity of the building. In addition to which all thresholds and fittings are designed to be suitable for both children and disabled users.
The public zones; café, advisory centre, and event spaces, are all located on the ground floor.

The first floor, which is accessed via a generously proportioned ramp, is given over to the child care centre which caters to 120 children. The rooms of the nine two-storey children's units build the southern, projecting tract of the complex. Each unit benefits from the full width balcony which provides direct access into the garden.

Apartments for seniors

The remaining storeys accommodate the living units for seniors which are sheltered from traffic noise by the protecting access balconies erected to the north. Each unit is designed for two residents; with separate entrance, foyer, bathroom and living space. The shared kitchen with dining area and the small south-facing conservatory are located between the two private bedrooms.

Construction

The range of uses accommodated within the building is reflected by the material selection and facade treatment. The residential tract is of massive construction, predominantly exposed concrete and glass; the walls of the access balconies and stairwells are emphasised in red while the external walls are clad in clinker face brickwork. The child day care centre is constructed of timber framework and also internally fitted out in timber.

Project Details
Usage: advisory centre, day care centre, assisted accommodation
Units: 10 shared living units for seniors 90 m²
Access: central corridor, access balconies
Internal room height: 2.5 m
Construction type: reinforced concrete, timber-frame
Total internal volume: 20,000 m³
Total floor area: 5,200 m²
Usable floor area: 4,200 m²
Total site area: 3,900 m²
Construction cost: 8.5 million Euros
Funding: Financial foundation
Construction time: 1999–2001

aa

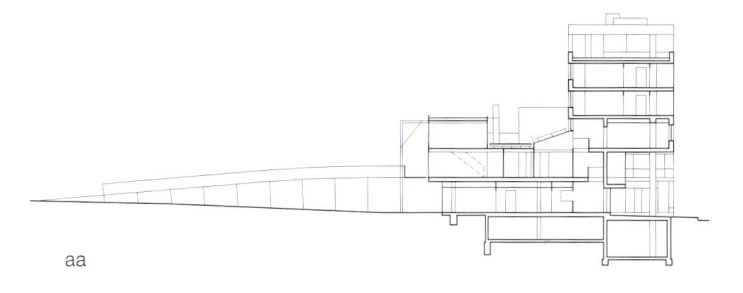

site plan
scale 1:2500
section · floor plans
scale 1:750

A ground floor
B first floor
C second floor
D third floor

1 foyer
2 info-bar
3 cafeteria
4 kitchen
5 gymnastic room
6 service office
7 day care unit
8 sleeping room
9 roof terrace
10 group room
11 senior living unit

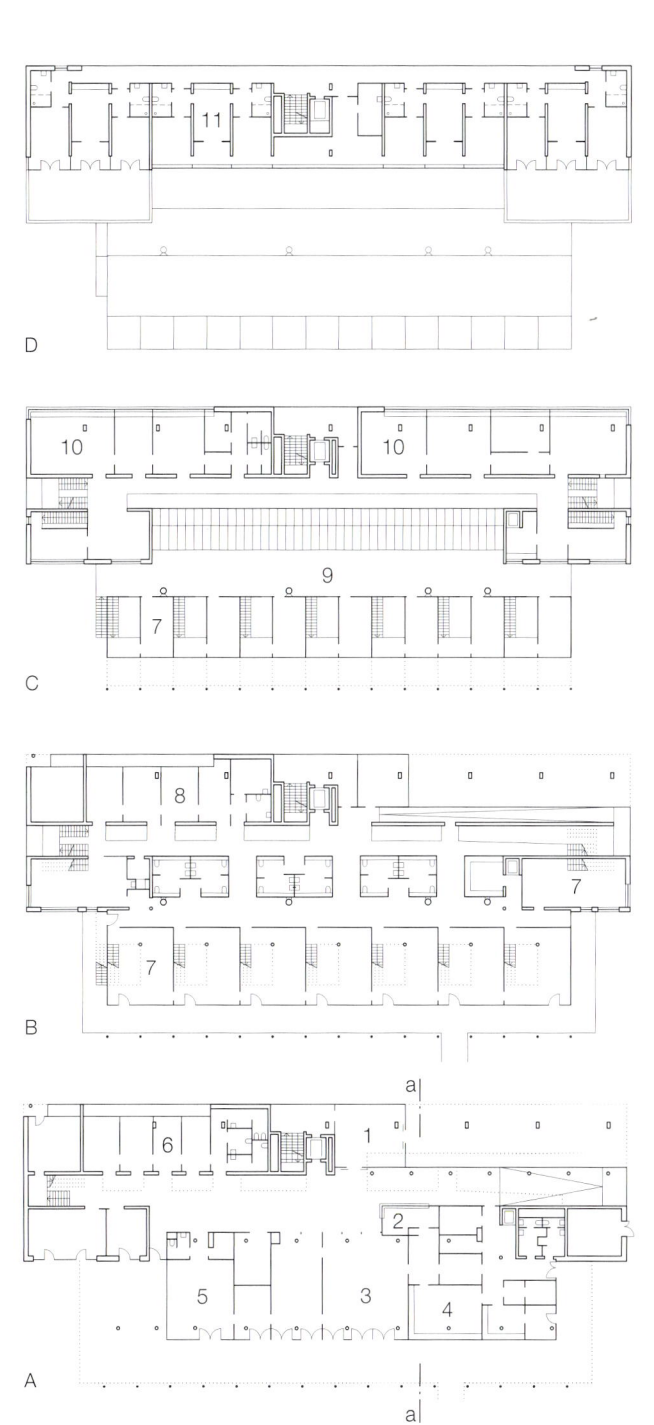

senior living unit floor plan
scale 1:200

1 access balcony
2 entrance
3 bathroom
4 living room
5 kitchen
6 conservatory

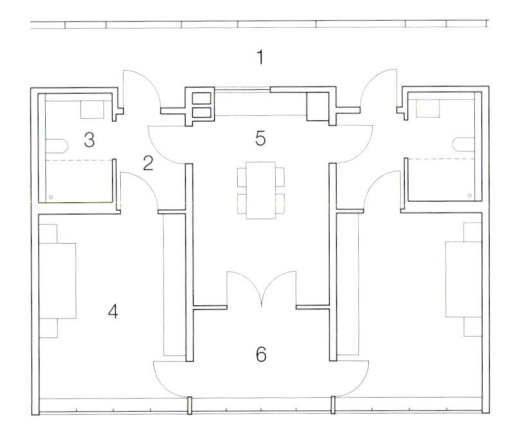

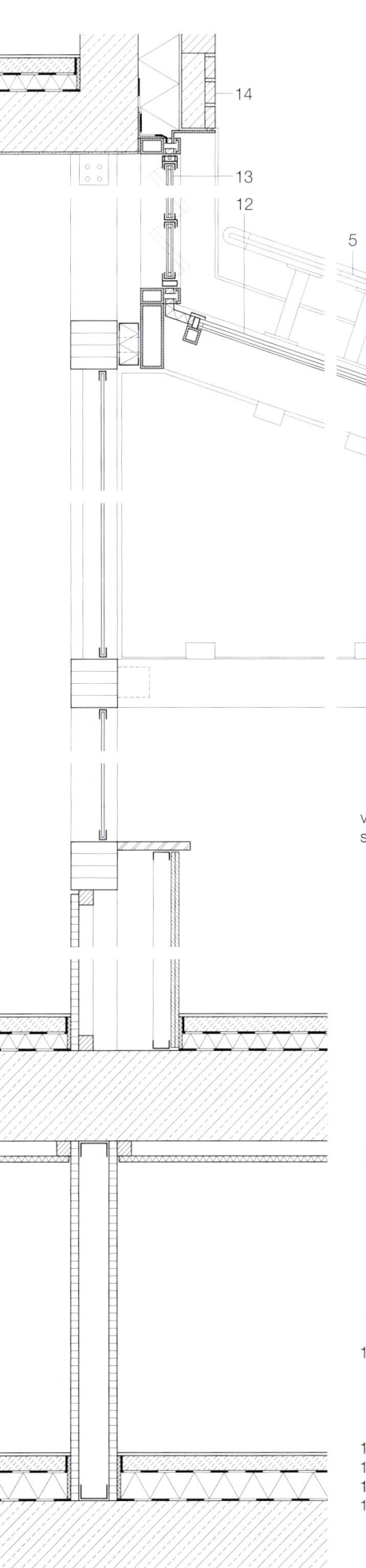

vertical section
scale 1:20

1 roof construction:
  89 × 38 mm Douglas pine planks
  scantling on metal substructure
  10 mm rubber granulate matting
  double layer bituminous membrane
  thermal insulation, with fall
  bituminous vapour barrier
  bituminous separation layer
  36 mm particle board, 50 mm battens
  25 mm timber-wool acoustic panel
  200 × 240 mm laminated timber rafter
2 Ø 114 mm galvanised steel downpipe
3 100 mm steel I-beam
4 120 mm steel I-beam
5 sun shade guide rail
6 rear building wall construction:
  24 mm red cedar cladding
  35 mm battens, 35 mm counter battens
  diffusion-pervious membrane
  thermal insulation between
  140 mm timber-frame wall
  vapour barrier, 20 mm plywood
7 timber window with double glazing
8 metal grid
9 89 × 38 mm Douglas pine plank
10 floor construction:
  10 mm linoleum, 30 mm dry screed
  polyethylene separation layer
  50 mm impact sound insulation
  PE vapour barrier, 300 mm r.c. slab
11 60 × 10 mm steel RHS climbing protection
12 double glazing
13 ventilation louvers
14 wall construction:
  115 mm clinker face brickwork
  10 mm ventilation cavity, 140 mm insulation
  200 mm reinforced concrete element

34

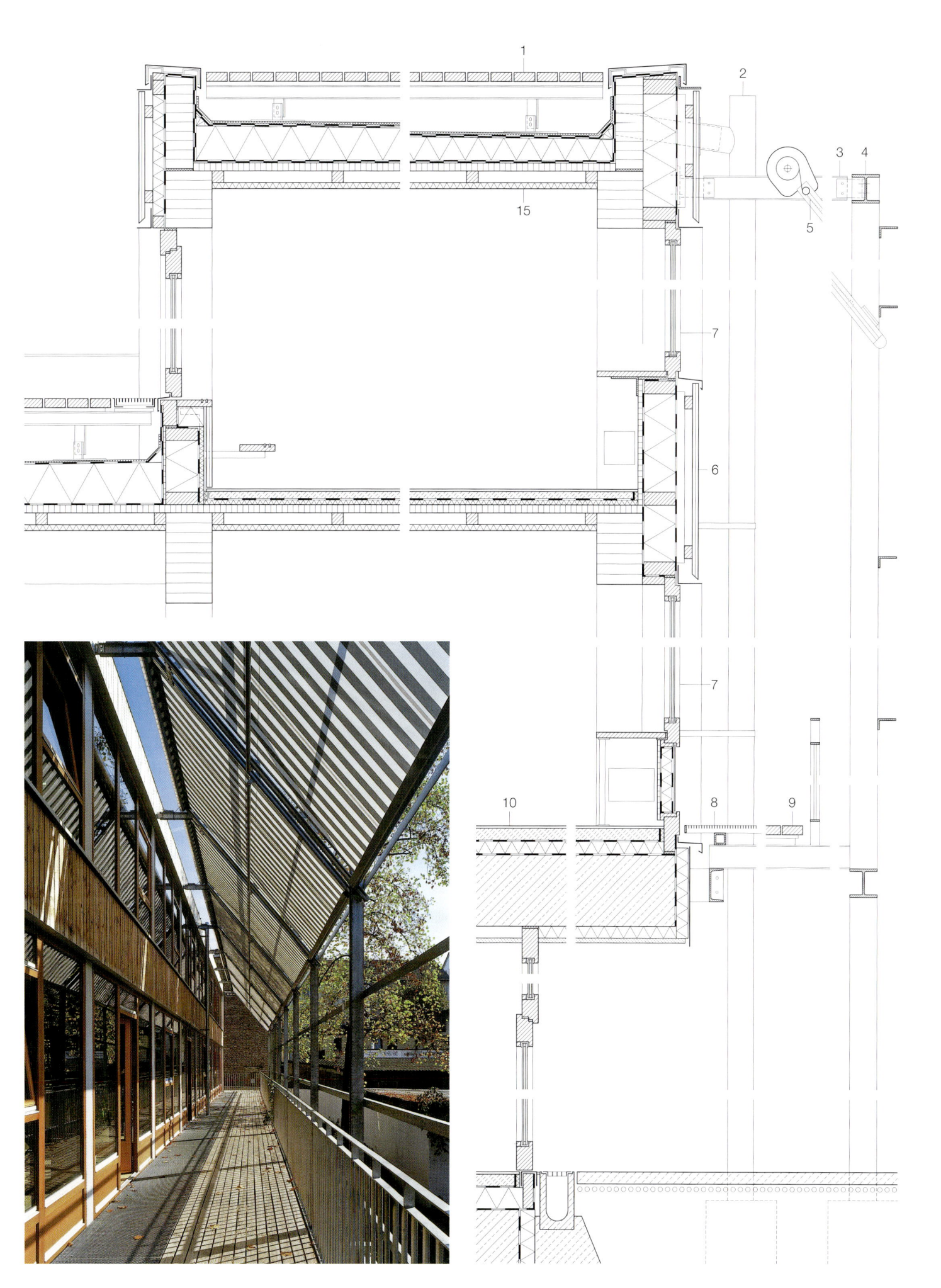

35

Multi-generational Housing in Vienna

Architects: Franziska Ullmann and Peter Ebner, Vienna

District centre with public facilities
30 assisted-living dwellings
12 mini-lofts for temporary accommodation

"We are taking our parents with us", is the motto of this multi-generational housing development in southern Vienna. Taking on the role of a district centre, it has a tightly-woven structure of shops, medical practices and various dwelling types for all generations.

Urban environment
With their urban framework of five to seven storey high peripheral constructions, the architects have reconciled the opposite street frontage of high-rise constructions from the 1970s and a public park to the South. Dual office constructions facing the busy thoroughfare shelter the residential constructions behind. The five storey multi-generational building is set back from the street, creating a public open plaza which indicates the commencement of the urban district. Various businesses front onto the plaza providing residents with their daily needs, while the café enhances and animates the square. A semi-private courtyard is encompassed by the development. Open stairwells punctuate the corners of the development, creating views and providing through drafts. The residential alternatives; single storey apartments, maisonettes, assisted living for the elderly and short-term mini-lofts, all face the lively internal courtyard space and are accessed by open walkways.

Mini-lofts with customised fittings
The first floor is constructed with greater internal ceiling heights than standard, 3.15 metres, in order to accommodate the technical requirements of the medical practices in the western wing of the development. In the opposite wing this situation also benefits the mini-lofts which are designed to provide temporary accommodation for students or relatives caring for other residents. Although the areas of the lofts are restricted, specifically designed, built-in furniture optimises and rationalises the spaces. The kitchen unit is set on a 72 cm high timber platform, the side walls of which also function as shelving, and below which the bed – including bedding – is slid during the daytime. From the elevated position of the platform the residents have generous views through the large-format glazing into the surroundings and via a skylight in the bathroom, to the walkway.

Assisted living
The dwellings are organised in pairs in the upper levels, the access walkways create timber-clad bays which accommodate the kitchens. Small corner windows provide views out into the interconnecting walkway. Private niches shelter the entry doorways and 45 cm wide metal grids create psychological screens in front of the windows. The actual layouts of the apartments are open in structure, allowing even bed-ridden residents to take part in daily life. It is also possible for residents to take advantage of the in-house Red Cross care services, when necessary.

Project Details	
Usage:	shops, café, offices, medical practices, apartments
Units:	30 assisted living apartments (51.46 m²)
	12 mini-lofts (31.39 m²)
	6 maisonettes (98.65 m²)
	26 2-room apartments (54.72 m²)
	13 3-room apartments (78.81 m²)
Access:	access walkways
Internal room height:	3.65 ground floor
	3.15 m first floor
	2.76 m second-fifth floors
Construction type:	reinforced concrete
Total internal volume:	34,312 m³
Total floor area:	2,040 m²
Residential area:	4,905 m²
Total site area:	6,000 m²
Construction cost:	800 Euros/m² usable area (excl. basements)
Construction time:	1998–2001

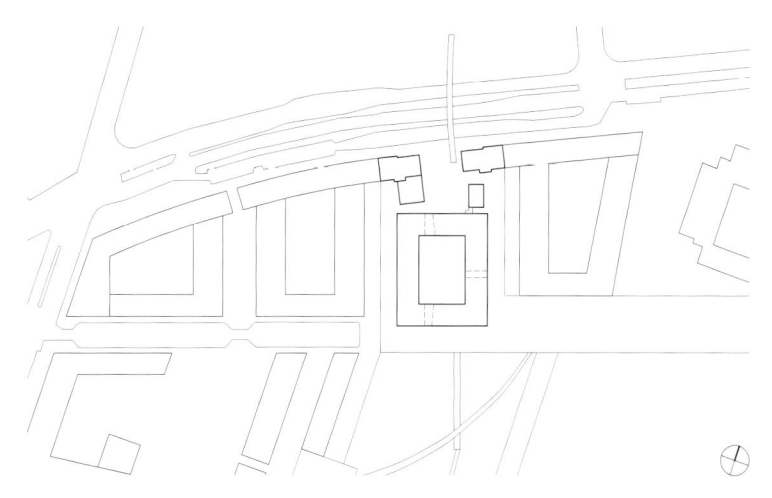

site plan
scale 1:4000

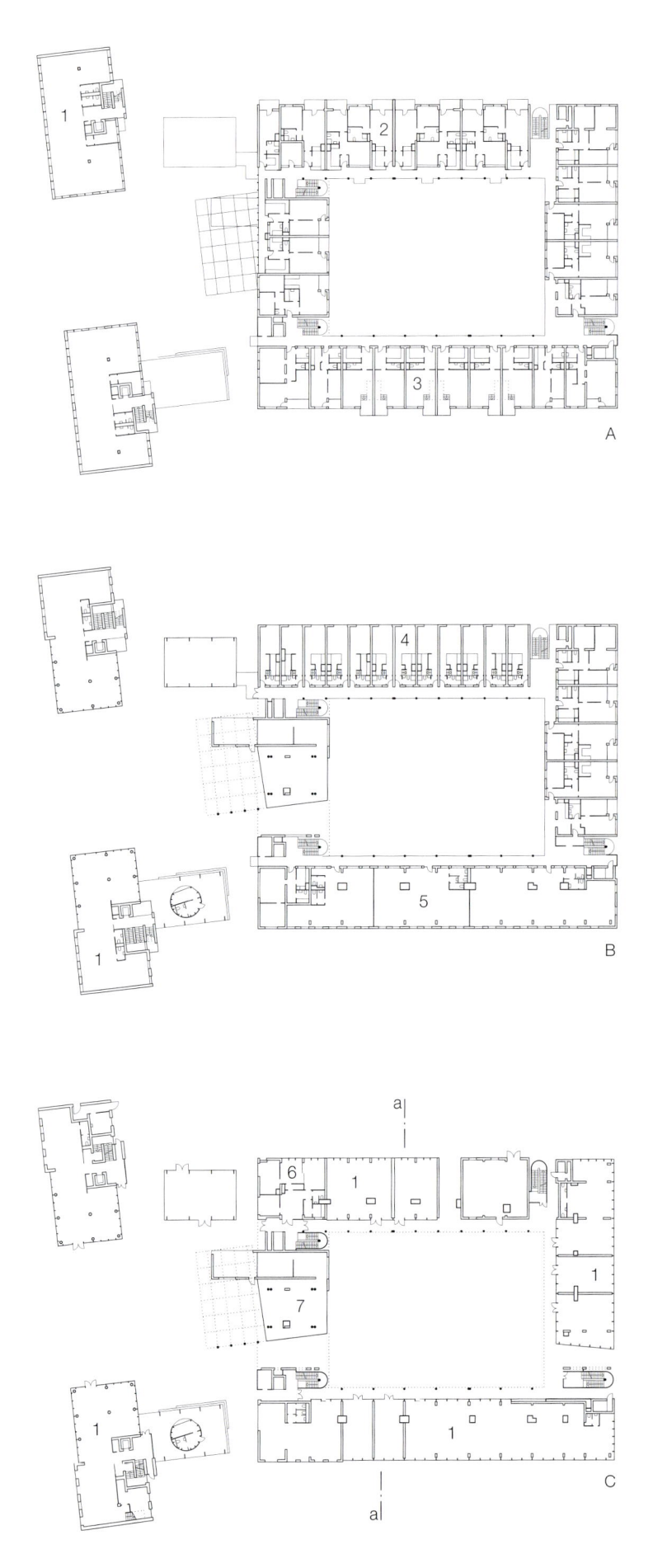

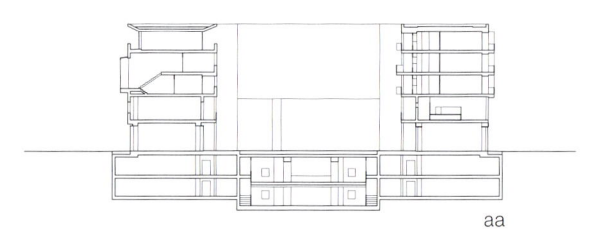

A

B

aa

C

floor plans · section
scale 1:1000
floor plans apartments
scale 1:200
A ground floor
B first floor
C second floor

1 office first floor/shop ground floor
2 assisted living apartment
3 family maisonette
4 temporary apartment
5 medical practice
6 Red Cross care station
7 café

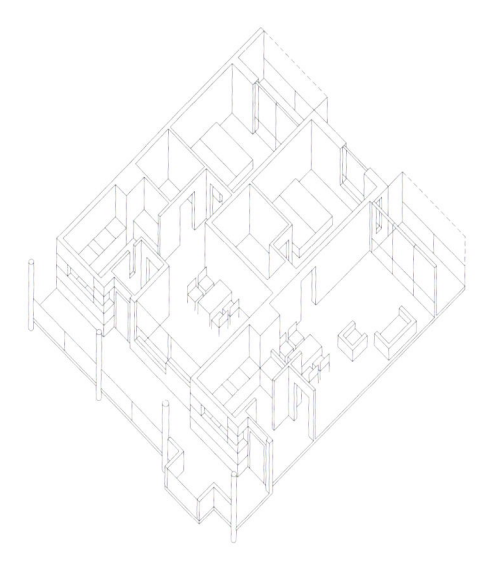

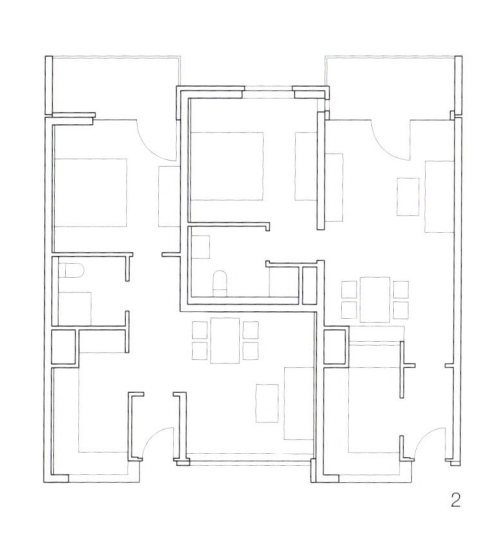

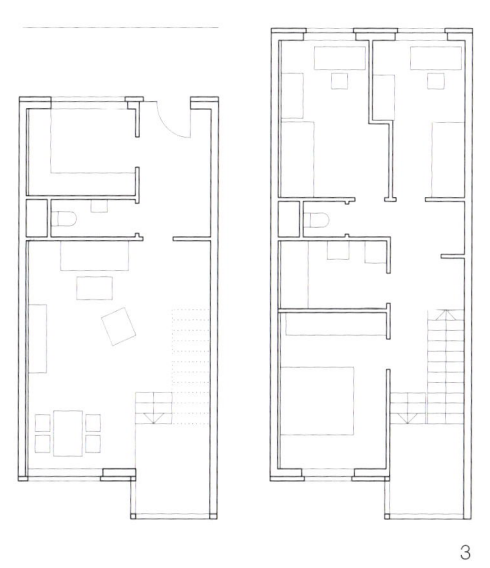

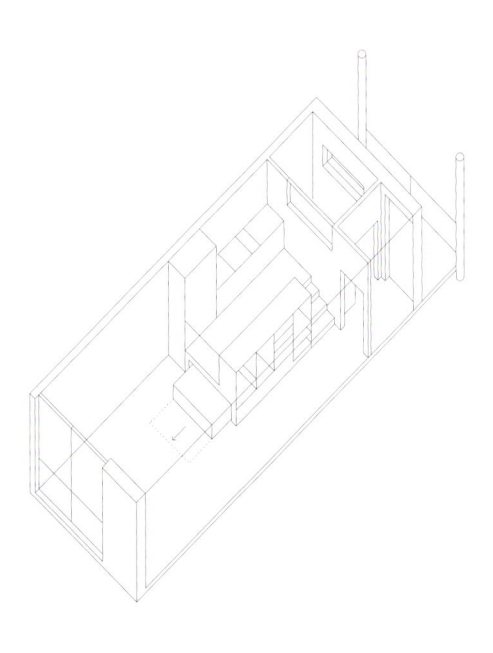

Isometric mini-loft
floor plan alternatives built-in furniture
scale 1:200

section access walkway/kitchenette
scale 1:20

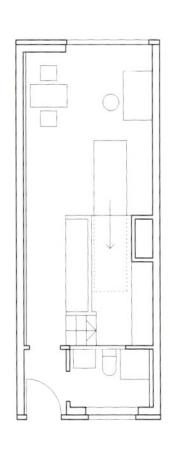

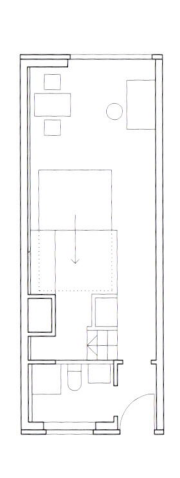

4

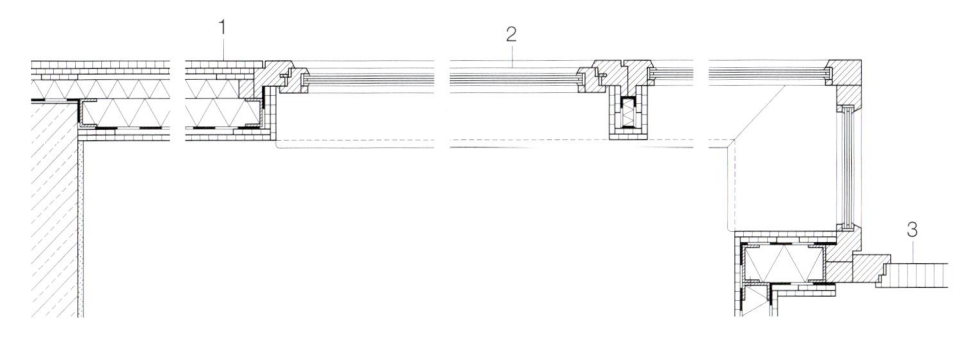

1 wall construction:
  20 mm waterproof birch particleboard
  15 mm calcium silicate board
  15 mm calcium silicate strips
  50 mm mineral fibre thermal insulation between
  50 × 40 mm timber battens
  75 mm mineral fibre thermal insulation between
  40 × 75 mm steel channels
  vapour barrier
  15 mm calcium silicate strips
  15 mm calcium silicate board
2 insulating glass in timber frame
3 entry door
4 double-layer synthetic membrane
5 stainless steel drip
6 floor construction kitchen:
  18 mm parquet, 55 mm screed
  vapour barrier
  30 mm impact sound insulation
  25 mm levelling course
  200 mm reinforced concrete slab
7 15 mm cement fibreboard
8 access walkway:
  190 mm pre-fabricated r.c. element

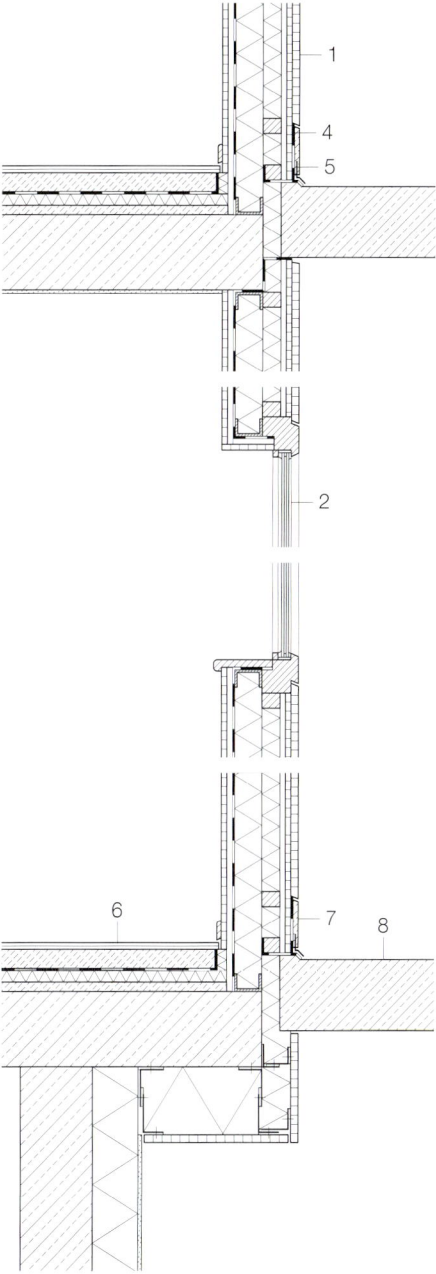

Apartment Building in Vienna

Architects: PPAG Architects, Vienna

Project Details
Usage: single storey apartments
Units: 32 apartments
2 to 4-room apartments (60.9–103.1 m²)
temporary shared accommodation for teenagers
4 1-room apartments (10.7–21.1 m²)
Development type: 5 unit layouts
Internal room height: 2.5 m
Construction type: reinforced concrete and brickwork
Total internal volume: 13,419 m³
Total floor area: 4567 m²
Total residential area: 2,655 m²
Total site area: 942 m²
Construction cost: 3.16 million Euros
Heating consumption: 32.4 kWh/m²a
Construction time: 2003–2006

Social housing with integrated shared accommodation for teenagers
Window variations based on standard modules

Located within the 20th district of Vienna, this apartment building is surrounded by municipal buildings with flat, punctuated facades dating from the post-war era. The construction completes the north-western corner of the peripheral development and creates an intimate internal courtyard. A vibrant, animated impression is created by the variations in the window sizes which are spread rhythmically, yet staggered, across the facades. Projections and recessions, in addition to the set back loggias, articulate the volumes. The pigmented silicate render shimmers through colour nuances from silver to dark grey according to the quality of the light.

Access

The glazed entrance to the north-east allows views from the street into the generously dimensioned foyer. The individual apartments, which are arranged five per storey, are accessed via the centrally located stairwell, while variations in the colour treatment of the levels simplify orientation within the eight storey building. The loggias, which are located to the side of the living rooms, have glazed rear walls providing natural illumination to the corridors. These resultant ventilation and light wells interconnect the different storeys and provide visual links.

In order to strengthen the individuality of the apartments the locations of the windows, in relation to both the apartments and the facades, vary. This results in differing illumination patterns within, and diverse views from the apartments.
The 32 single-storey apartments vary in size from two to four-room layouts. Generous entry areas accommodate enough space for ample storage. Bedrooms, bathrooms and WCs form core units within the apartments. The living rooms, with associated loggias, are orientated towards either the internal courtyard or the roadway. A communal roof terrace has been provided for the benefit of all residents.

Temporary shared accommodation for teenagers
A 206 m² maisonette apartment, with independent access, has been incorporated on the north-eastern side of the building. This apartment is intended to provide temporary accommodation for eight teenagers up to the age of 15 years.
The city council of Vienna has decided to reduce the number of larger homes for children and youths, in favour of more smaller shared accommodation facilities. These facilities are to be spread across the city, thereby allowing the children to remain in their familiar surroundings. The bedrooms each accommodate two young people, while the communal kitchen and dining area remains the focal point of the dwelling. The adjacent courtyard with private access provides an area of relaxation and communication for all residents.

floor plans · section
scale 1:500

A ground floor
B first floor
C standard floor

1 access to shared accommodation
2 communal room
3 room
4 access to apartments
5 passage
6 internal courtyard
7 apartment
8 ventilation well
9 loggia

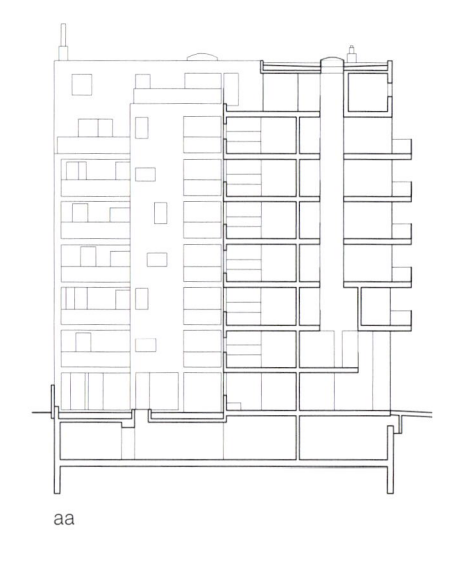

aa

A B C

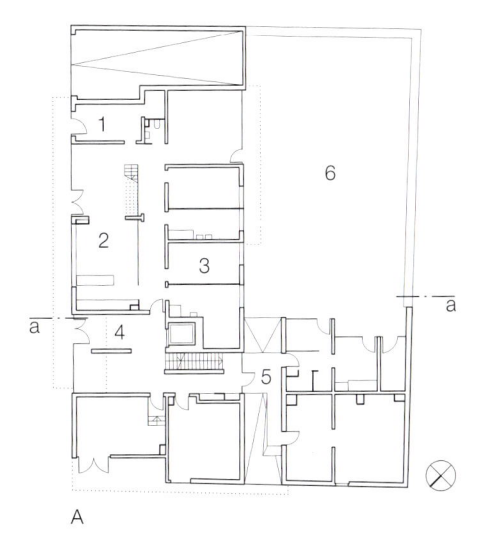

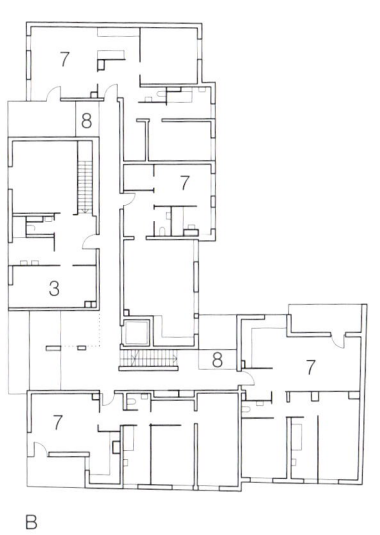

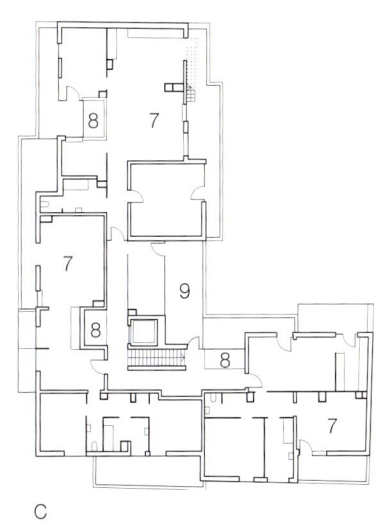

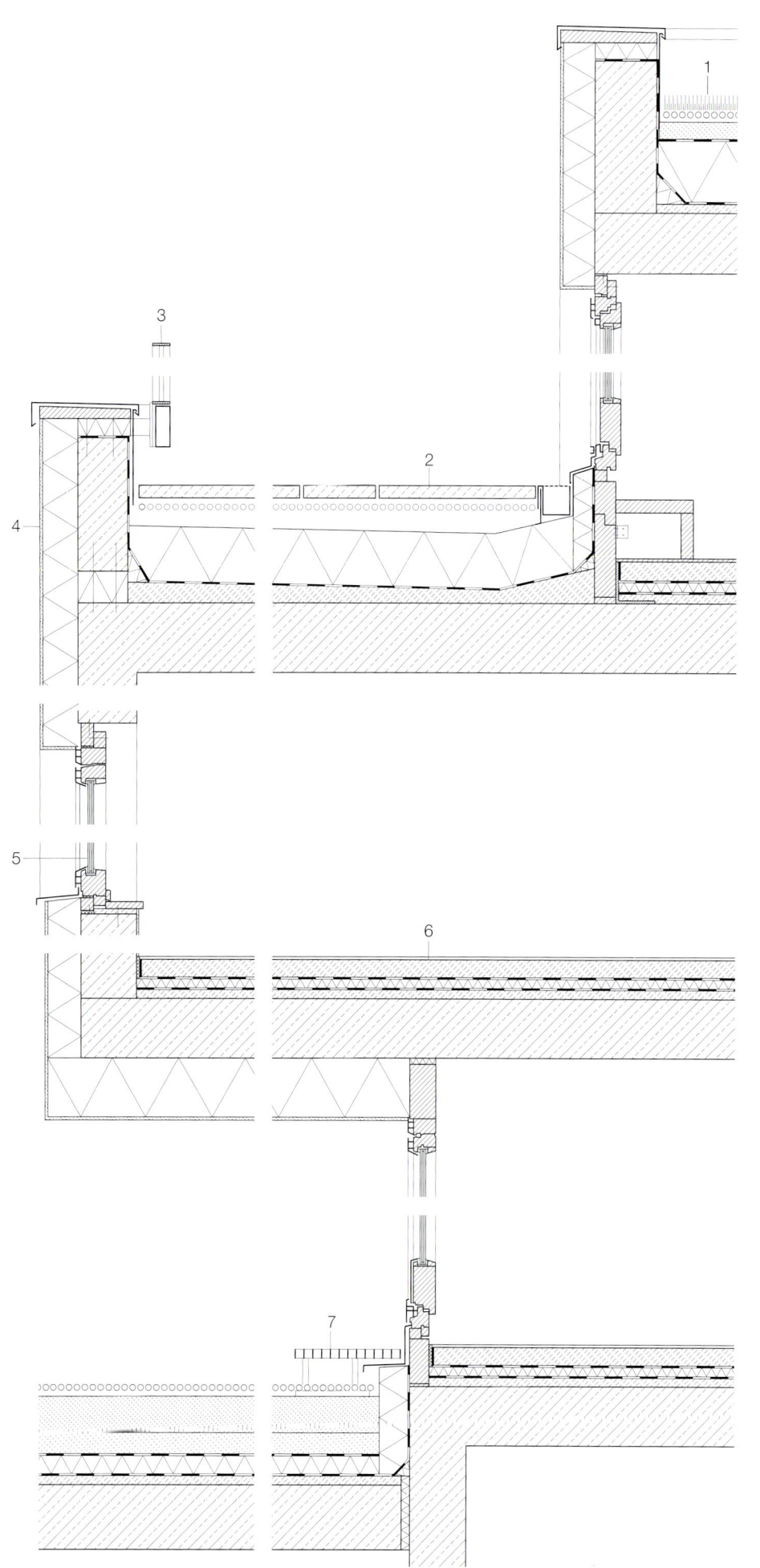

vertical section
scale 1:20

1 roof construction:
   100 mm vegetation layer
   filter matting, 10 mm drainage layer
   separation layer
   root protection layer
   20 mm triple-layer bituminous membrane
   200 mm thermal insulation
   10 mm vapour barrier
   10 mm moisture equalising layer
   30 mm min. concrete, with fall
   200 mm reinforced concrete slab
2 roof terrace construction:
   40 mm washed concrete pavers
   30 mm gravel bed, fibre matting
   180 mm thermal insulation
   20 mm triple-layer bituminous membrane
   30 mm min. concrete, with fall
   200 mm reinforced concrete slab
3 balustrade: 4 mm steel flat
4 composite thermal insulation system:
   12 mm silicate render with
   transparent glitter top-coat
   120 mm mineral fibre thermal insulation
   200 mm reinforced concrete
5 floor construction:
   2.5 mm carpet
   60 mm cement screed
   separation layer
   30 mm impact sound insulation
   vapour barrier
   37 mm fill
   200 mm reinforced concrete slab
6 double glazing
7 concrete pavers

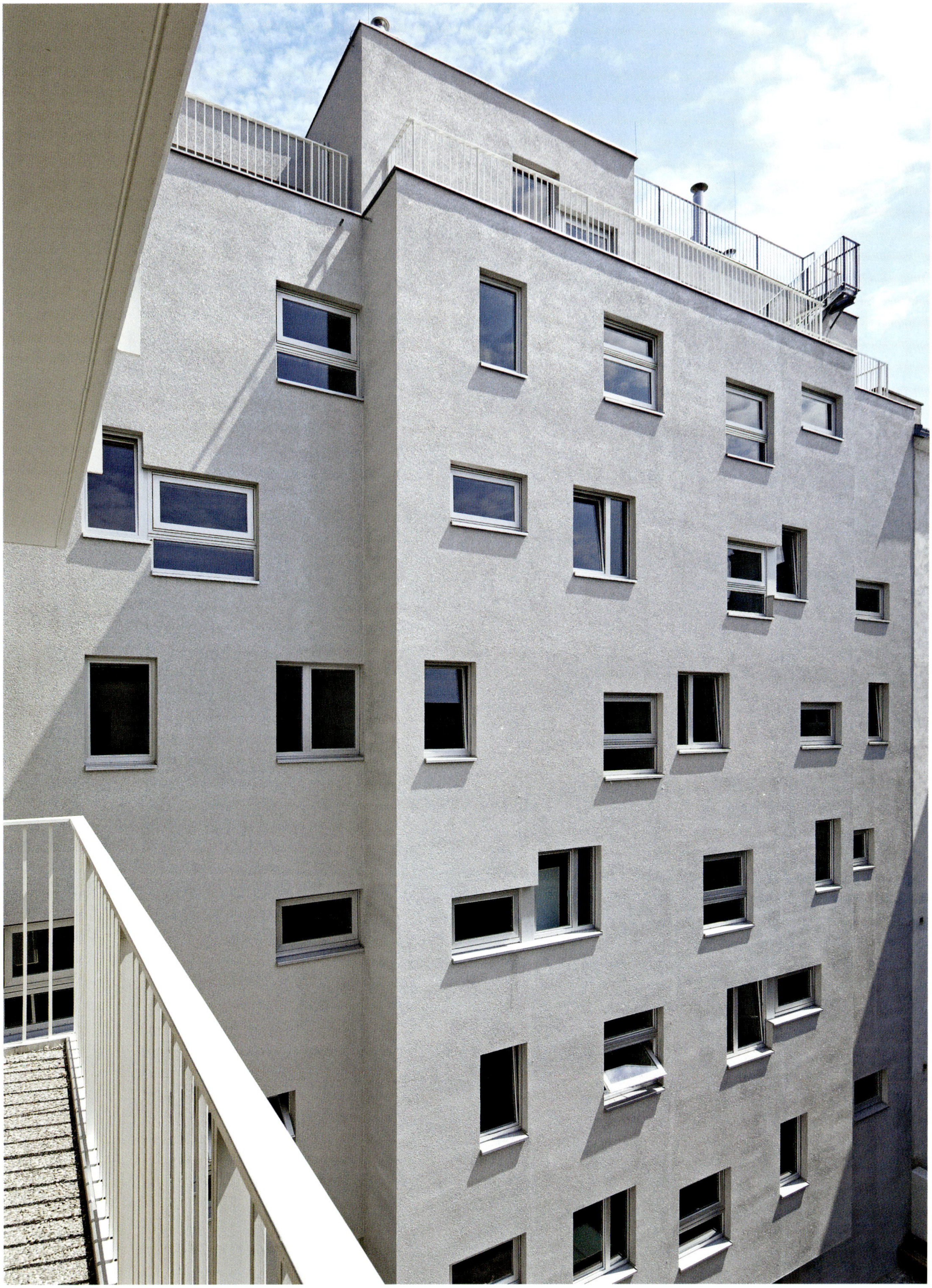

Renovation of a Department Store in Eschweiler

Architects: BeL, Cologne

Barrier-free living in former department store
Function room, retail, gastronomy
Communal roof terrace
Shared accommodation for seniors
Internal courtyard for each apartment

The original department store was constructed in Eschweiler in 1899. After being destroyed in the Second World War, its reconstruction on the same site was conducted by the architect Hellmuth Müller. The design of the four-storey department store, reminiscent of the formal language of similar buildings by Erich Mendelsohn, is based upon a reinforced concrete skeleton with an open-plan layout. The most noticeable feature of the building is the rounded corner.

User concept
The four storeys of the building have each been allocated different uses. The ground floor is still available for retail usage, while the first floor has been given over to a so-called "urban living" function room; a recreational space with gastronomic facilities for the use of both residents and the public intended to encourage communication and interaction. The second and third floors are the residential storeys; a total of eight apartments benefit from the open floor plans, 3.6-metre-high ceilings and the 35 metre long south-facing facade. The residents are older people who wish to transfer their lives to a more urban environment and still enjoy the advantages of barrier-free living. The building offers lift access and wide corridors, the dimensions of which have been determined by wheelchair turning circles in both the dwellings and the corridors. All rooms within the apartments are designed to be threshold-free, the doorways are one metre wide and the generously-sized bathrooms are fitted with floor-gullies for the showers. Independent living is thus an achievable goal.

Individual living and community
Free-standing sanitary cells and sliding, rotating wall partitions subdivide the floor plans in such a way as to leave the historical structural system undamaged and unspoiled. Simultaneously, planning flexibility for changes in future usage is retained. The usage of the second floor is reserved for one wheelchair-friendly apartment and a 210 m² shared accommodation facility for six seniors. Five private rooms; four single rooms and one double room each with a private bathroom, are arranged around an 80 m² living area and three internal courtyards.

All apartments benefit from private internal courtyards. With the exception of the corridor wall, where the fire-rated doors to the apartments are incorporated, the courtyards are fully glazed with ceiling-high glass panels and doors in timber frames.

The courtyards are cut into the concrete structure. Not only do the courtyards provide natural daylight and fresh air, but they also allow each resident to develop his or her own private space. These visually protected intermediate zones can either be used as semi-public front gardens or more introverted private patios. In addition to the private outdoor zones the communal roof terrace, measuring almost 100 m², is accessible via both the stairs and lift.

site plan   scale 1:4000
section • floor plans   scale 1:500

A third floor
B second floor
C first floor

1 function room, gastronomy and retail
2 shared accommodation for six seniors
3 wheelchair-friendly apartment
4 apartment for disable user
5 private courtyard
6 communal roof terrace
7 area for retail outlet

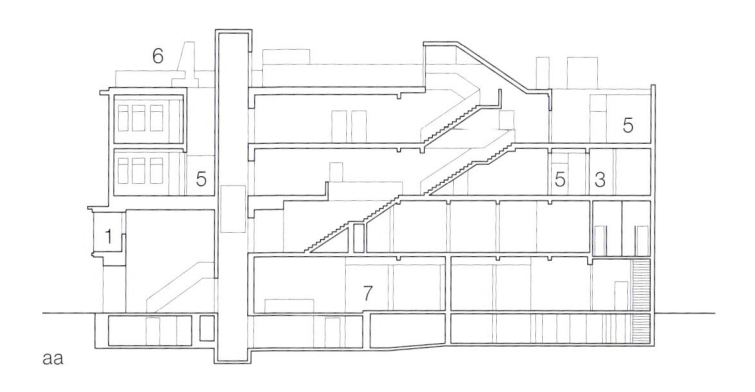

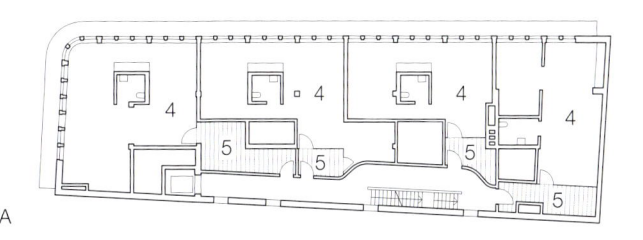

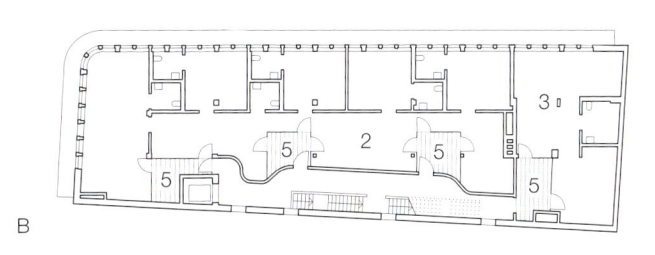

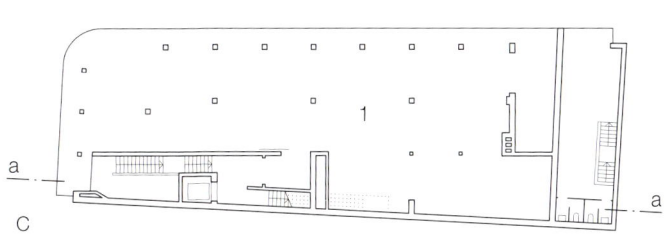

Project Details	
Usage:	retail, barrier-free apartments
Units:	2nd floor: 210 m² + 3 × 8 m² courtyards barrier-free shared accommodation for six residents
	67 m² + 8 m² courtyard, wheelchair-friendly apartment
	3rd floor: 4 apartments 56–78 m² + courtyards 5–15 m², barrier-free
Access:	unit construction
Internal room height:	3.6 m
Construction type:	reinforced concrete skeleton structure
Total internal volume:	7,338 m³
Total floor area:	2,314 m²
Usable floor area:	1,465 m² (1,330 m² internal + 135 m² external); 320 m² shops + 155 m² store/personnel rooms 330 m² function room 525 m² residential + 70 m² courtyards 65 m² roof terrace
Total site area:	442 m²
Construction cost:	1.2 million Euros (incl. tax)
Construction time:	July 2005 – May 2006

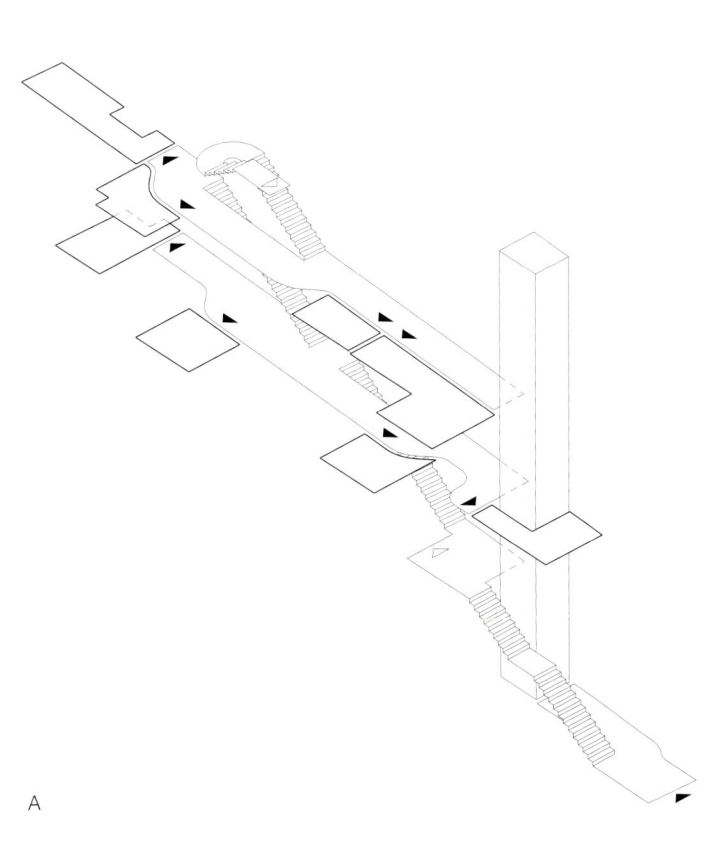

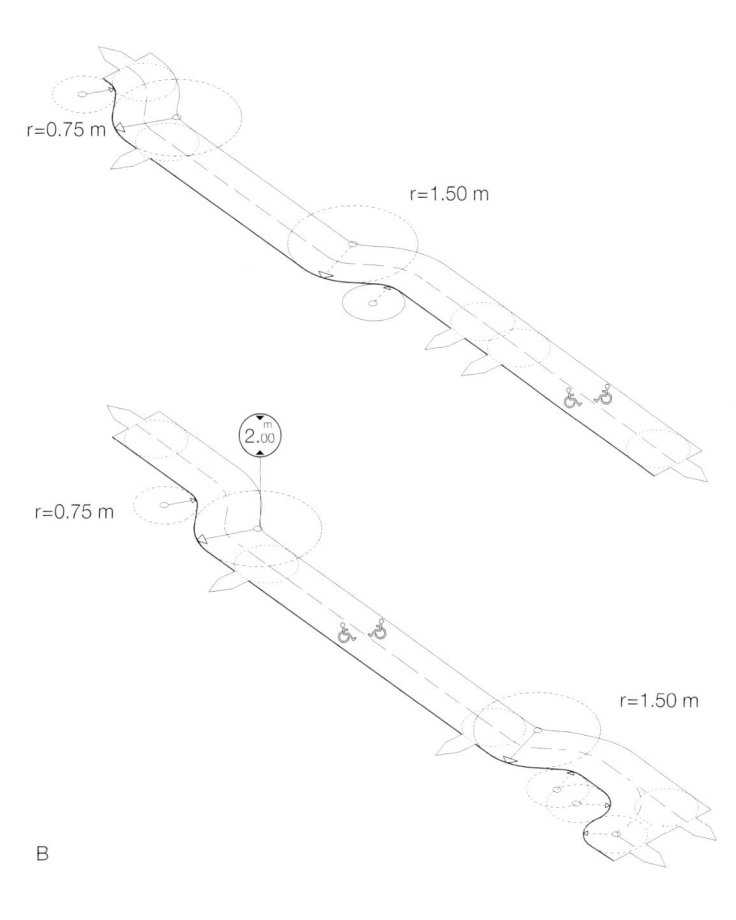

A

B

48

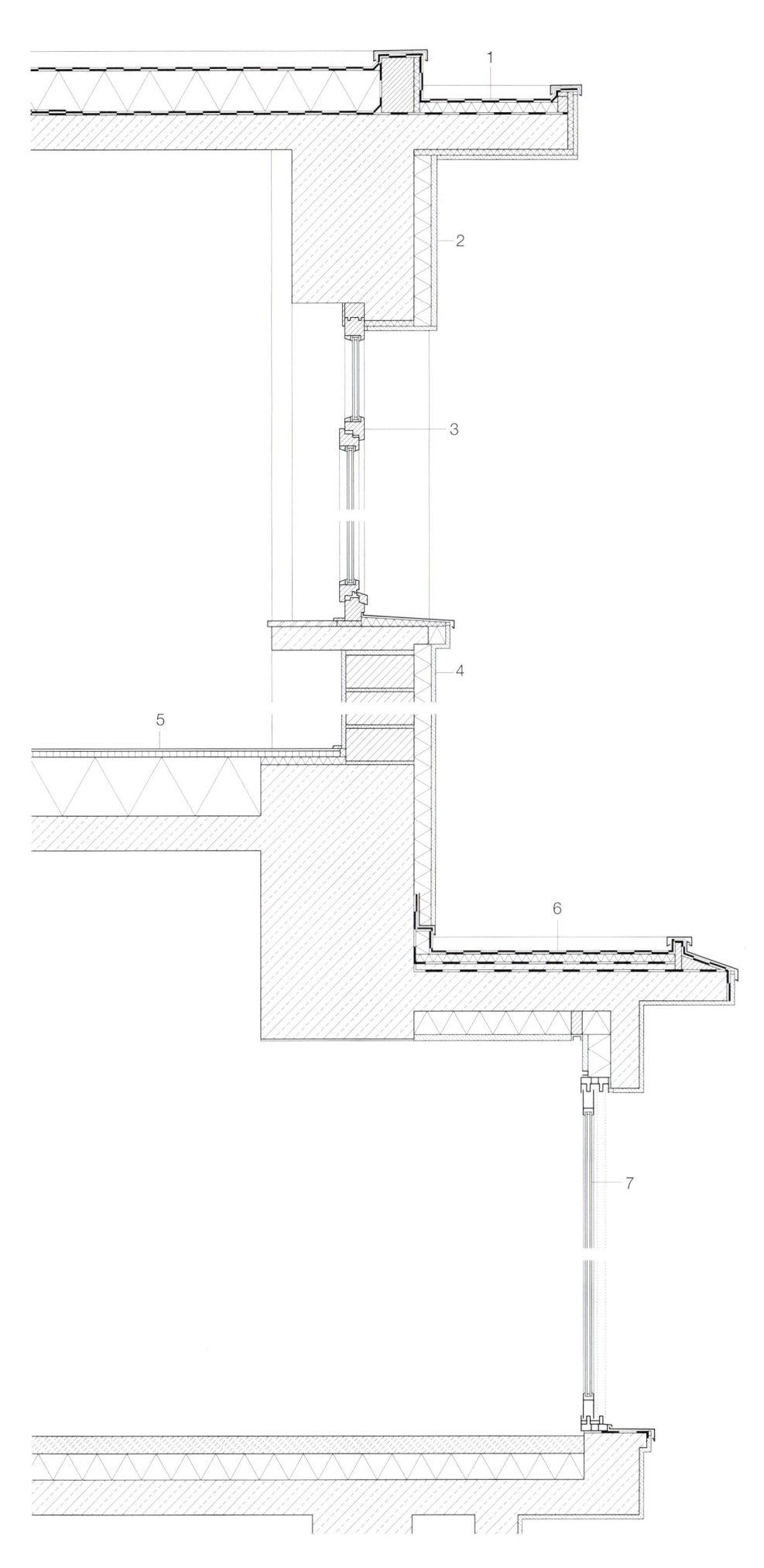

axonometric

A access via a single-flight stair parallel to the firewall and a lift
B access corridor dimensions are determined by wheelchair turning circles:
horizontal layout is influenced by turning circles in apartments and corridors

vertical section
scale 1:20

1 roof construction:
    waterproof membrane
    40 mm rigid foam insulation
    waterproofing, existing
    120 mm reinforced concrete slab, existing
    20 mm EPS insulation
    15 mm external render
2 lintel construction:
    20 mm external render
    60 mm EPS thermal insulation
    430 mm reinforced concrete external wall
3 timber window with sun-shading and double glazing
4 spandrel construction:
    15 mm external render
    60 mm EPS thermal insulation
    240 mm brickwork
    niche for heater
5 floor construction:
    8 mm parquet
    19 mm particle board
    203 mm mineral fibre insulation
    120 mm reinforced concrete slab, existing
6 roof construction:
    waterproof membrane
    30 mm rigid foam insulation
    30 mm screed, with fall
    waterproofing, existing
    130 mm reinforced concrete
    80 mm insulation
    20 mm render
7 sliding window in aluminium frame with sun shading and double glazing

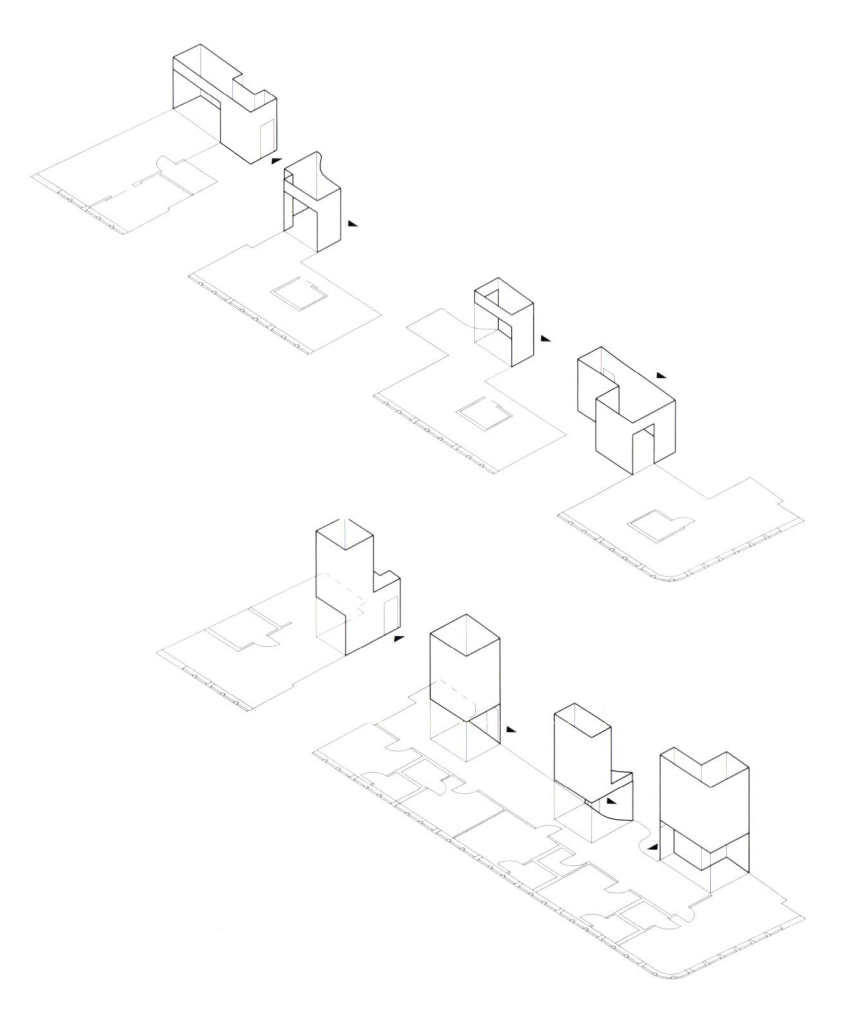

axonometric

Each apartment benefits from a protected, internal courtyard. Access to the apartments is provided from the corridor through the private courtyards. Within the shared accommodation for six seniors on the second floor are three courtyards and thereby three entrances. The courtyards are threshold-free.

detail sections
scale 1:5

1 floor construction corridor:
   60 mm washed terrazzo screed
   170 mm mineral fibre insulation
   120 mm reinforced concrete slab, existing
2 10 mm vapour barrier
3 100 × 120 mm timber block
4 metal flashing
5 courtyard door, steel sheeting
   with recessed weather strip
6 internal courtyard floor construction:
   28 mm Yellow Balau parquet
   60 × 62 mm timber base
   400 × 400 × 4 mm concrete pavers
   concrete levelling course
   protective matting
   roof membrane
   80 mm insulation, with fall
   vapour barrier
   120 mm reinforced concrete slab, existing
7 floor construction apartment:
   8 mm parquet
   19 mm particle board
   203 mm mineral fibre insulation
   120 mm reinforced concrete slab, existing
8 entrance door, timber and glass
9 aluminium threshold

51

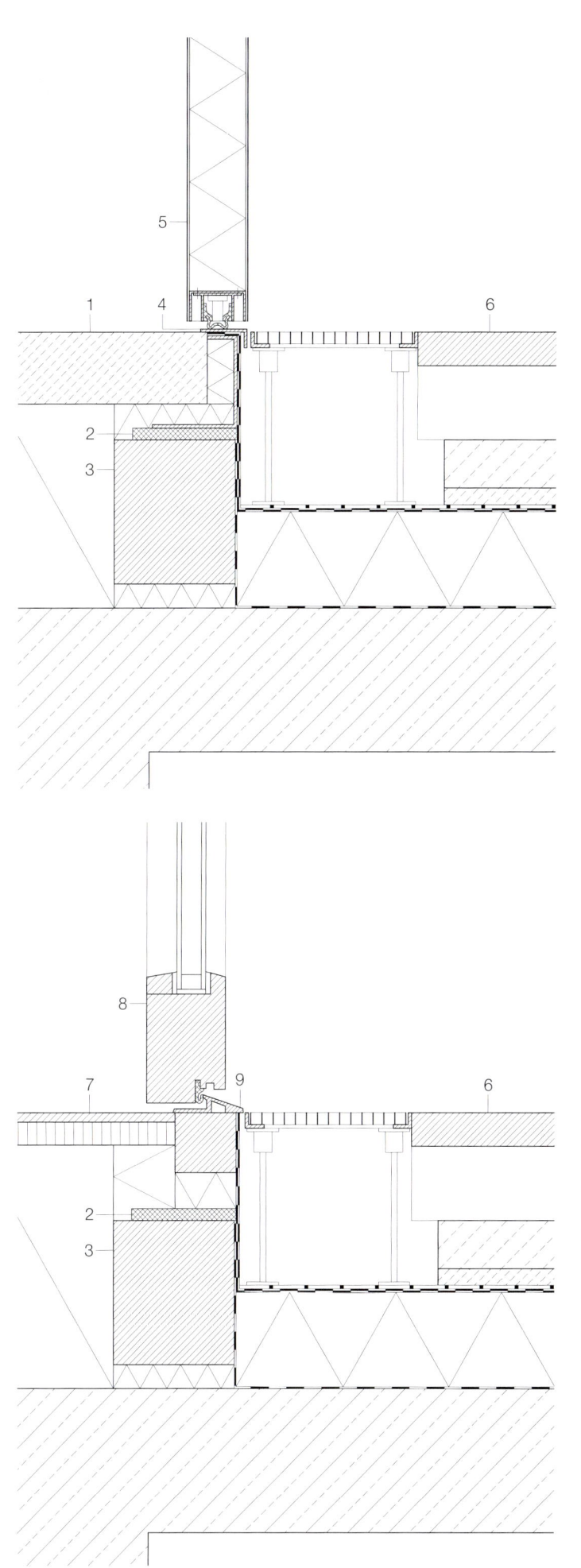

Community Centre in Stuttgart

Architects: Lederer + Ragnarsdóttir + Oei, Stuttgart

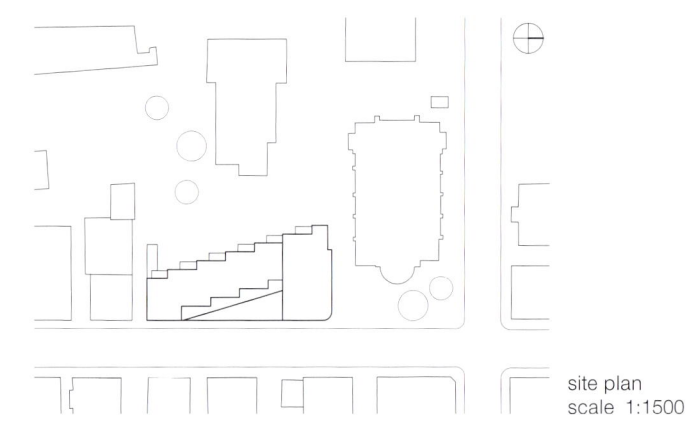

site plan
scale 1:1500

Public usage of ground floor
Barrier-free and wheelchair-friendly dwellings in the upper floors
Temporary accommodation for care personnel

The St. Antonius church with its prominent belfry, built in the early 20th century, and the neighbouring community centre are both highly visible landmarks in the suburb of Zuffenhausen, in Stuttgart. The newly completed community centre accommodates public facilities on the ground floor; community hall, fair-trade shop and the offices of a social welfare centre, while the upper levels are given over to 12 dwellings attuned to the special needs of the elderly.

Urban planning context

The semi-circular form of the church's choir has great impact on the structure of the streetscape and is reflected in the curved stairwell of the community centre to the south. An open plaza connects the two buildings. While the ground floor of the community centre is flush with the north-south roadway, the upper levels are set back from the lower facade and create open angles with the frontage. The coloration of the face brickwork harmonises with that of the church and other large neighbouring buildings. Tantalising views of the church and visual links with the city are created by the sophisticated cubature of the centre. Although the new construction is indeed larger than its secular neighbours it neither dominates nor overwhelms them.

Organisation

Beyond the generously proportioned entrance, the ground floor of the centre is almost entirely given over to the community hall, which opens out to the garden, and the associated foyer. The offices of the welfare centre are linked via a corridor. The vertical connection with the residential storeys, however, is from the vestibule via a double-flight stair, or lift for wheelchair users. From the stairwell residents are led onto two open access balconies. The apartments are located along the lengths of the balconies and stepped back to provide local seating niches which, in addition to various covered areas, provide ample opportunity for interaction and communication between residents and staff. Each storey accommodates one wheelchair-friendly apartment and five barrier-free apartments. The wheelchair-friendly apartments, located immediately opposite the lift, are appropriately fitted out for disabled residents and provide ample space for wheelchair mobility in kitchen and bathroom. Four of the barrier-free apartments follow in progression, their corner kitchen windows allowing views into the access balconies and to the church beyond. Located at the opposite end of each balcony is a barrier-free two-room apartment.
All living spaces open up to the west, with ceiling-high windows and threshold-free doors to the balconies, and benefit from a semi-private green zone.
A permanent apartment for the caretaker and another for temporary use by either residents' guests or care personnel are incorporated into the third upper level.

Project Details
Usage: community hall, social welfare centre, fair-trade shop and apartments
Units: 2 1-room wheelchair-friendly apartments (48 m^2)
8 1-room barrier-free apartments (43 m^2)
2 2-room barrier-free apartments (52 m^2)
1 caretaker apartment (95 m^2)
1 apartment for care personnel (32 m^2)
Access: access balconies
Internal room height: 2.8 m ground floor
2.45 m upper floors
Construction type: reinforced concrete
Total internal volume: 5,986 m^3
Usable floor area: 1,177 m^2
Total site area: 3,980 m^2
Construction cost: 2.65 million Euros
Funding: church funding
Construction time: 1999–2001

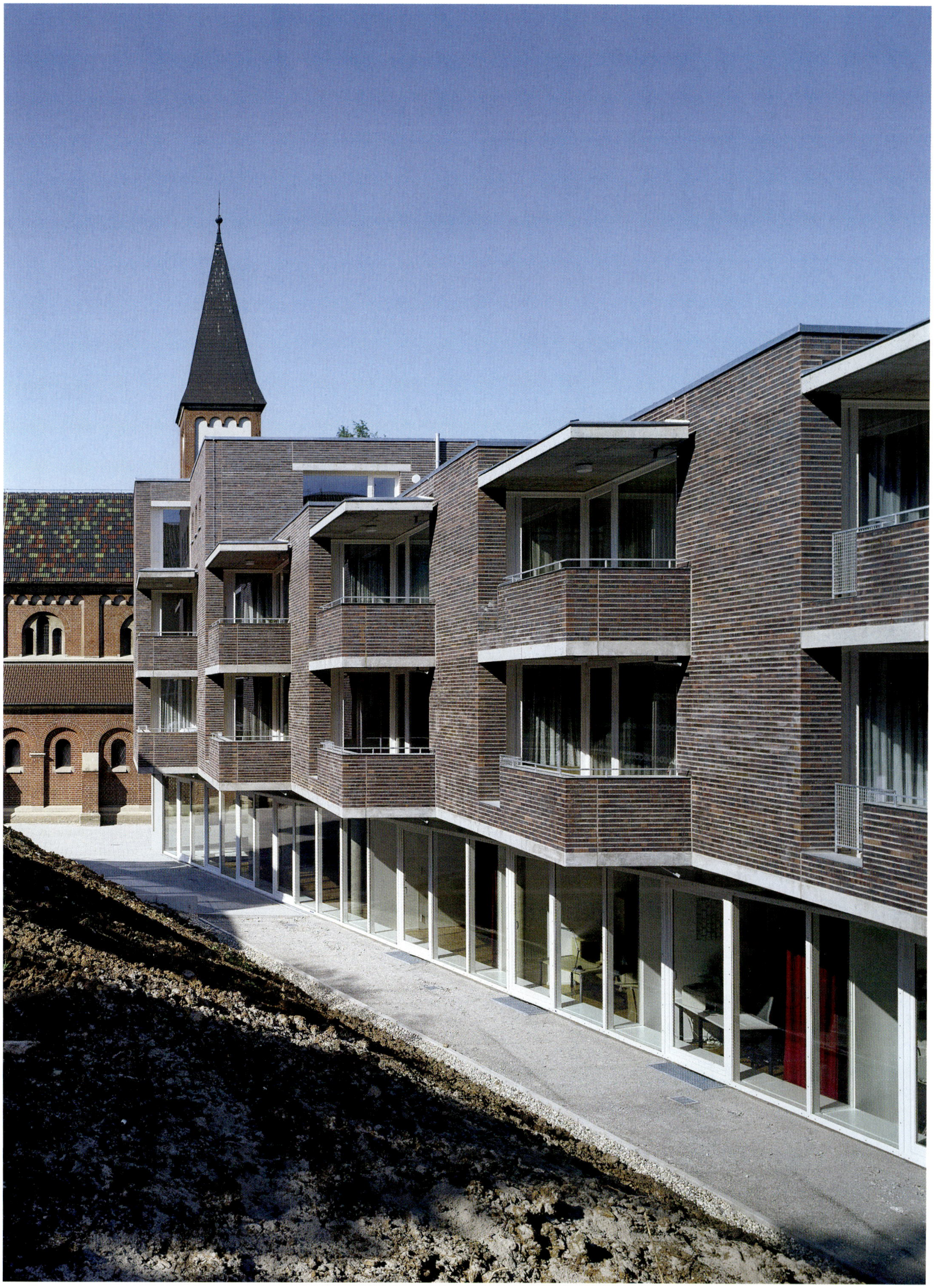

sections   floor plans
scale 1:400

1 community hall
2 social welfare centre
3 wheelchair-friendly apartment
4 1-room barrier-free apartment
5 2-room barrier-free apartment
6 caretaker apartment
7 apartment for care personnel

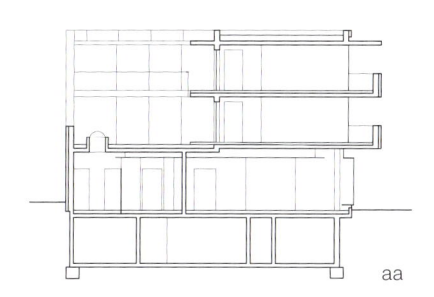

aa

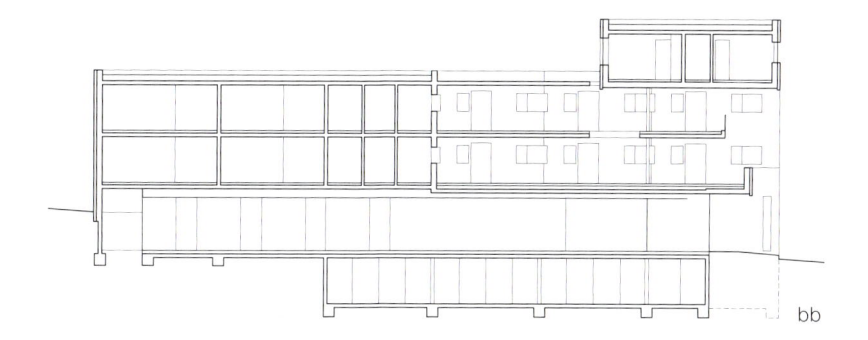

bb

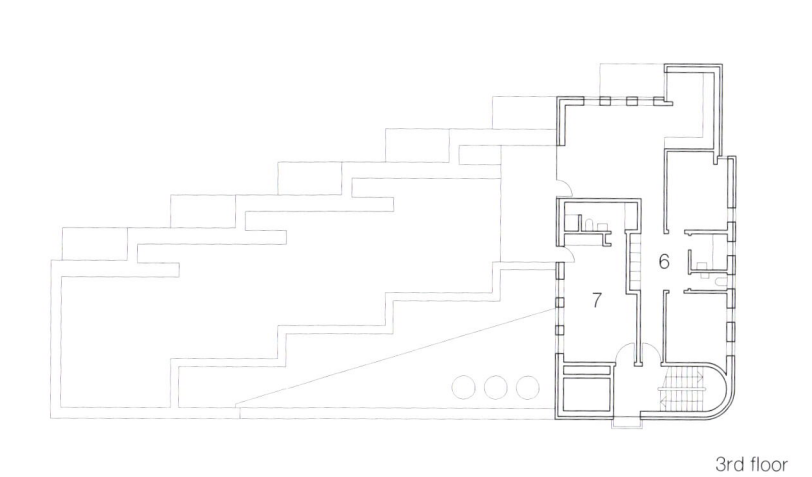

3rd floor

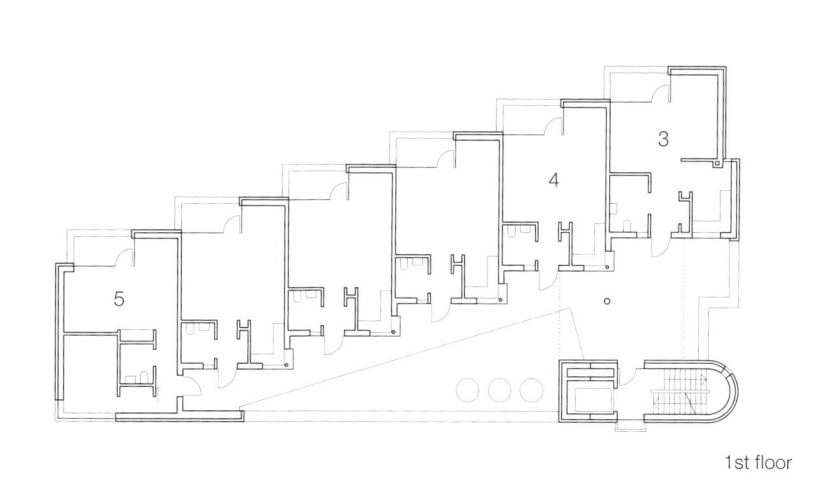

1st floor

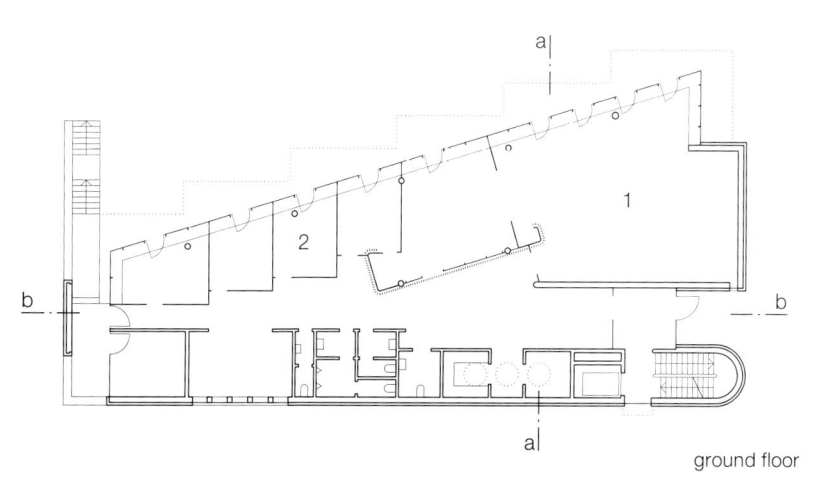

ground floor

55

1

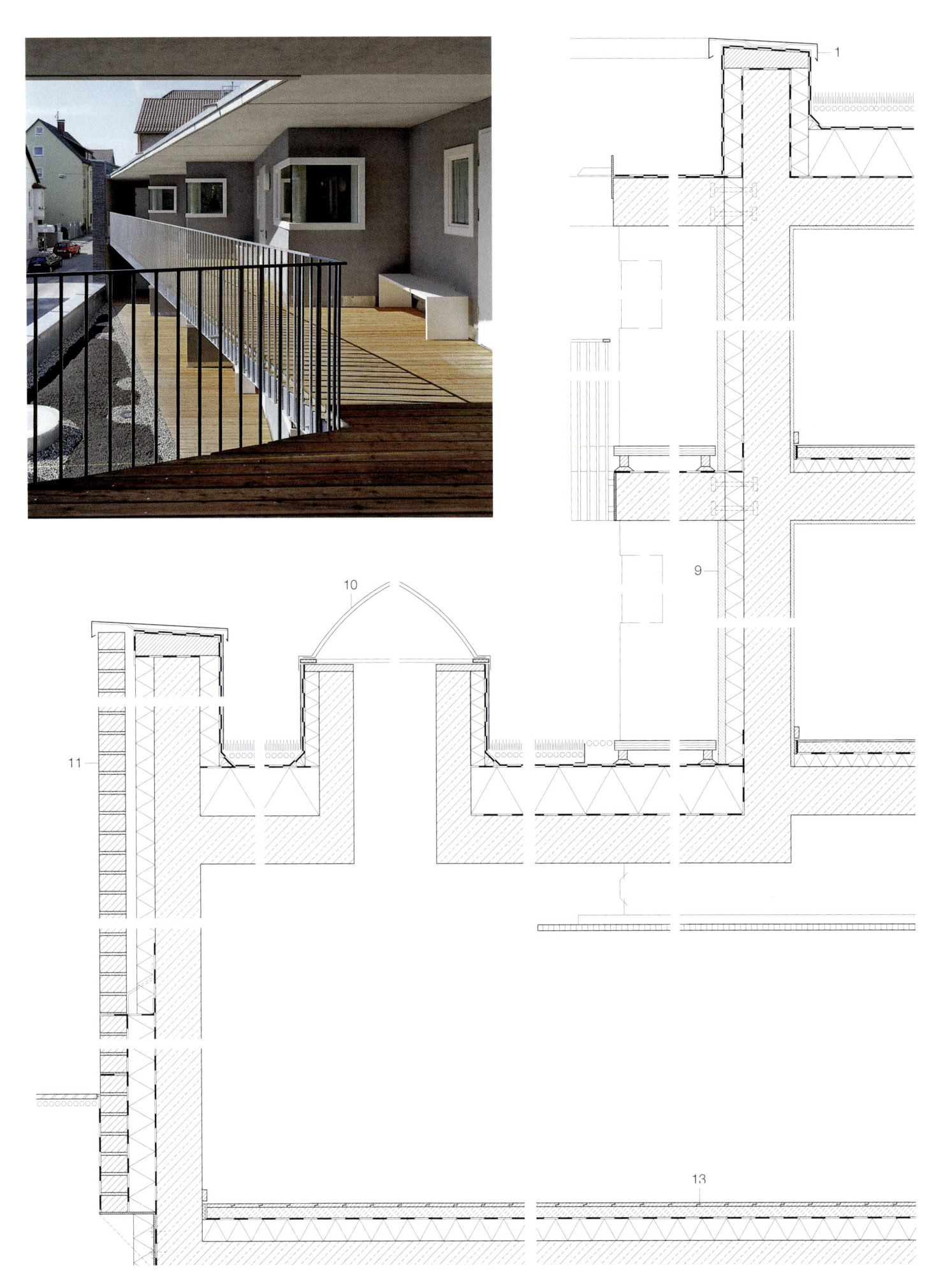

9

10

11

13

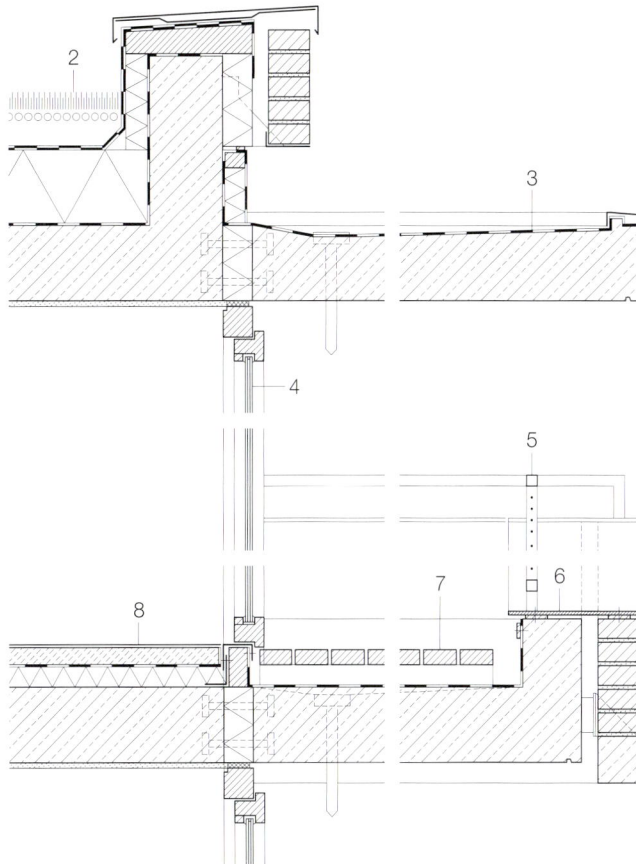

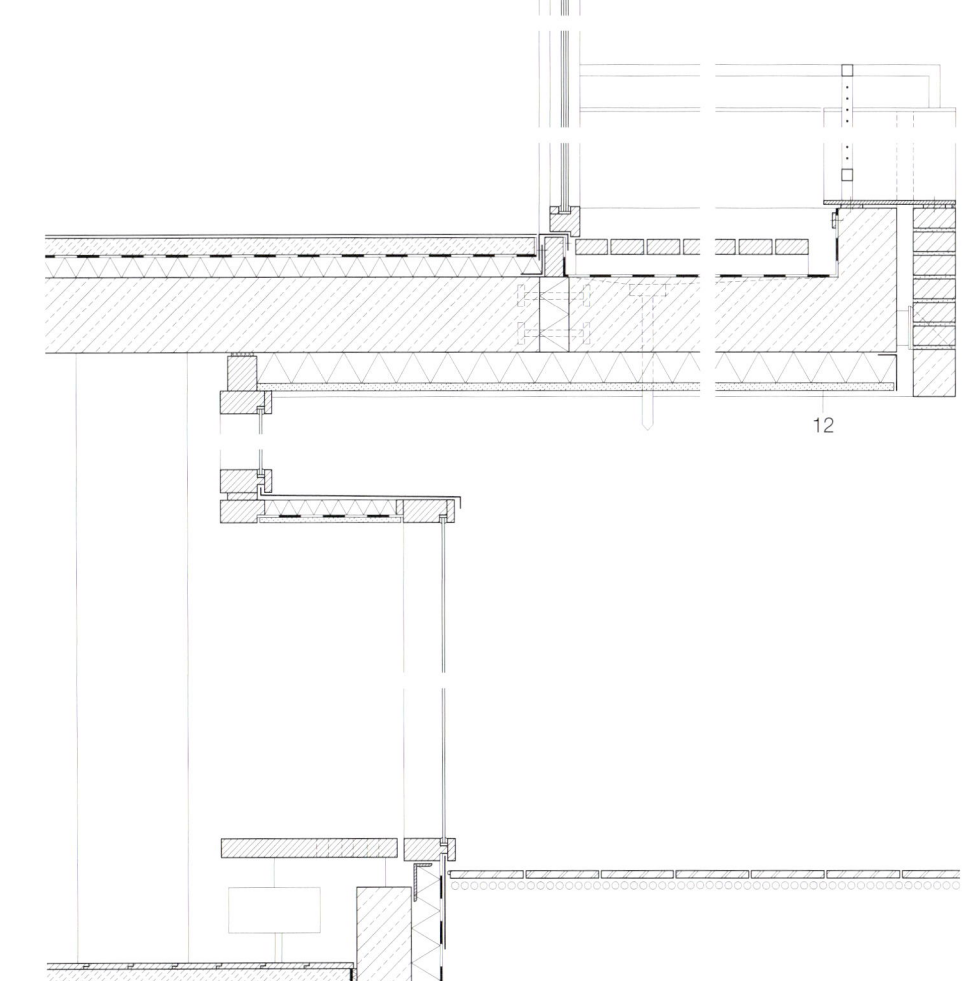

facade section
scale 1:20

1 0.7 mm titanium zinc flashing
 impermeable membrane 60 mm timber block
2 roof construction:
 120 mm extensive greening
 waterproof bituminous double layer,
 upper layer root-resistant
 190 mm polystyrene thermal insulation
 bituminous vapour barrier
 200 mm reinforced concrete slab
 15 mm internal render
3 balcony cladding:
 waterproof bituminous double layer
 170–200 mm reinforced concrete
4 insulating glass in timber frame
5 30 × 30 × 3 mm steel profile hand rail
6 8–10 mm steel cover plate,
 galvanised and coated black
7 douglas fir decking
8 upper floor construction:
 2.5 mm cork
 45 mm screed, separation layer
 45 mm impact sound insulation
 200 mm reinforced concrete slab
 15 mm internal render
9 wall construction:
 150 mm composite thermal insulation system
 200 mm reinforced concrete slab
 15 mm internal render
10 Ø 1300 mm 3-ply acrylic skylight
 screwed to timber framework
11 wall construction:
 290 × 115 × 52 mm face brickwork
 80 mm mineral fibre thermal insulation
 45 mm ventilation cavity
 200 mm reinforced concrete slab
12 100 mm composite thermal insulation system
13 ground floor construction:
 16 mm finger parquet
 45 mm screed
 90 mm thermal and impact sound insulation
 200 mm reinforced concrete slab

Seniors' Residence in Zurich

Architects: Miller & Maranta, Basle

"Collective house" with hotel character
Apartments for independent living
Aged care facilities with roof-top views
Public café on ground floor

This seniors' residence welcomes visitors and residents alike with an atmosphere comparable to a hotel. A semi-contained courtyard leads into the timber-panelled reception area, which includes a café and a fireplace lounge. The café is instrumental in drawing public life into the complex while internal spaces and informal communication and interaction zones ensure that the daily lives of the residents remain varied and interesting.

Urban structure

This polygonal, six-storey construction plays a central role in the determination of the heterogeneous urban fabric of the district. The compact northern and southern building elements are interconnected by a central tract. To the southeast, this narrower element embraces the open forecourt and a public entrance to the pedestrian passage, while behind a quieter, more private courtyard garden has been created. The northern facade is integrated into the streetscape of the busy nearby thoroughfare. The spandrel elements, which articulate the elevations, are constructed of sand-blasted in-situ concrete, pre-mixed with Jurassic lime to create a warm pale colour. The dark brown window frames, which alternate in height, contrast with the otherwise light-coloured facades.

Internal spaciousness

The ground floor accommodates the community rooms, while the set-back roof level houses the care facilities where 18 single rooms are arranged in a horseshoe-shaped layout around a communal recreation room with adjacent roof terrace. The four remaining storeys are given over to small apartments for independent living. The central corridors, which connect 17 apartments per storey of varying size, widen near the stairwells to form seating niches with views over the entry courtyard. The two-room apartments, with bathroom and kitchen, are accessed via small entry areas which incorporate built-in wall cupboards. The two rooms are connected via the kitchen area; by opening the intermediate sliding doors the individual spaces flow into one another. Storey-high glass doors allow the interior spaces to merge with the outdoor seating area, while the low-set window sills allow uninterrupted views to the outside.

Project Details
Usage: single-storey apartments, aged care facilities, café
Units: 8 1-room apartments (26 m^2)
56 2-room apartments (47–51 m^2)
4 3-room apartments (59 m^2)
18 single rooms (19–25.5 m^2)
Access: central corridor
Internal room height: 3.5 m ground floor
2.55 m upper floors
Construction type: reinforced concrete
Total internal volume: 30,843.5 m^3
Total floor area: 9,289 m^2
Total site area: 2,811 m^2
Construction cost: 798 CHF/m^3
Construction time: 2004–2006

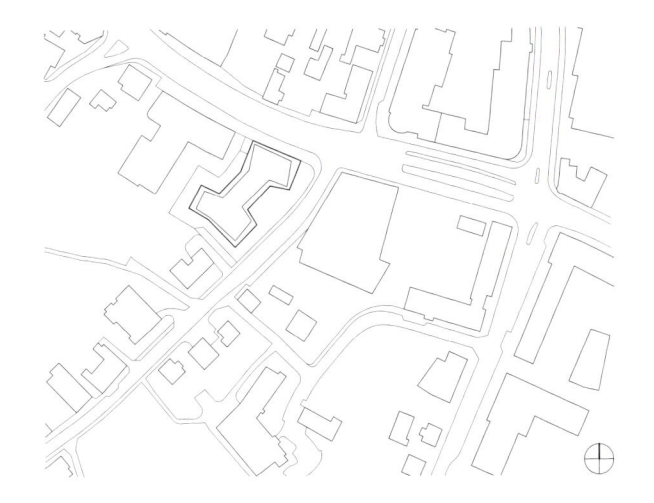

site plan
scale 1:4000

sections
floor plans
scale 1:500

A roof level
B upper storey
C ground floor

1 single room
2 recreational room
3 nursing station
4 3-room apartment
5 1-room apartment
6 2-room apartment
7 seating niche
8 dining room
9 office
10 gym
11 work room
12 hair dresser
13 laundry
14 meeting room
15 library
16 entrance
17 café
18 forecourt
19 garden courtyard

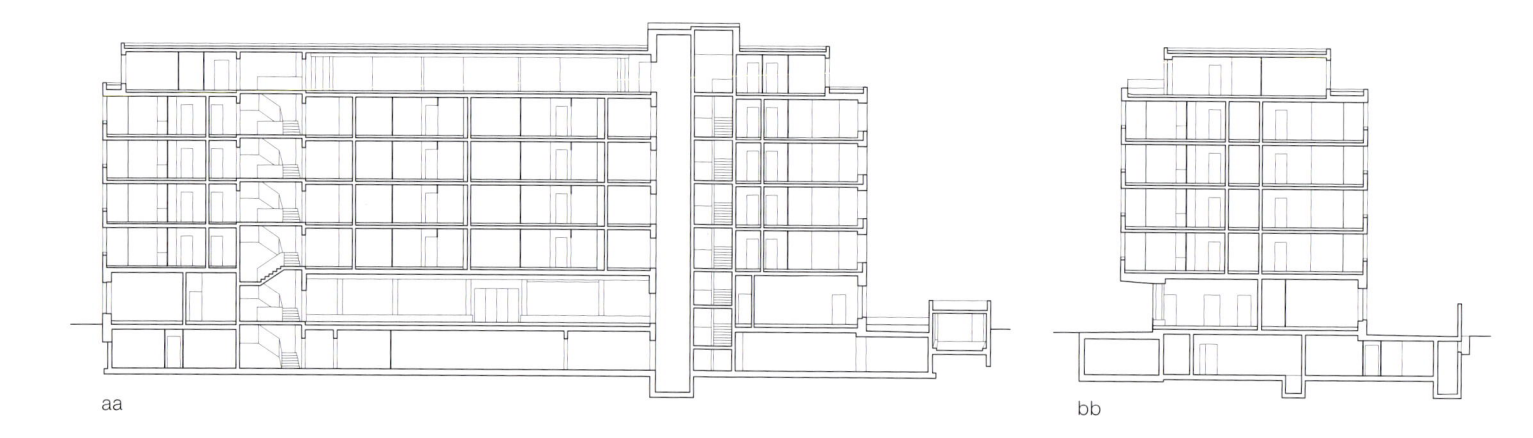

aa

bb

60

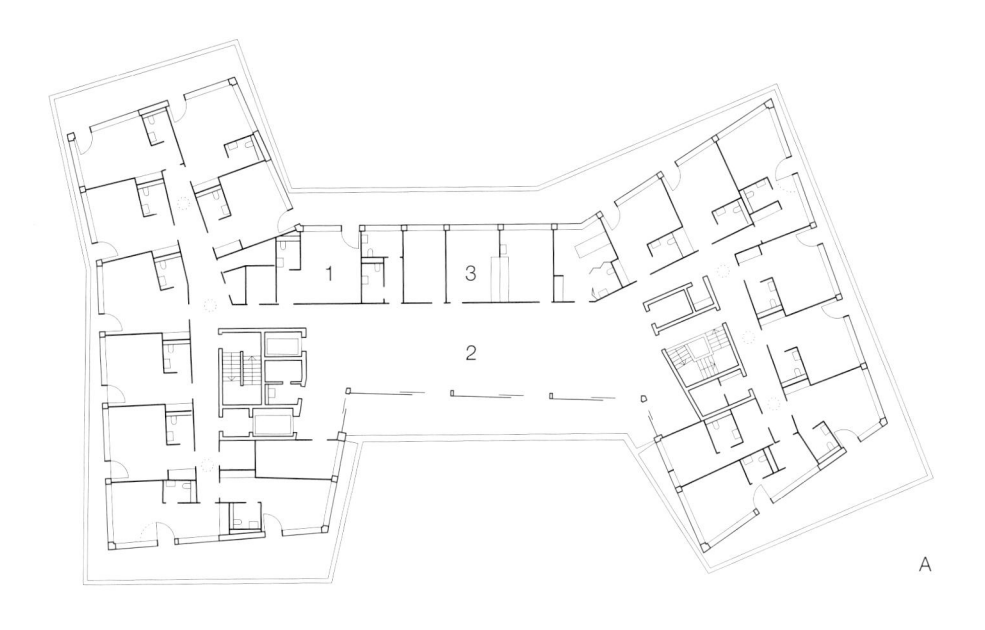

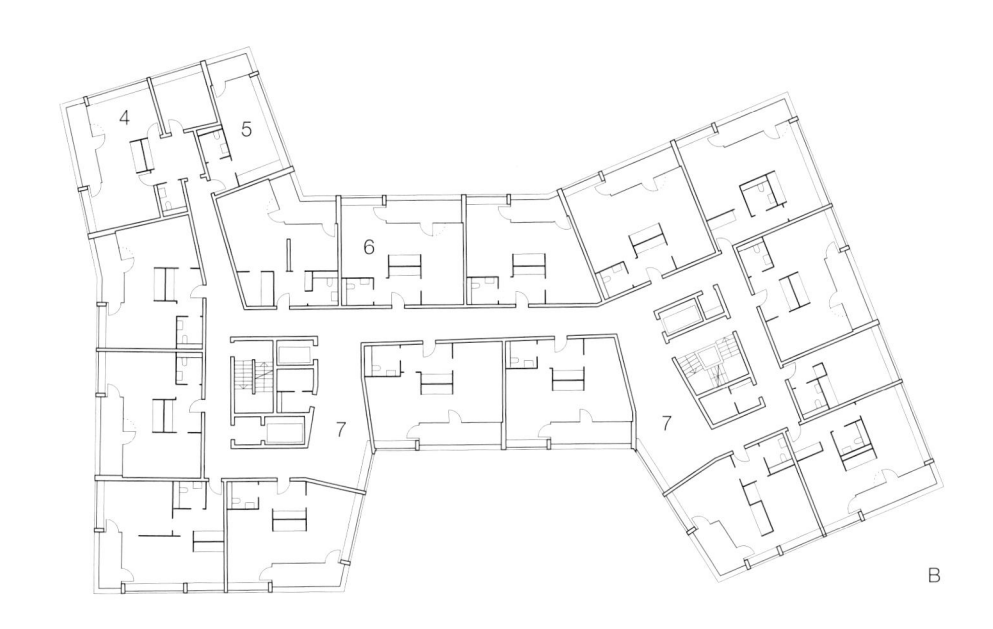

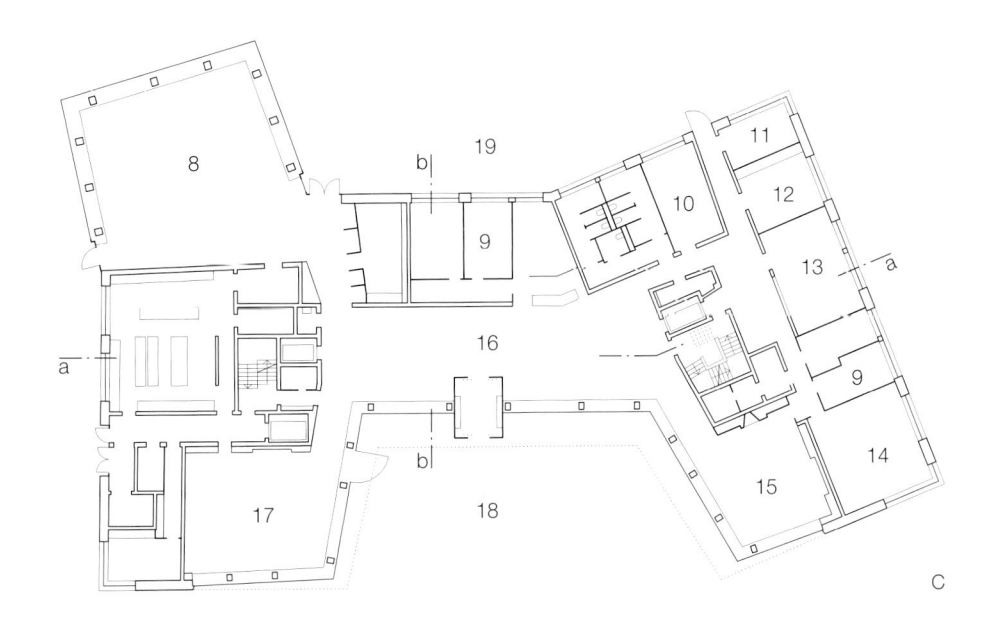

A

sections
floor plans
apartment 4th floor
scale 1:200

1 room (16.8 m²)
2 kitchen (6.4 m²)
3 loggia (6.8 m²)
4 room (17.8 m²)
5 entry (5.6 m²)
6 bathroom (3.0 m²)

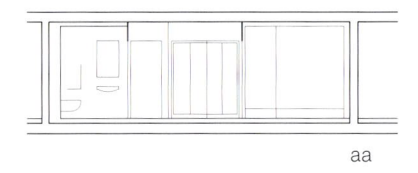

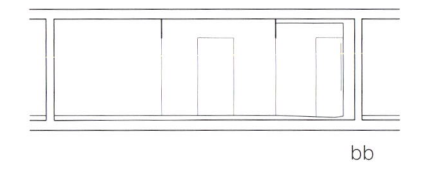

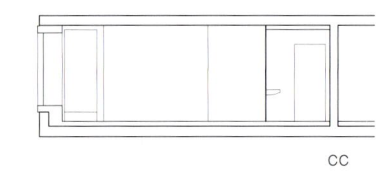

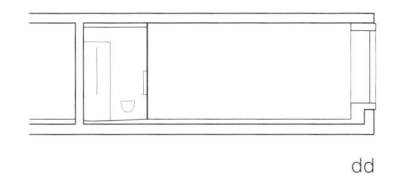

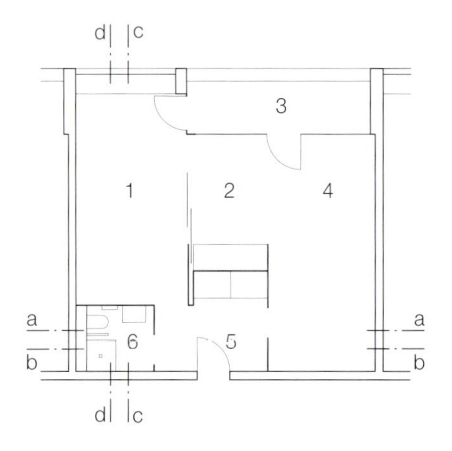

aa

bb

cc

dd

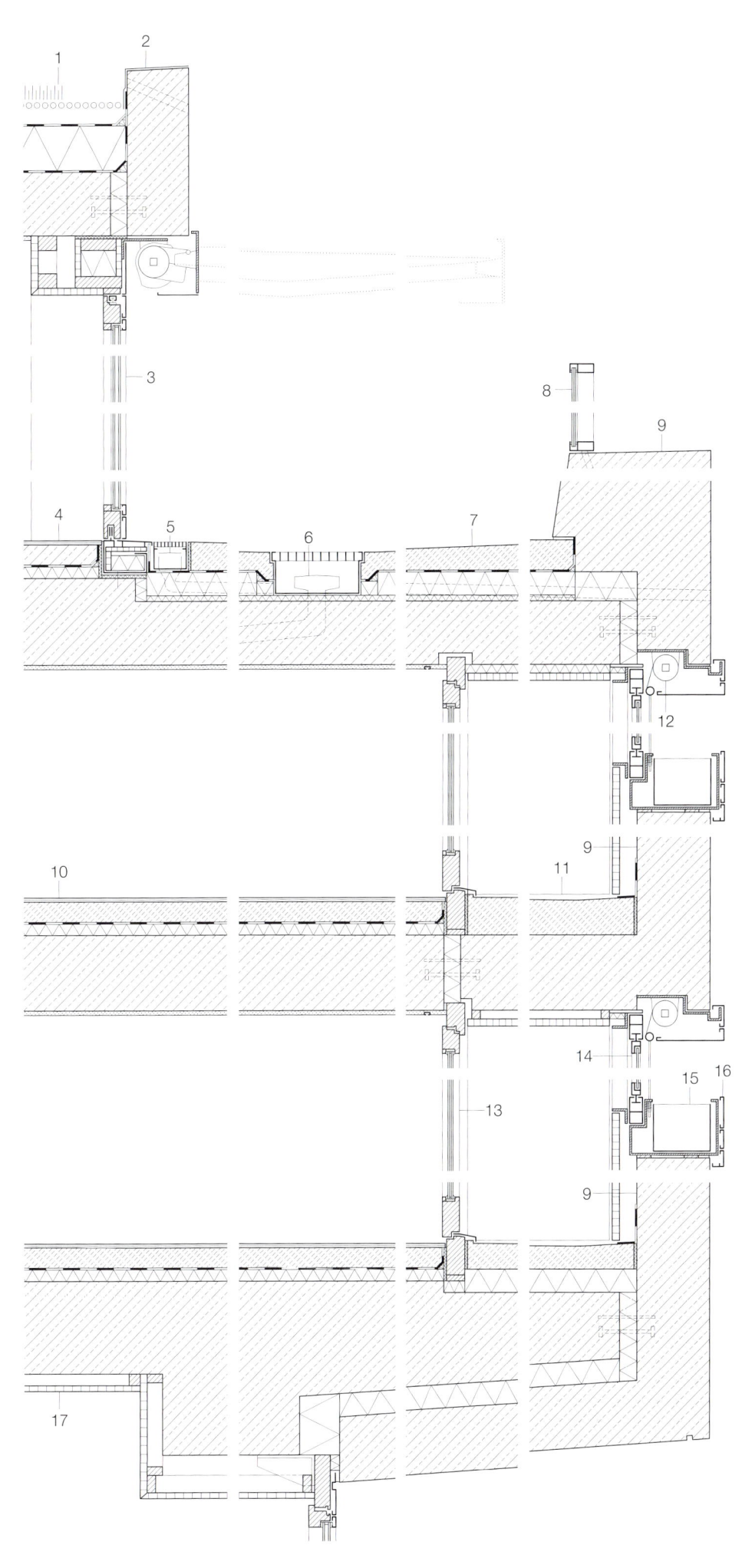

facade section
care accommodation
scale 1:20

1. roof construction:
   80 mm gravel fill, protection layer
   root-proof membrane, separation layer
   double-layer bituminous membrane
   160 mm rigid core thermal insulation
   vapour barrier
   220 mm reinforced concrete slab
2. fluid polyurethane sealant
3. sliding glass door:
   insulating glass in aluminium timber frame
4. recreation room floor construction:
   14 mm oak parquet
   76 mm screed, separation layer
   40 mm impact sound insulation
   300 mm reinforced concrete
   15 mm internal render
5. overflow integrated into gutter
6. gully
7. roof terrace floor construction:
   69–90 mm pigmented screed with fall
   separation layer
   double-layer bituminous membrane
   80 mm foam-glass thermal insulation
   20 mm impact sound insulation
   220 mm reinforced concrete slab
   30 mm thermal insulation
   21 mm MDF soffit with elm veneer
8. glass spandrel panel:
   2× 6 mm laminated safety glass in
   30 × 85 mm steel profile
9. reinforced concrete element with Jurassic lime additive
10. single room floor construction:
    14 mm oak parquet
    76 mm screed, separation layer
    40 mm impact sound insulation
    260 mm reinforced concrete
    15 mm internal render
11. loggia floor construction:
    80–90 mm pigmented screed with fall
    260 mm reinforced concrete slab
    21 mm MDF soffit with elm veneer
12. vertical awning
13. door: insulating glass in timber frame
14. loggia glazing with folding/sliding elements
15. balcony boxes: 3 mm aluminium
16. 3 mm anodised aluminium profile
17. entry hall ceiling:
    acoustic panels with micro-perforations
    20 mm elm veneer panels on 70 mm battens

Multengut Seniors' Residence near Bern

Architects: Burkhalter Sumi Architects, Zurich

Three different dwelling types and care accommodation for varying types of living Numerous communal spaces

The stately manor house which lends its name to this development in Muri near Bern completes the vista created by the two 90 metre long, parallel building tracts. The two apparently discrete buildings of the Multengut Seniors' Residence are in fact connected by an underground basement level. The intermediate courtyard space serves as both arrival and outdoor recreational zone, while the vertical access routes within each building are centrally located.

Accommodation

The residential tract is made up of four identical storeys, predominantly providing 3-room apartments for the more independent residents. The first floor of the main building houses the care accommodation, above which additional apartments are located.

Three different apartment types and sizes are available. Type I is subdivided by wall panels and organised into narrow strips which establish the spatial sequence. Type II is organised by the centrally located core, consisting of cloakroom, bathroom and kitchen, within the otherwise open-plan apartment. The corner apartments, type III, are a combination of the two and, as a result, of more generous proportions. Every apartment benefits from an internal window overlooking the communal corridor, which encourages interaction between neighbours and precludes the risk of anonymity. The apartments open out to the balconies through generously proportioned sliding doors and large flower windows. Running the full length of the buildings, the balconies are subdivided into individual, private zones by red, full-height storage cupboards. When a more secluded outdoor area is required, the residents can simply let the sun-shades down to the level of the balcony balustrade. The rails of the balustrades are set higher than standard requirements and are placed at larger intervals in the upper zone allowing views. By recessing the gardens in front of the ground floor apartments the privacy of the residents is retained, in addition to equalising the slope of the site.

Communal areas

Various communal spaces are located within the ground floor of the main building. The glass facade, with large casement windows, and the terrace stretch the length of the building. The continuous, perforated-timber suspended ceiling and parquet flooring allow the interior and exterior spaces to merge with one another. The internal flooring flows uninterrupted out to the level of the raised timber decking of the terrace, which can be accessed from the lower level of the internal courtyard via either steps or ramps. The basement level of the main building incorporates a wellness area for the benefit of the residents.

Colour concept

The vibrant colour scheme of the seniors' residence is designed to concur with the sensual perception of the elderly. Stairwells are illuminated blue and easily recognisable, while the red corridors are differently decorated on each level to assist orientation.

The undersides of the balconies are also blue, contrasting with the vertical articulation of the red outdoor cupboards.

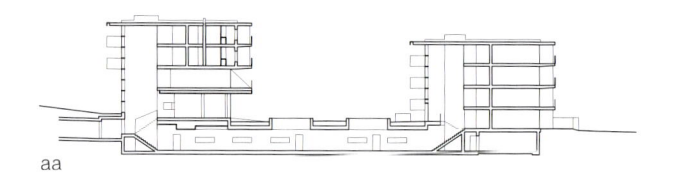

aa

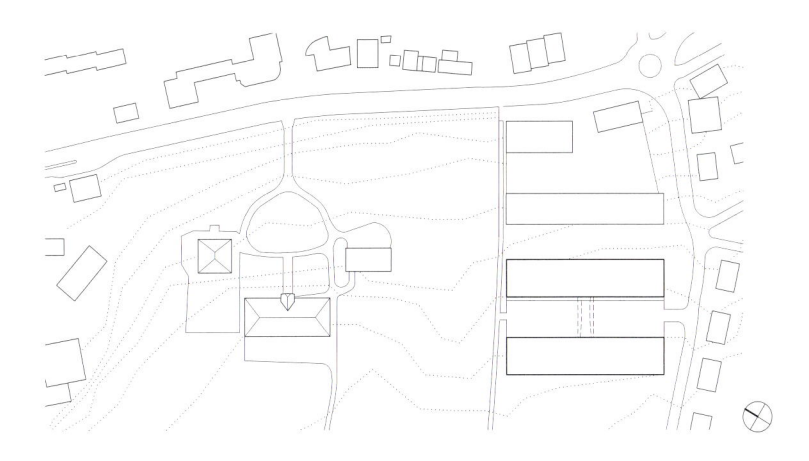

site plan	Project Details	Internal room height:	3.2 m ground floor
scale 1:4000	Usage: 98 apartments		2.4 m first floor
section	26 care accommodation rooms		2.7 m basement
scale 1:1000	Units: 24 4-room corner apartments	Construction type:	reinforced concrete
	4 4-room strip-type apartments	Total internal volume:	51,200 m³
	44 3-room strip-type apartments	Usable floor area:	10,851 m²
	22 3-room core-type apartments	Total site area:	8,700 m²
	4 2-room core-type apartments	Construction cost:	28.9 million CHF
	Access: central corridor	Construction time:	2002–2004

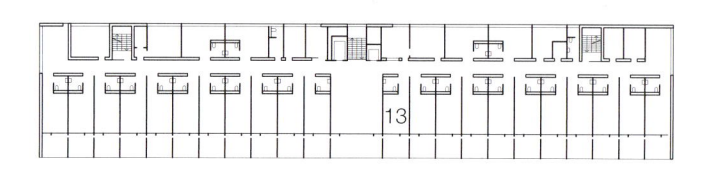

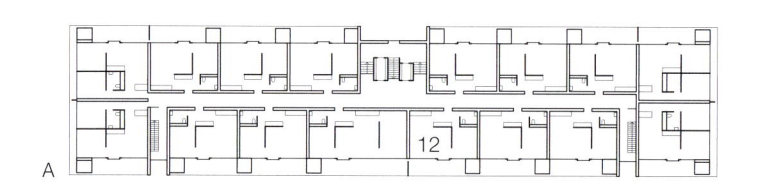

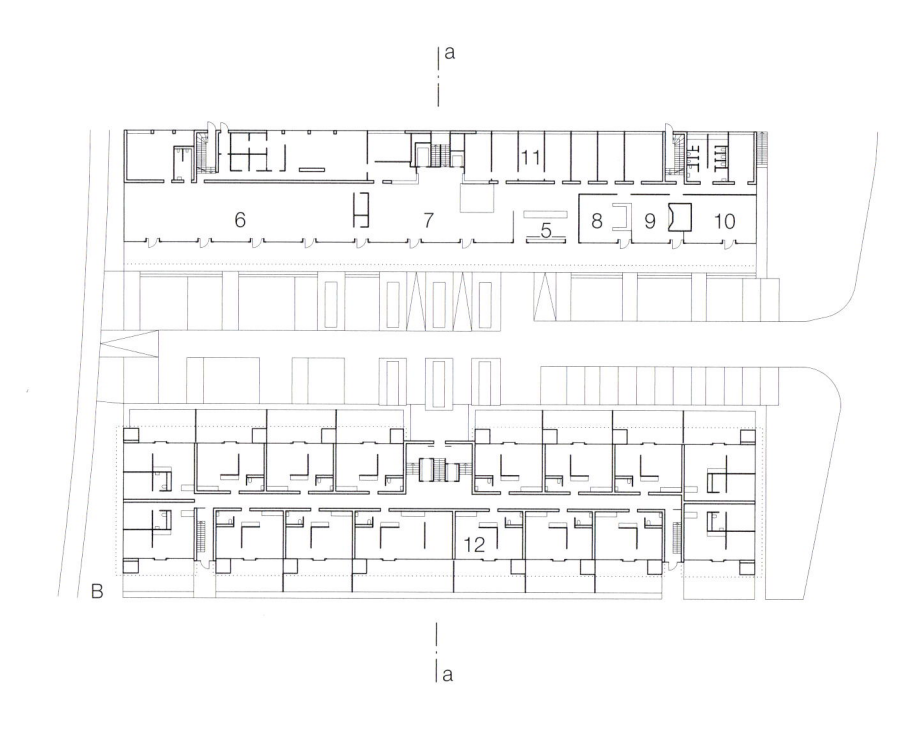

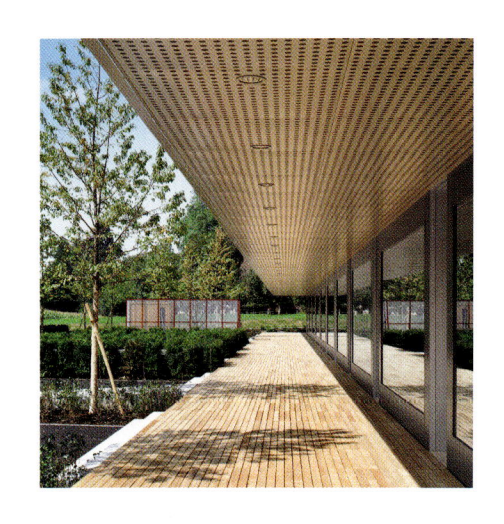

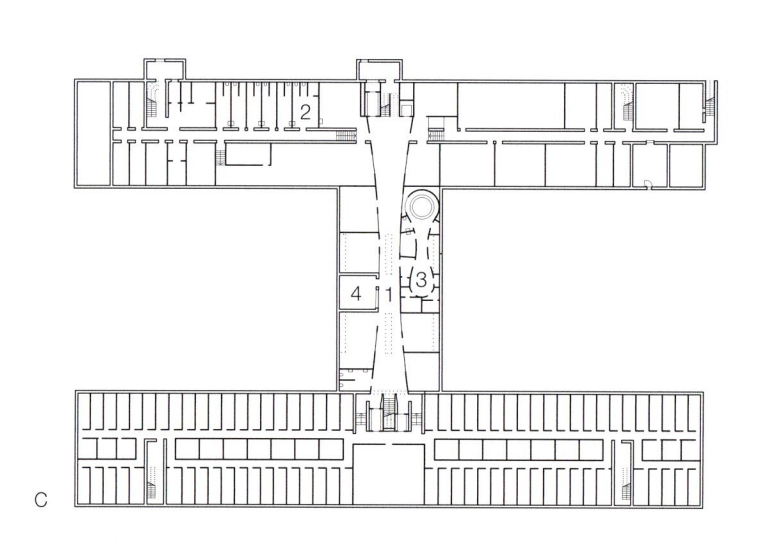

A

B

C

floor plans
scale 1:1000

apartment type plans
scale 1:200

A first floor
B ground floor
C basement
D care accommodation
E 3-room type I
F 3-room type II
G 4-room type III

1 corridor
2 change room
3 wellness area
4 music room
5 entrance
6 dining room
7 lounge
8 library
9 inglenook
10 lecture room
11 administration
12 apartments
13 care accommodation

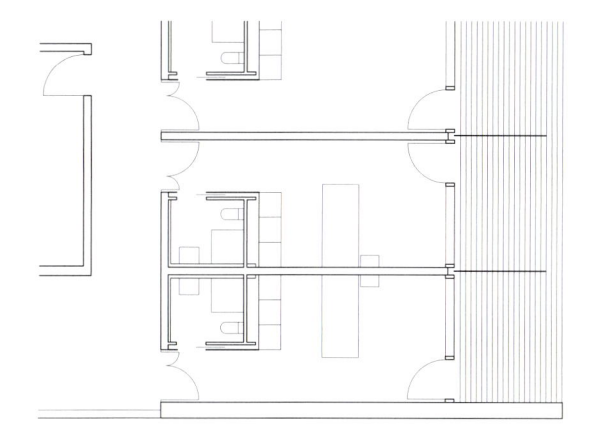

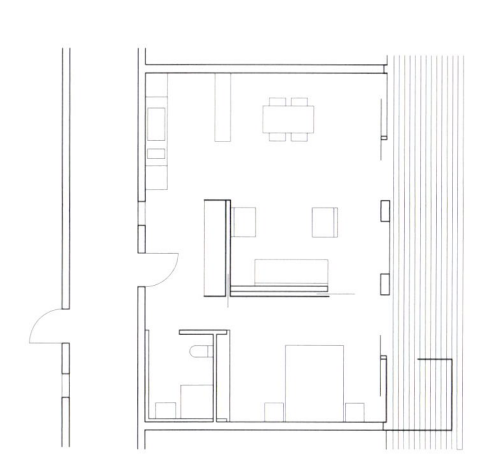

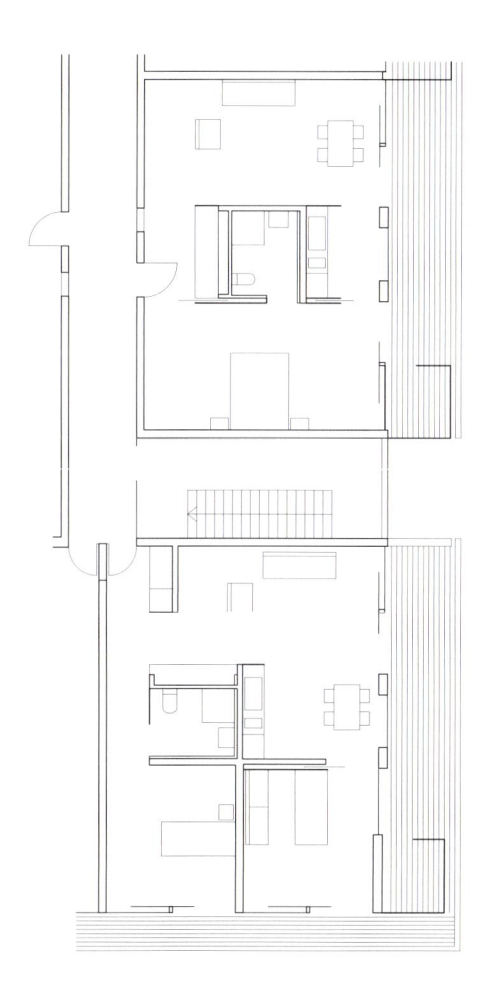

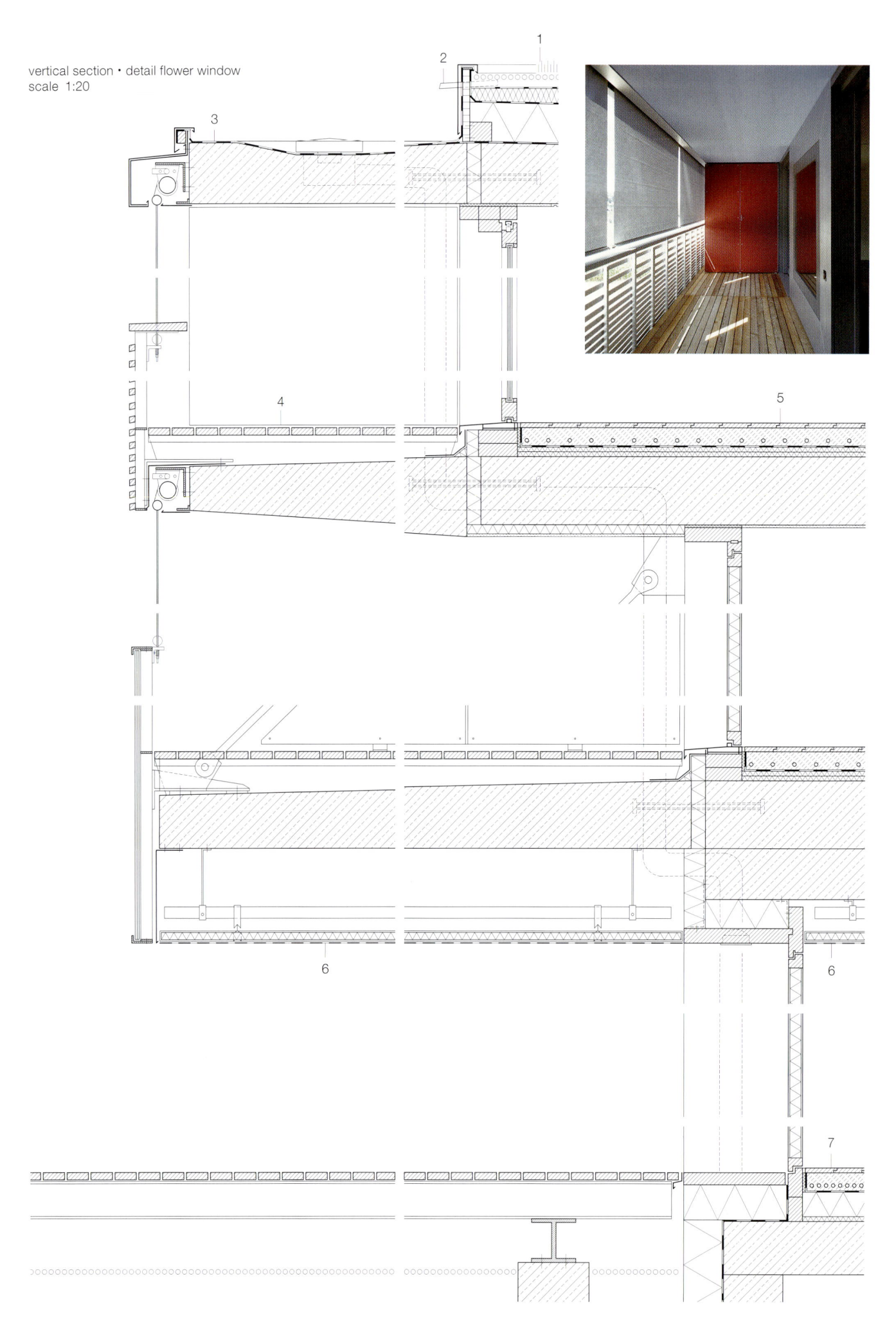

vertical section · detail flower window
scale 1:20

68

1 roof construction:
  extensive substrate greening
  filter and drainage matting
  bituminous membrane
  160 mm polyurethane foam thermal insulation
  bituminous vapour barrier
  220 mm reinforced concrete slab
  10 mm smooth gypsum plaster undercoat
2 30 × 100 × 250 mm RHS titanium zinc overflow
3 200–250 mm in situ concrete projecting roof
4 balcony decking construction:
  90 × 30 mm larch decking with 5 mm spacing
  timber sub-construction
  180–330 mm reinforced concrete with fall
5 floor construction apartment:
  20 mm parquet, 80 mm screed
  polyethylene separation membrane
  20 mm thermal insulation
  20 mm impact sound insulation
  220 mm reinforced concrete
  1 mm smooth white plaster
6 suspended perforated metal ceiling;
  1 mm galvanised steel sheeting with
  Ø 40 mm perforations
  50 mm acoustic backing, black
7 ground floor construction:
  20 mm oak parquet, 80 mm screed
  polyethylene separation membrane
  100 mm solid foam thermal insulation
  20 mm impact sound insulation,
  220 mm reinforced concrete
8 flower window:
  silver painted timber cladding
  integrated rigid foam thermal insulation
  prefabricated concrete element with
  30 × 30 mm timber frame with ventilation cavity
9 6 mm toughened glass shelving
10 double glazing in grey painted timber framing

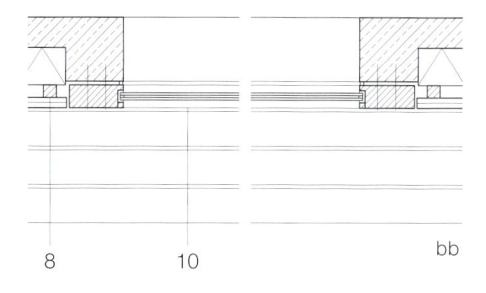

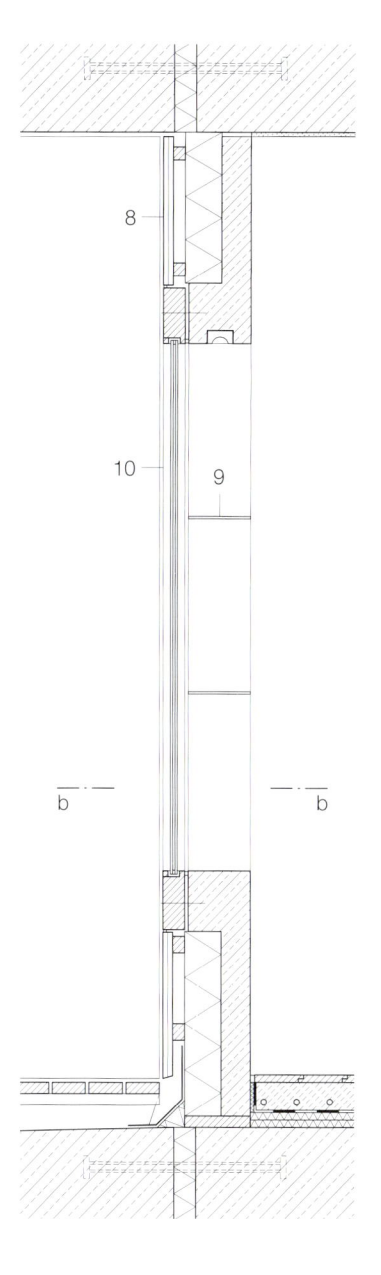

Housing Development and Aged Care Centre in Alicante

Architect: Javier García-Solera Vera, Alicante

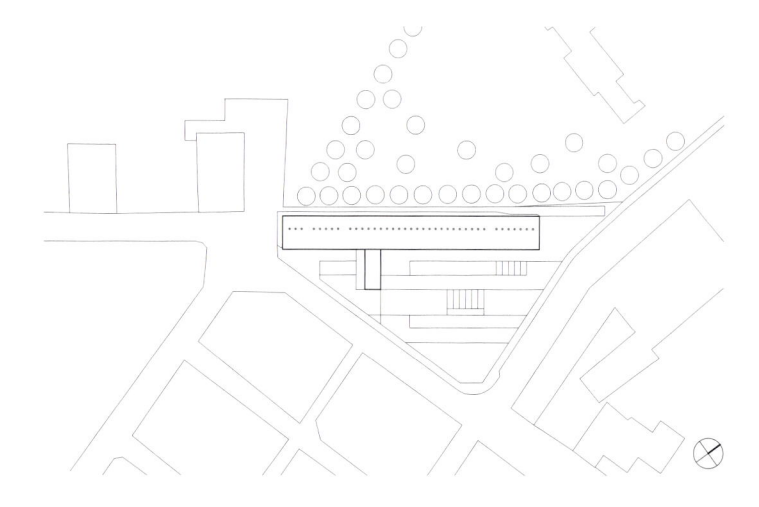

Apartments for independent living
Care centre and community facilities
Access walkway as connecting element

North of Alicante, this housing development seems to hover above the ground at the base of the hospital. The flat, elongated building tract is partially buried into the gently sloping hillside at the edge of a small pine forest. Although the original development plan for this triangular site called for a six-storey construction, the successful final design by the architect was based upon a recreational, urban parkland zone – much to the relief of the neighbours.

The two storey building is 140 metres long and almost 18 metres deep yet projects a mere 3.3 metres above the level of the park, the lower level being set into the ground. A narrow, courtyard-like area to the rear provides access to the parking bays and storage spaces. A small walkway leads to the traverse tract which projects into the park with ceiling-high glass walls, and accommodates the aged care centre and community facilities.

The 39 slender dwelling units on the upper level; three of which are designed to be wheelchair-friendly, are approached from an access walkway to the south. Here neighbours can meet and stroll along the urban promenade; strengthening social interaction and avoiding isolation. The continuous concrete upstands of the roof and floor slabs emphasise the horizontal articulation of the scheme, while the set-back, dividing elements reinforce its structure.

The apartments are entered via a covered loggia with a shaded seating area. Ceiling-high glazing gives way to a dwelling of 12 metres in depth which is subdivided by the off-centre placement of the sanitary cell. The living space with integrated kitchen is orientated to the south; whereas the bedroom opens out to the north, via a French window and private balcony, to the pine forest beyond.

Project Details
Usage: aged housing, day centre, community facilities
Units: 36 2-room apartments (40 m²)
3 2-room wheelchair-friendly apartments (40 m²)
Access: access walkway
Internal room height: 2.8 m ground floor, 2.5 m first floor
Construction type: reinforced concrete
Total internal volume: 7,490 m³
Total floor area: 2,674 m²
Total site area: 4,979 m²
Construction cost: 2.19 million Euros
Construction time: 2005

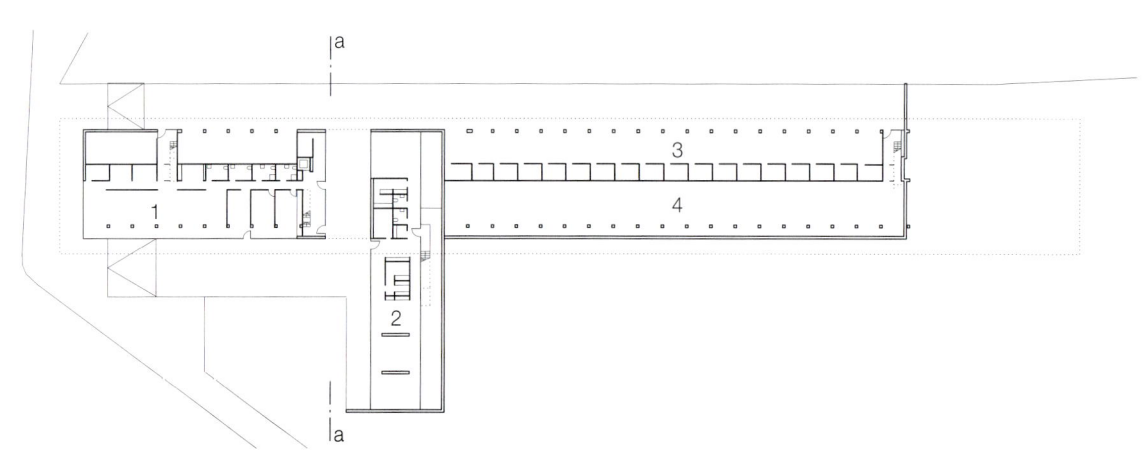

site plan
scale 1:4000
floor plans
cross section
scale 1:1000

1 community room
2 day centre
3 parking bay
4 storeroom

71

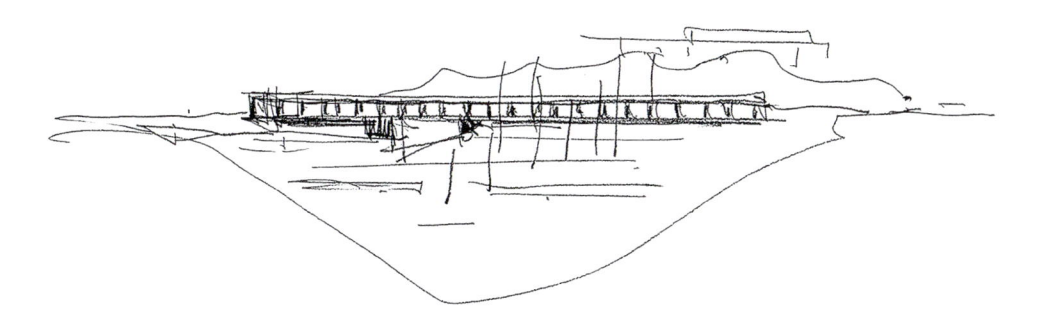

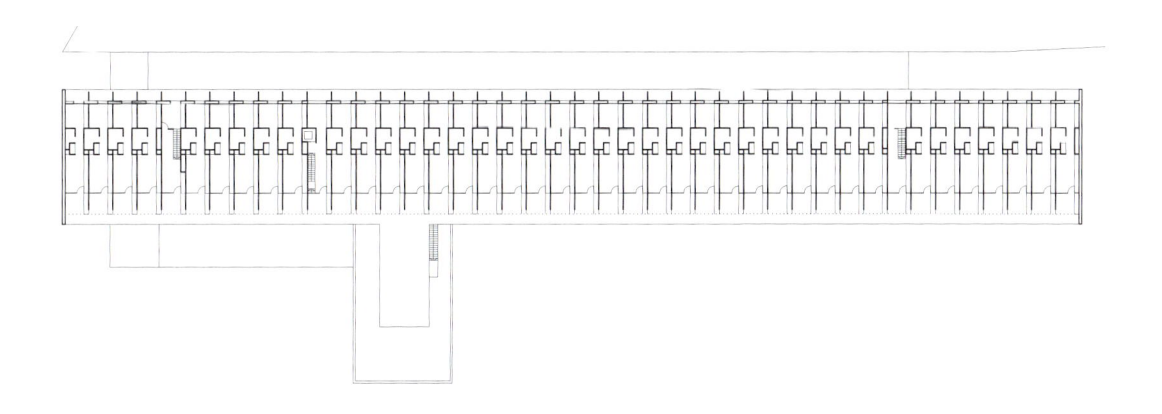

aa

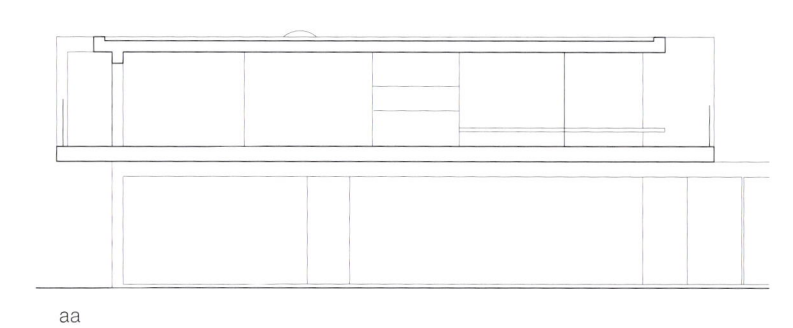

cross section aa
apartment floor plan
scale 1:200

1 bedroom (8.5 m²)
2 bathroom (4.5 m²)
3 living (21.0 m²)

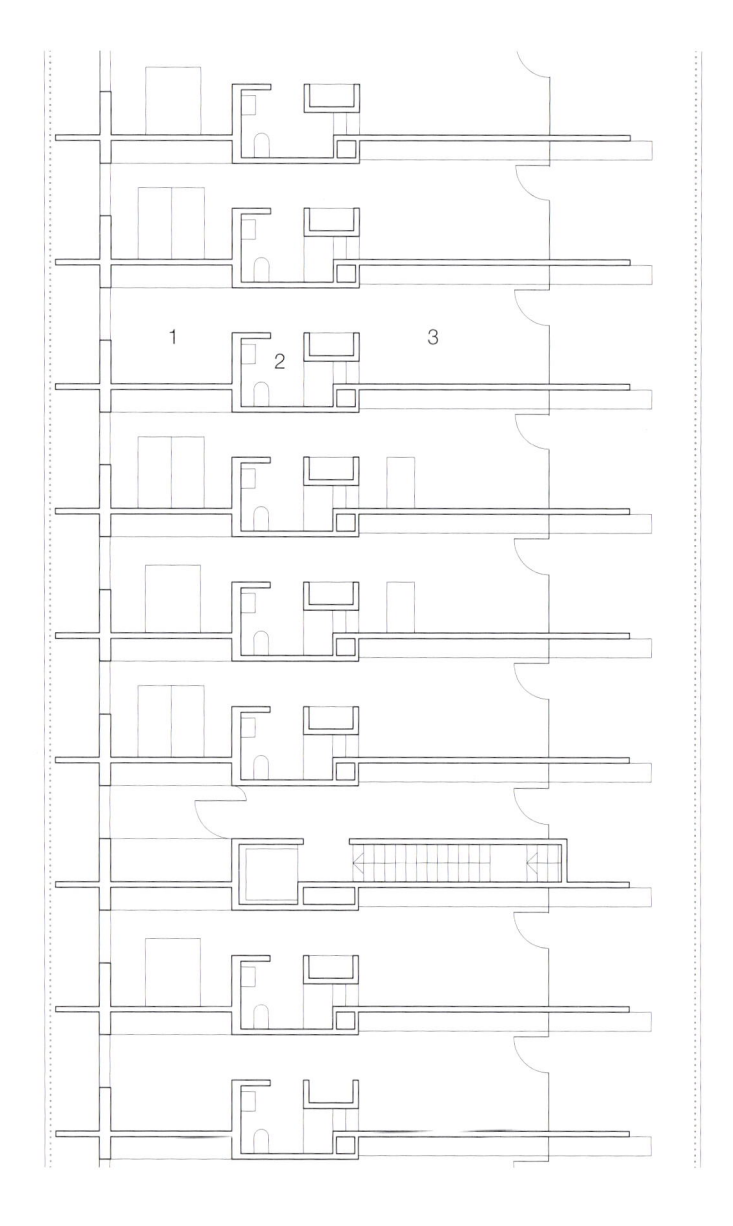

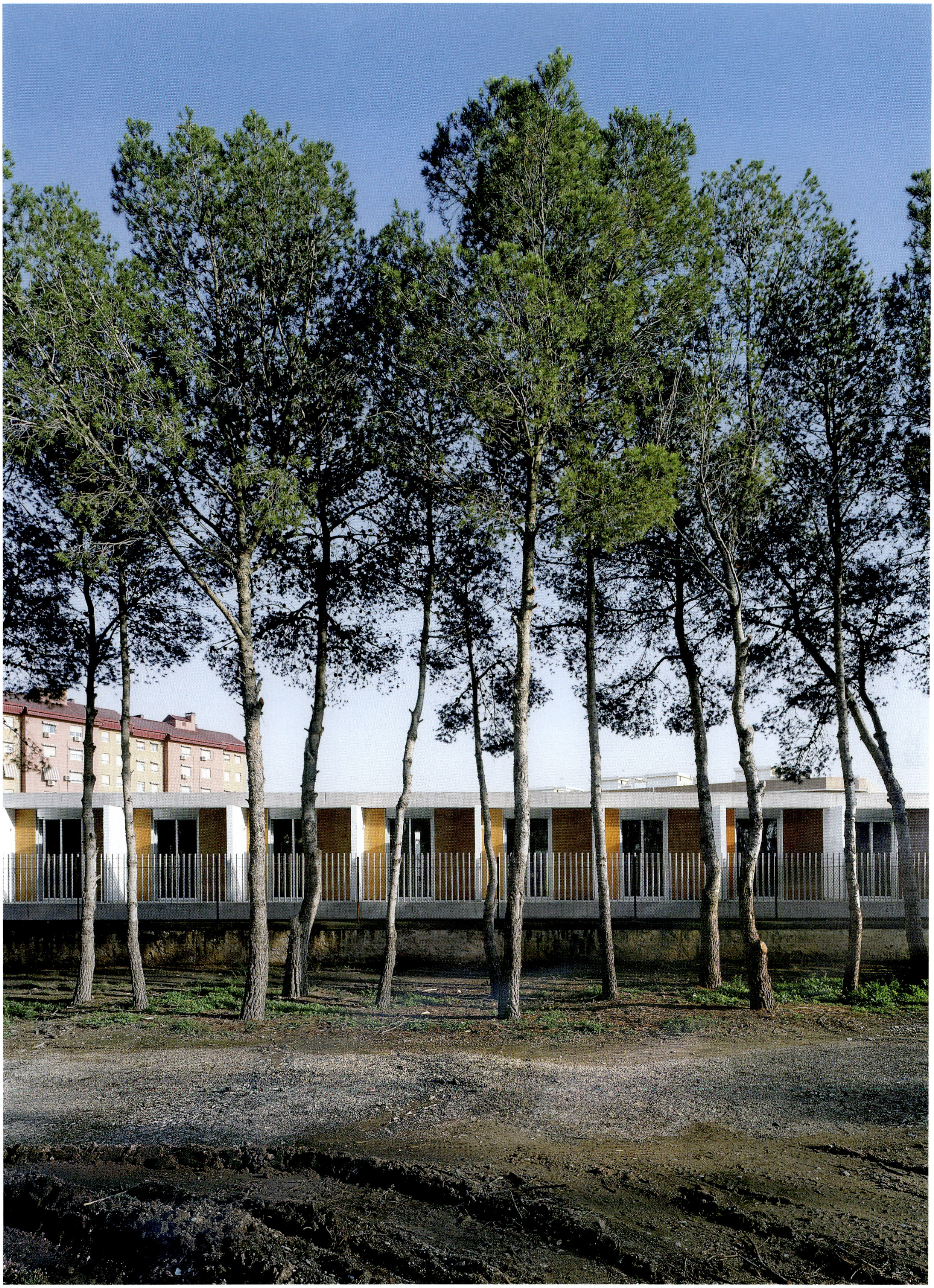

High-rise Apartment Building in Rotterdam

Architects: Arons en Gelauff architecten, Amsterdam

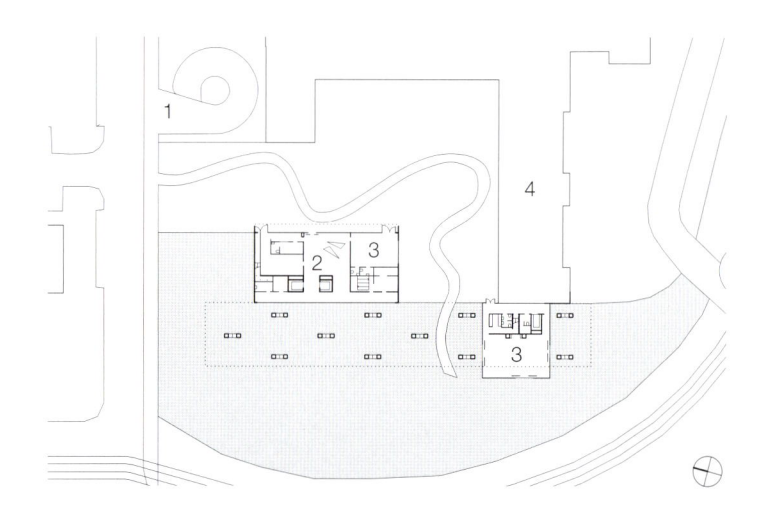

Rotated and reflected building forms
104 wheelchair-friendly apartments
Three-dimensional and coloured glass facades

This striking high-rise apartment building, with 104 dwellings for seniors, is located in IJsselmonde, a suburb of Rotterdam. The formal language and colour treatment are such that it is almost impossible to discern the function of the building. This construction of 17 storeys which is mounted on V-shaped columns and appears to hover 11.4 metres above the surface of the water, reflects the changing demands of the over 55's.

Urban environment

The suburb of IJsselmonde is a planned garden city dating from the post-war years. In order to resolve the lack of an adequate town centre, a master plan was developed encompassing 340 new constructions of various functions. This particular apartment building is connected to an existing nurses' residence, capable of providing medical or care personnel. A large open area is located at the base of the block; the asphalt pathway, which is suitable for mobility impaired residents, leads down to the water's edge, and a community room is located beneath the horizontal building element.

Rotated building structure

The two building elements have similar proportions and are rotated in relation to one another. The floor plans are one-sided and the apartments are reflected in the opposite building element. The corridors join and widen to become a mutual communication area.
At 9.8 metres, the structural grid enables generous apartments to be conceived and allows for future alterations. It is possible to separate off a room from the standard model which already accommodates bedroom, living room, kitchen and bathroom. All apartments are wheelchair-friendly and have individual storage spaces. Space has also been provided on the ground floor for walking frames and wheelchairs.

Facade execution

The contrasting building elements have dissimilar facade treatments which correlate to the functions behind. The storey-high glazed facades are emphasised by vibrant coloured coatings which range through 200 shades of colour from yellow to red. The balcony facades are reserved and cool, yet eye catching in their three-dimensional treatment. The balcony slabs and party walls oscillate and the impression of mobility is emphasised by the flowing curves of the balustrades.

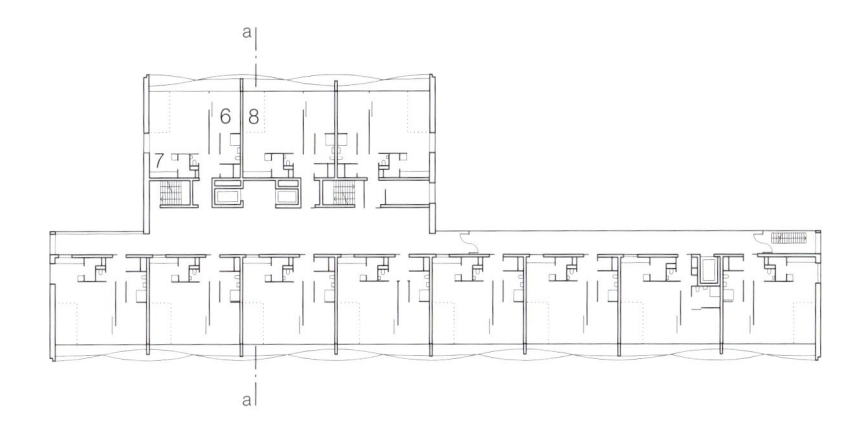

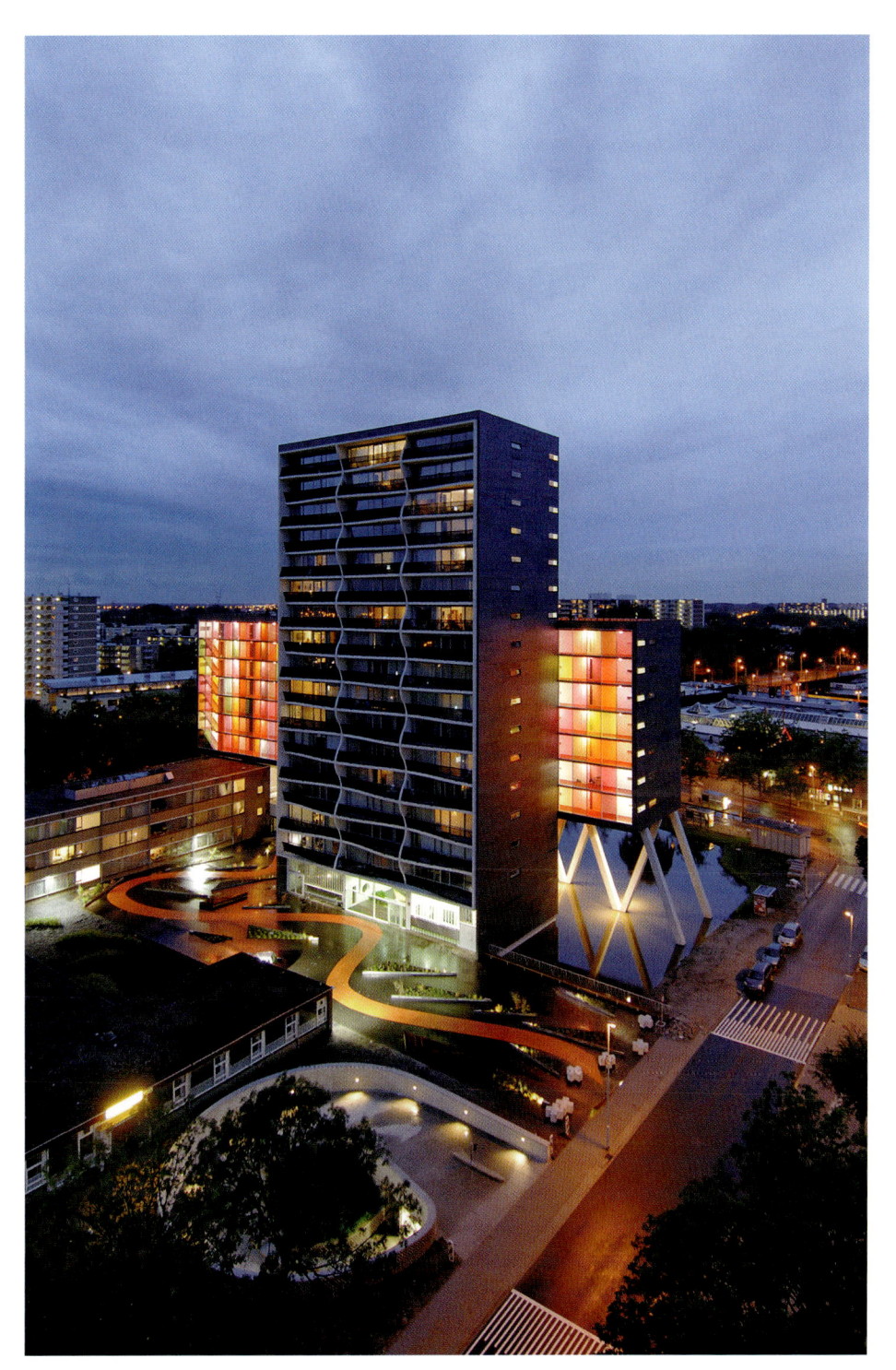

ground floor plan
scale 1:1500
standard storey floor plan · section
scale 1:750

1 driveway to underground parking
2 entrance hall
3 community room
4 existing nurses' residence
5 living room
6 bedroom
7 kitchen
8 additional room

Project Details
Usage:	apartment building for seniors
Units:	104 apartments
Access:	central corridor, one-sided
Internal room height:	2.6 m
Construction type:	reinforced concrete
Total internal volume:	47,232 m³
Total floor area:	15,678 m²
Residential floor area:	11,924 m²
Total site area:	4,167 m²
Built site area:	1,577 m²
Construction cost:	15.1 million Euros
Construction time:	2001–2006

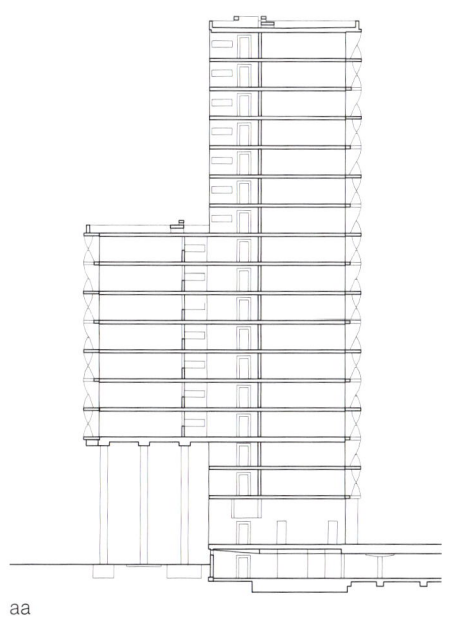

aa

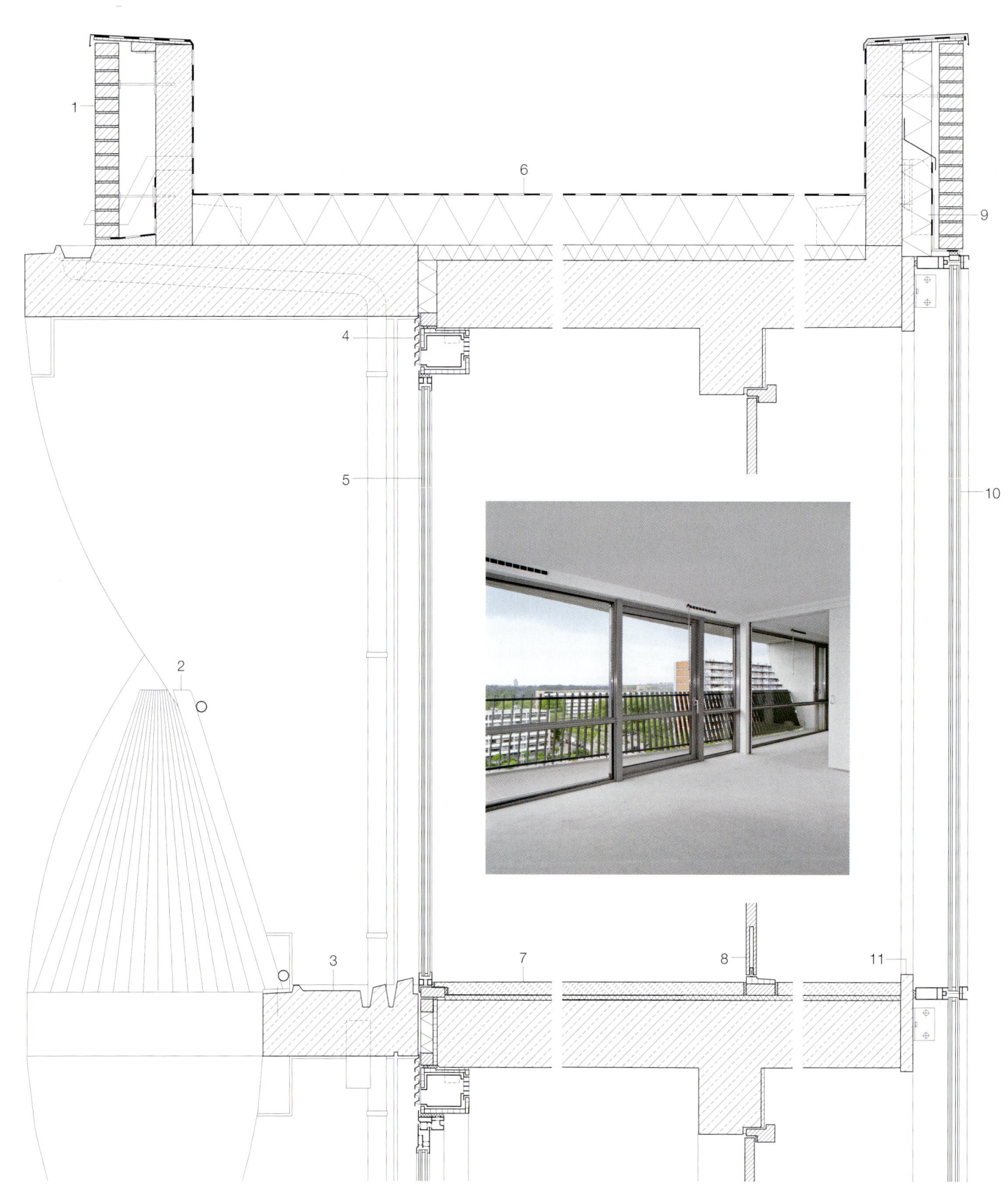

vertical sections   scale 1:20
1 parapet construction
   100 mm brickwork
   152 mm ventilation cavity
   150 mm pre-cast
   reinforced concrete element
2 handrail flat steel, warped:
   70 × 4 mm steel flat
   Ø 40 mm steel rod handrail
3 250 mm prefabricated concrete balcony slab
4 aluminium ventilation louvers
5 aluminium window with double glazing
6 roof construction:
   impermeable membrane
   235 mm thermal insulation
   270 mm reinforced concrete slab
7 floor construction:
   50 mm screed
   20 mm impact sound insulation
   270 mm reinforced concrete slab
8 timber entry door
9 spandrel anchor
10 glass facade:
   toughened glass with photocatalytic coating
   lam. saf. glass with coloured PVB-membrane
11 50 × 370 mm prefabricated
   concrete slab edge

76

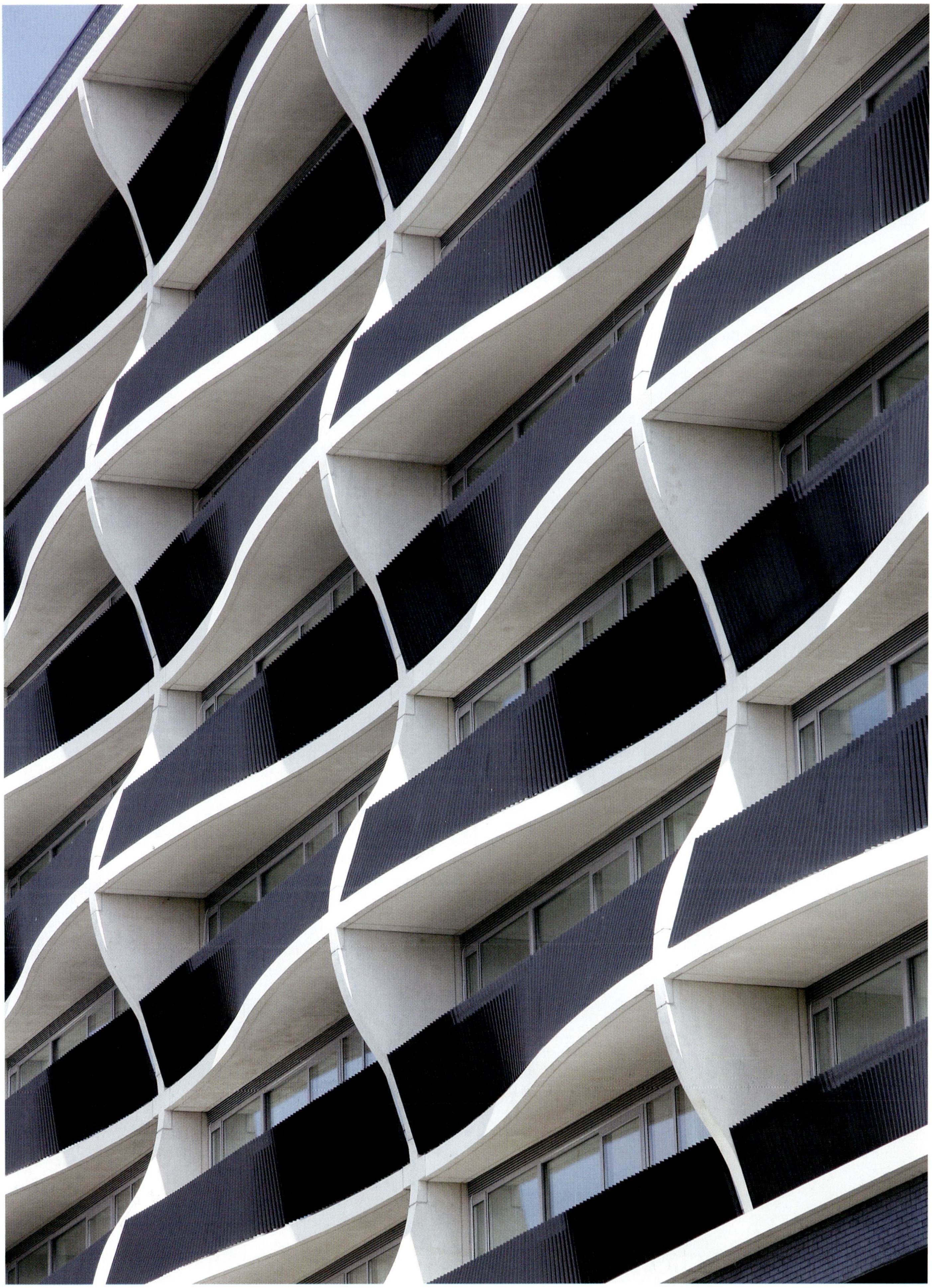

Senior Dwellings in Domat/Ems

Architect: Dietrich Schwarz, Domat/Ems

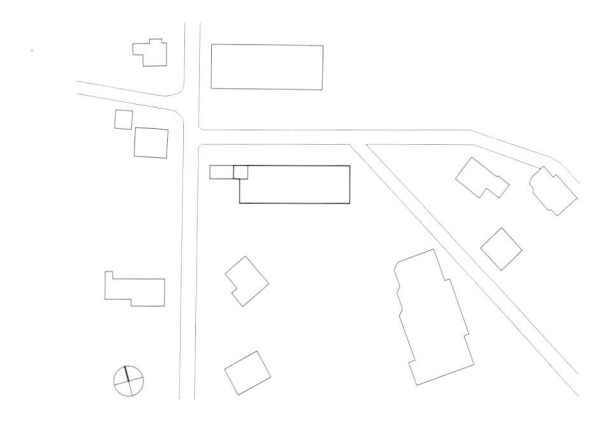

Open planning for independent living
Communal communication zone
Solar facade with latent heat storage modules

Located on the southern boundary of Domat/Ems in the Swiss canton of Graubünden, this four storey residential hostel is positioned immediately adjacent to an existing nursing home for the elderly. Extending the range of options, it provides an alternative for those wishing to live independently, while care services remain accessible. The northern side of the grey rendered cube is dominated by large window openings whereas the southern facade is fully glazed.

Compact built structure

The floor plan is divided into three zones; the northern access zone acts simultaneously as puffer and communication space. While interconnecting the individual storeys, the off-set, cascading staircases generate a spatial fluidity. Recreational and communication areas are layered allowing a variety of interactive alternatives for the residents. Lift access is provided on one side, enabling wheelchair bound residents to fully interact with their neighbours. Each level incorporates 5 two-bedroom apartments of 57 m². All 20 apartments stretch through the depth of the building from the puffer zone, and are of identical layout, being symmetrically reflected and horizontally translated, according to the organisation of the storey. Kitchen and dining areas are only separated from the communication zones and stairwell by fire-proof windows, allowing interaction between residents. The southern sides of the apartments are entirely made up of loggia-style spaces, which act either as glazed conservatories or open air seating spaces as desired, and illuminate the living areas and bedrooms. Threshold free doorways are achieved through the application of sliding doors. Each apartment is provided with a storage space on the same level, rather than in the cellar. Although the budget was restricted, it remained possible to construct a low-energy building.

Solar energy application

The building is constructed of reinforced concrete slabs and sand-lime brickwork. The insulated external walls are 20 cm thick, meeting Swiss passive house standards.
The southern, checkerboard facade has been conceived as a large solar gain element; translucent, triple-layer, insulating glass panels were specifically developed for this project and are incorporated into the elevations of the bedrooms. Prismatic glass sun-shading elements are located within the outer cavity of the window construction, reflecting the rays of the summer sun while allowing the lower rays of the winter sun to enter the building. Grey polycarbonate panels filled with a phase change material (PCM) have been inserted within the second window cavity. This material, a salt-hydrate, acts as a latent heat storage element, melting when warmed by the sun and absorbing energy. Later, as the building cools, the warmth is released back into the building, creating a comfortable internal climate. By simultaneously activating the ceiling slabs, additional warmth is produced in winter and cooling in summer. Fresh air is provided by both a 24-hour ventilation system, and from the internal communication zone. The heating system and warm water are provided by two discrete pumps and supported by a solar system. The entire heating system is contained in three compact rooms in the top storey.

Project Details
Usage: single storey apartments
Units: 20 2-room apartments (57 m²)
Provisions: lift
 storage space allocated to each apartment
Access: access walkways
Internal room height: 2.46 m
Construction type: reinforced concrete
Total internal volume: 6,050 m³
Usable floor area: 1,680 m²
Total site area: 1,233 m²
Construction cost: 3.9 million CHF
Funding: privately funded
Construction time: Sept. 2003 – Nov. 2004

site plan
scale 1:2500

schematic sections
solar gain facade
A summer sun
   angle of incidence > 40°
   total reflection of sun's rays
B winter sun
   angle of incidence < 35°
   melting of PCM
   uninterrupted admission of sun's rays

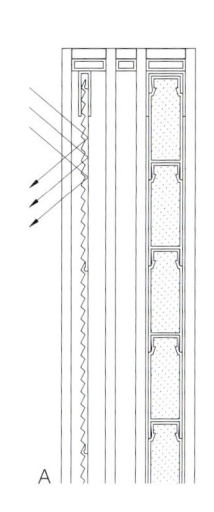

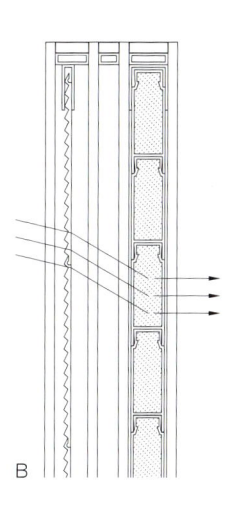

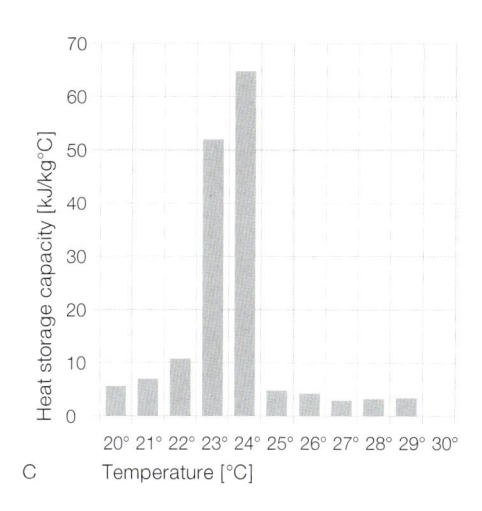

sections
floor plans
scale 1:500
A second floor
B first and third floors
C ground floor

1 room
2 loggia
3 living room
4 kitchen
5 storage space
6 seating area

aa

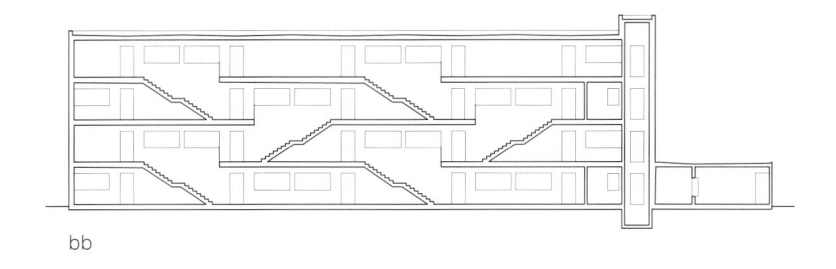

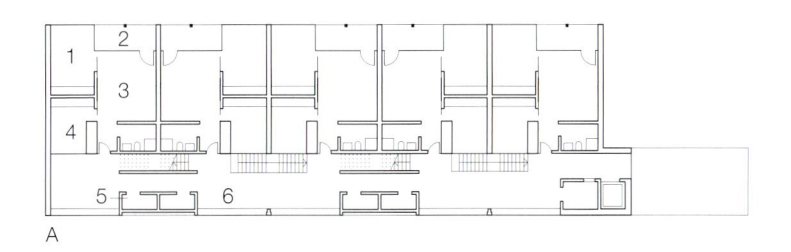

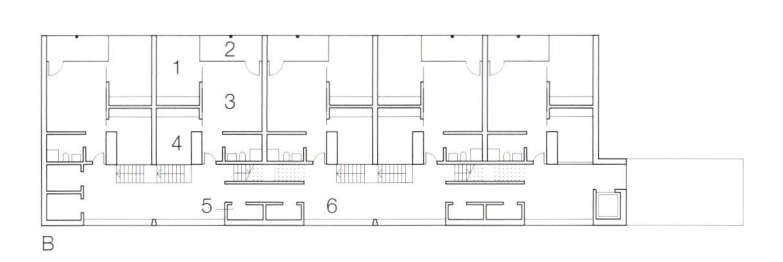

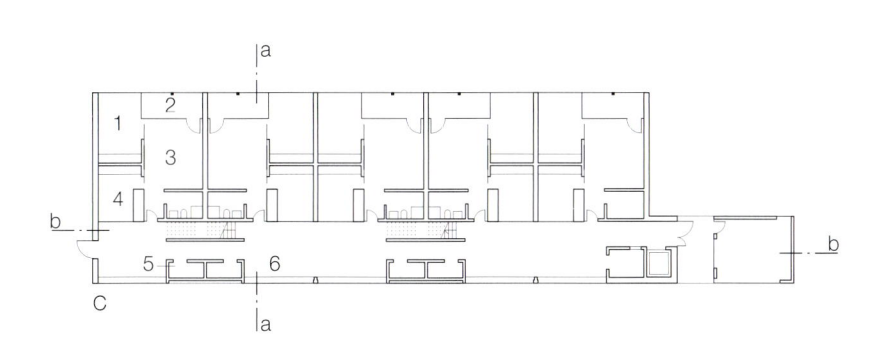

bb

A

B

C

81

vertical and horizontal section south facade
scale 1:10

1. 1.5 mm powder-coated sheet metal flashing
2. roof construction:
   80 mm gravel
   bituminous-polymer roof membrane,
   double layer
   bituminous-polymer matting
   180 mm rigid foam thermal insulation
   vapour barrier, undercoat
   330 mm r. c. slab
   5 mm plaster
3. 490 × 120 mm glulam rafter, waterproof
4. 90 mm composite thermal insulation system
5. handrail: 60 × 12 mm steel flats
6. winter garden double sliding window:
   5 mm toughened glass + 18 mm cavity +
   5 mm toughened glass in aluminium frame
7. vertical awning
8. winter garden floor construction:
   3 mm synthetic resin
   33 mm screed
   separation layer
   40 mm impact sound insulation
   250 mm r. c. slab
   5 mm plaster
9. insulating glass in timber frame
   1000 mm clear opening
10. 246 × 87 mm glulam rafter, waterproof
    100 × 65 × 4 mm aluminium angle
11. solar facade (U = 0.48 W/m²K)
    6 mm toughened glass + 20 mm cavity with
    6 mm prismatic panels +
    6 mm toughened glass +10 mm cavity +
    6 mm toughened glass +
    24 mm cavity with latent heat storage
    modules + 6 mm toughened glass
    with ceramic screen print
12. room floor construction:
    10 mm parquet
    60 mm underfloor heating screed
    separation layer
    20 mm impact sound insulation
    250 mm reinforced concrete slab
    75 mm thermal insulation composite system
13. double leaf thermally separated party wall
14. fixed insulating glazing in timber frame
15. sliding door stop
16. welded stainless steel column:
    60 × 4 mm flange, 60 × 12 mm web,
    60 × 3 mm flange

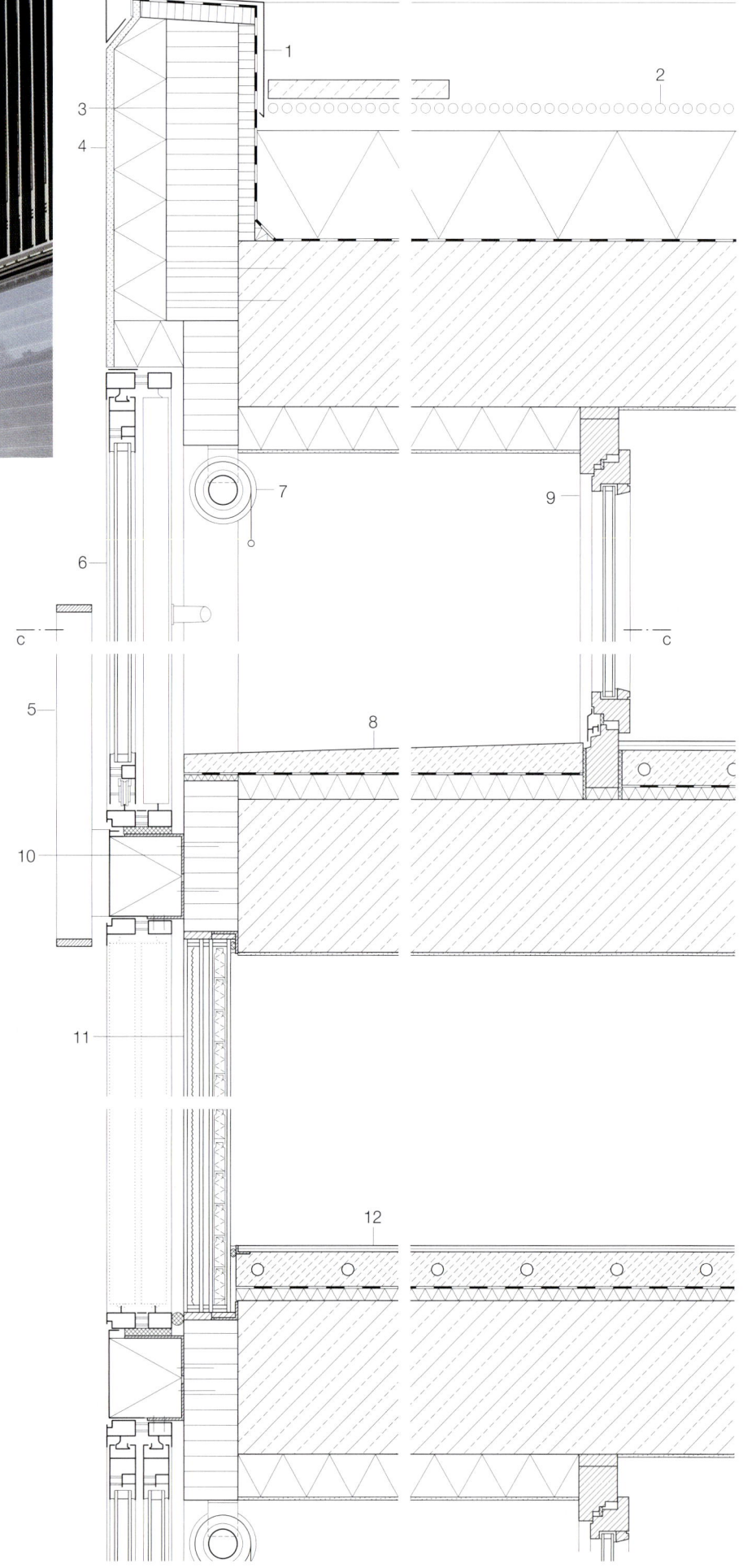

cc

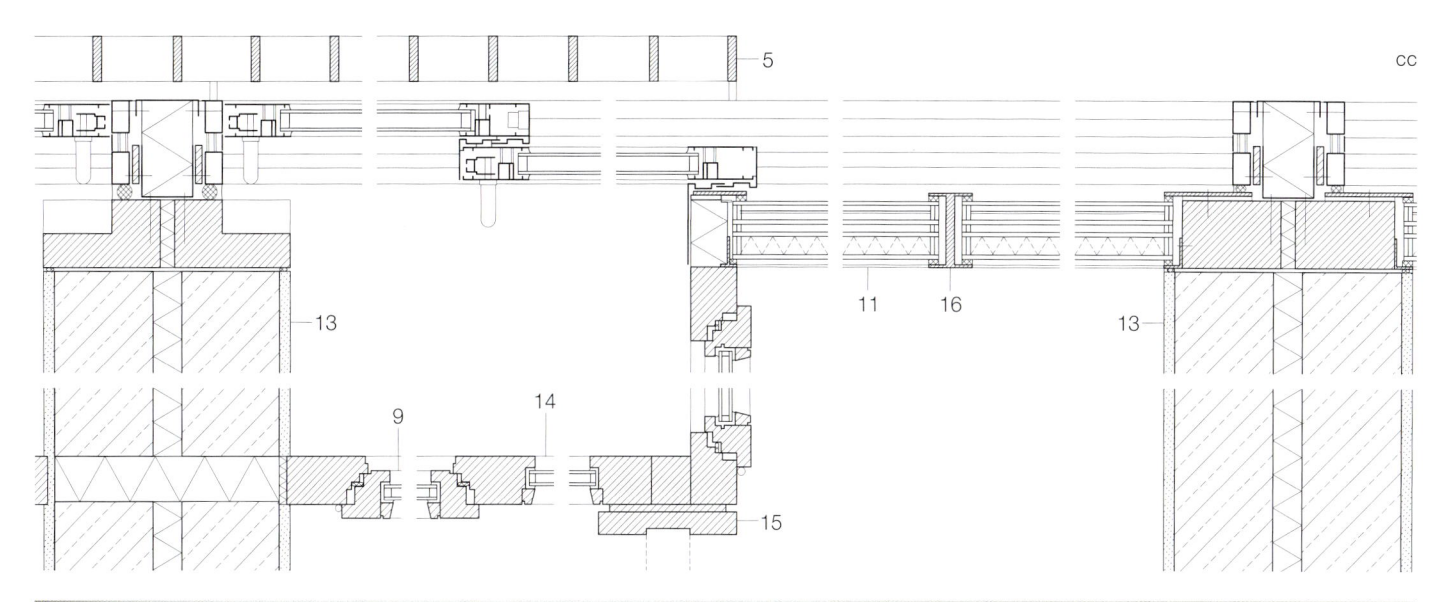

5

13

9 14

11 16

13

15

Centre for Seniors in Lich

Architects: Pfeifer Roser Kuhn, Freiburg

Assisted and independent living
Domestic units for residents with dementia
Small scale cluster structure

This centre for seniors in Lich was erected as part of a programme, initiated by the state of Hesse, dedicated to improving the standard of living of the elderly. The guiding principle is to provide the residents, many of whom suffer from dementia, with as much normality and independence as possible. A concept of interactive domestic units was developed.

Urban planning context

Subdivided into three sections, the centre for seniors is located immediately adjacent to the palace gardens. Two U-shaped buildings accommodate the assisted living units while the tract of apartments, which completes the development to the south, provides the independent housing. A trapezoidal courtyard forms the centre of the development, providing access to a café, administration facilities and a small chapel. All internal routes, fixtures and fittings have been designed to be barrier-free; for example the application of wheelchair accessible kitchen benches and height-adjustable bathtubs. Compatibility with the surrounding two and three storey timber-framed constructions and network of medieval streets has been addressed by the architects through proportion, spatial arrangement and material selection.

While the domestic units are of mixed construction of reinforced concrete and masonry with the facades clad in larch boarding, the independent living tract is of timber-framed construction with reinforced concrete floor slabs.

Domestic units

All of the domestic units are ranged around internal courtyards; they are accessed via small entry foyers and are individually arranged on single levels. Eight residents combine to make up one unit. The focal points of the units are the generously proportioned kitchen-living areas with the associated balconies or terraces. The day-to-day living is centred around these spaces; cooking, washing and ironing, the residents being involved at all times. In a communal wing, the private rooms for the residents are individually accessed from a central corridor. Fixed glazing opens up the rooms to generous external views, while set-backs in the facade structure produce an expansive appearance.

Independent living for the elderly

The 27 apartments, which are connected via northern access balconies, are located in the elongated independent living tract. They are spread out over two storeys. Opening out from the living room to the southern loggia, the two-room apartments benefit from uninterrupted views of the palace gardens. The adjacent zones of kitchen and bathroom facilities provide puffers between the residents and the access balconies.

Project Details
Usage: independent and assisted living
Independent living: 27 2-room apartments (50.9 m²)
Assisted living: 56 rooms (24.3 m²) organised into seven groups of eight residents each
Access: access balconies, central corridor
Internal room height: 2.5 m
Construction type: masonry with larch cladding, reinforced concrete slabs, timber-framed construction
Total internal volume: 21,320 m³
Total floor area: 7,002 m²
Usable floor area: U-shaped 2,039 m², tract 1,160 m²
Total site area: 1,551 m²
Construction cost: 9.03 million Euros
Construction time: 1998–2003

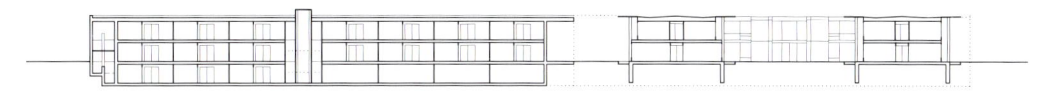

section · floor plan
scale 1:1000

aa

1 entrance hall
2 communal courtyard
3 internal courtyard
4 communal space
5 independent apartment
6 single room
7 administration
8 café
9 chapel

85

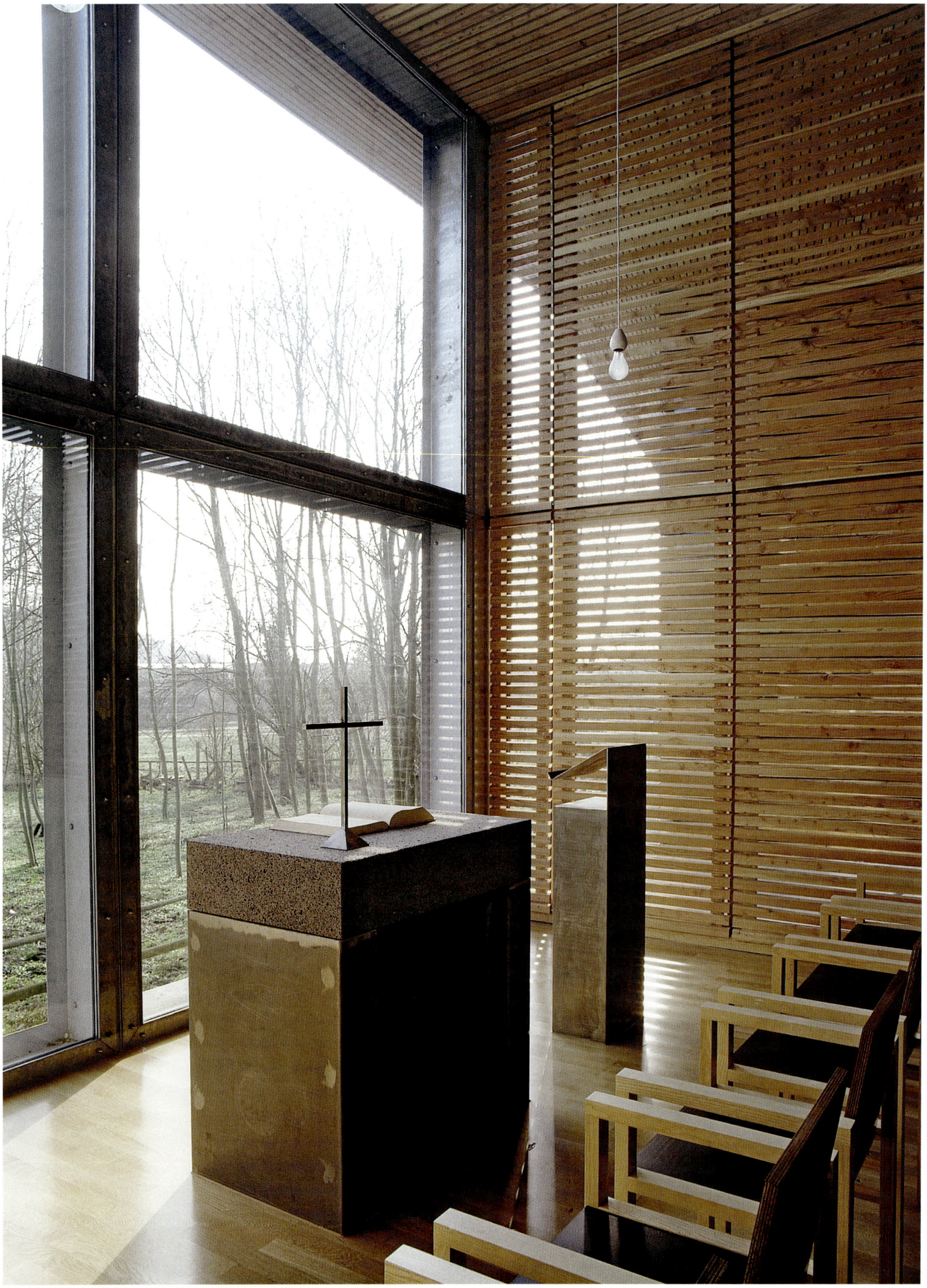

bb

A

B

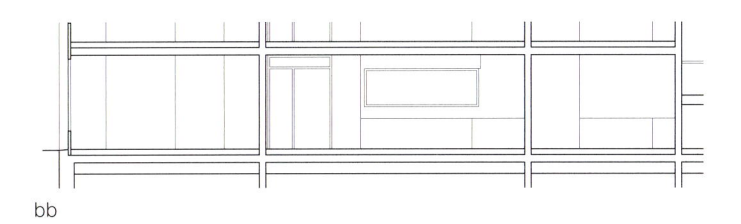

C

section
floor plans
scale 1:200

A communal area
B care accommodation (24.2 m²)
C 2-room apartment (50.9 m²)

1 care accommodation
2 2-room apartment
3 communal kitchen
4 pantry
5 utility room
6 living
7 terrace

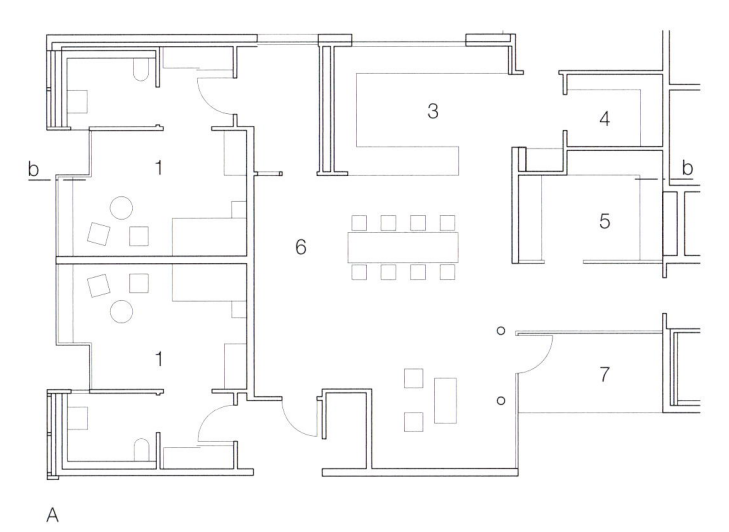

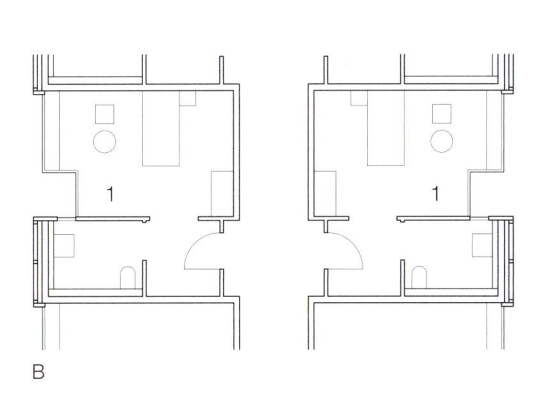

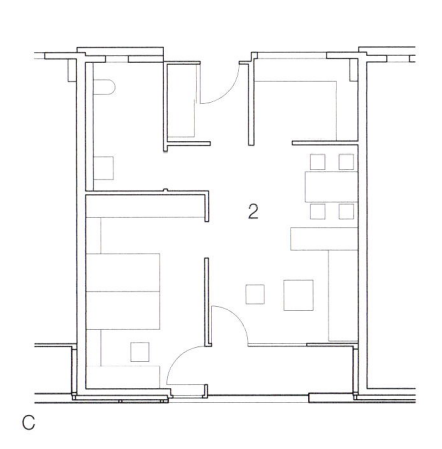

87

vertical section
horizontal section
scale 1:20

1 flashing
2 cantilever:
   waterproofing
   25 mm timber construction panel
   60 × 100–130 mm framing timber
   30 × 50 mm timber counter battens
   diffusion porous membrane
   20 × 50 mm larch cladding, screw fixed
3 100 mm steel I-beam
4 100 mm steel channel section
5 roof construction:
   vegetation layer
   double-layer bituminous barrier
   280–200 mm insulation, with fall
   vapour barrier
   200 mm reinforced concrete slab
6 fixing for steel profile
7 200 × 25 mm reveal
8 timber window frame with double glazing
9 4 mm RHS window sill
10 spandrel panel:
   10 mm larch 3-ply board
   15 mm insulation
   10 mm larch 3-ply board
11 floor construction:
   10 mm linoleum
   40 mm screed
   separation layer
   60 mm levelling insulation
   40 mm impact sound insulation
   separation layer
   200 mm reinforced concrete slab
12 wall construction:
   20 × 50 mm larch cladding
   ventilation cavity, 95 × 60 mm battens
   diffusion porous membrane
   120 mm thermal insulation between
   120 × 80 mm counter battens
   175 mm sand-lime masonry
   15 mm internal render
13 partition wall:
   40 × 40 mm steel channel
   2× 12.5 mm plasterboard,
   mounted to one side
14 spandrel:
   50 × 300 mm plywood

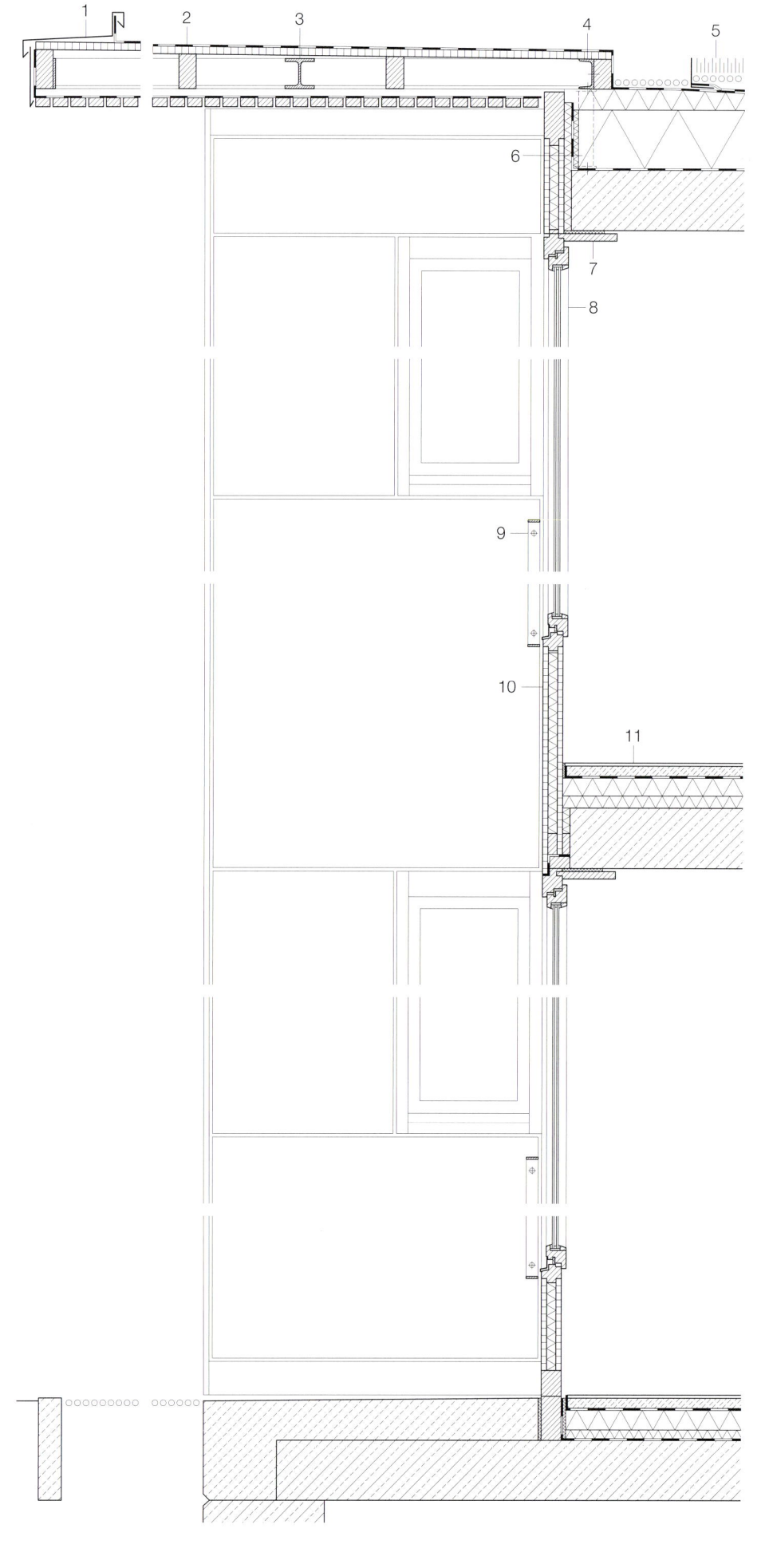

88

13

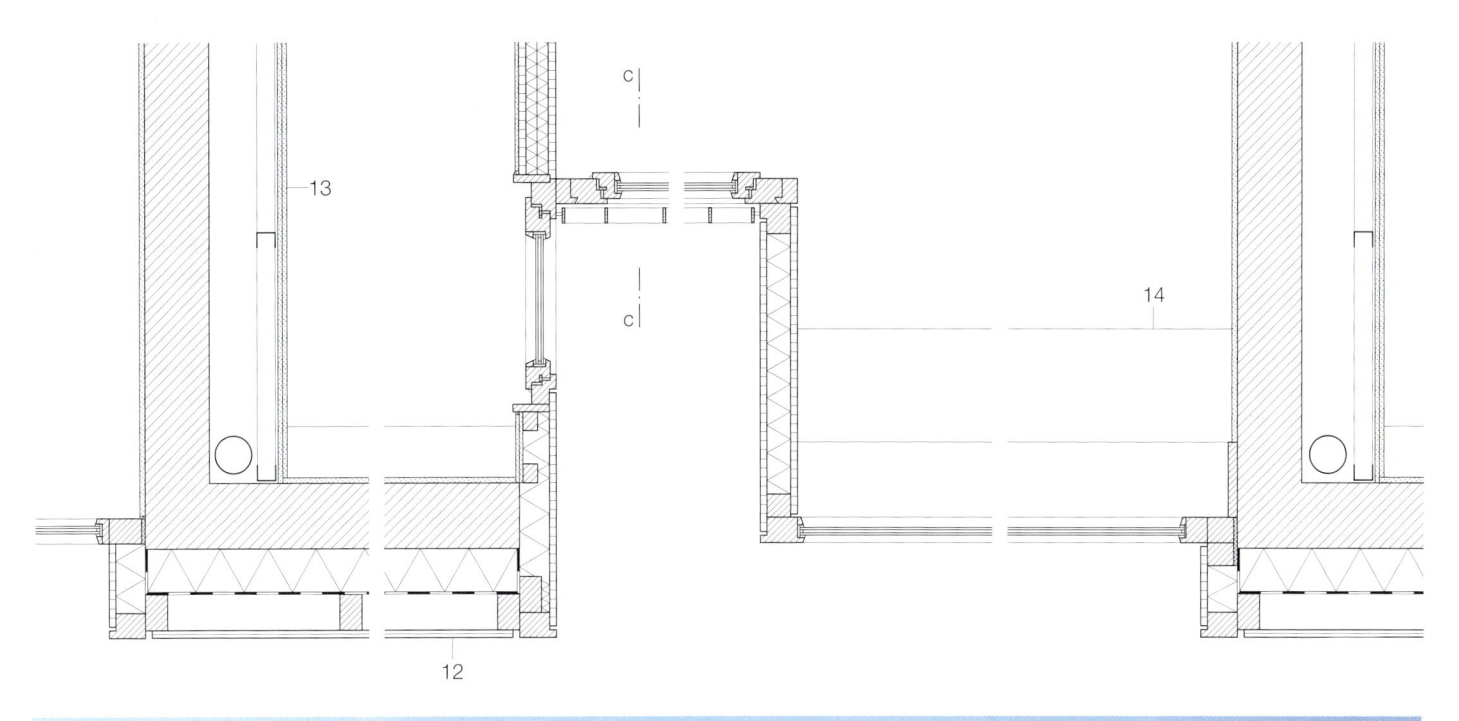

14

12

Long House on Henza Island

Architects: Kawai Architects/Toshiakii Kawai, Kyoto

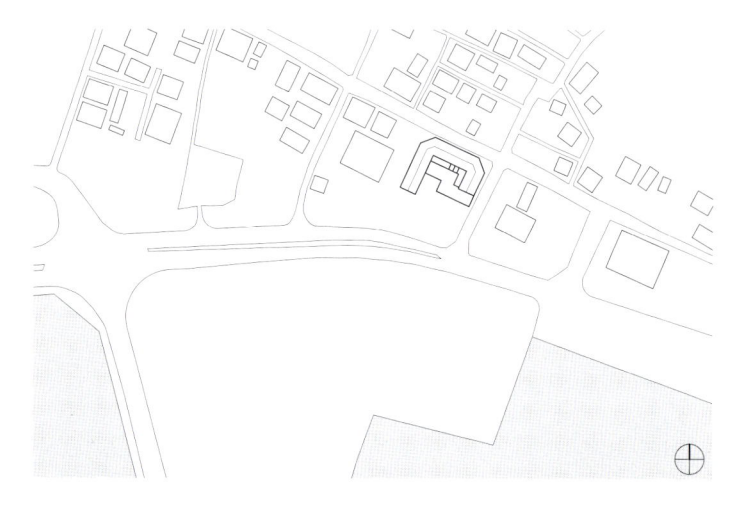

Ambulant and Care Accommodation
Natural Building Materials

Henza, a small Japanese island in the Pacific Ocean, is the location of the "Long House", a care facility for both ambulant and permanent aged residents in need of care. The subtropical climate in the region produces an annual mean temperature of 22.5 °C. The incidence of typhoons and lack of natural building materials have led to the predominance of reinforced concrete structures on the island.

Two functions under one roof

The ambulant day-care facilities of the "Long House" are located on the ground floor, while the upper level is given over to long-term care accommodation for 20 residents. From the main entrance one approaches the generously proportioned communal space, with café and dining room, as well as the nearby relaxation room and washing facilities. The stairwell, with lift, is accessible from either a covered external space or directly from the garages at the rear of the building.
The sense of community, and communication between residents are enhanced by a wide corridor in the care accommodation area. As much space, in fact, is allocated to the communications corridor as to the accommodation of 16 single-rooms and two double-rooms.
Outdoor spaces vary greatly in their treatment; articulated by paths of differing surfaces and garden beds on both levels, they extend and augment the recreational areas.

Construction for a comfortable internal climate

Reinforced concrete is well-known to be an effective heat accumulator; unfortunately this is a negative aspect in hotter climates. Natural materials were selected in order to balance the effects of the construction.
The ventilated facade is clad with timber; in the interior, untreated timber acts as thermal insulation while also regulating internal humidity levels.
The entire pitched roof is planted, insulating the building and simultaneously storing moisture. Water is pumped by an irrigation system from a subterranean tank to the ridge beam and distributed over the entire roof. Due to the continuous breezes, the water continually evaporates and the reinforced concrete roof is naturally cooled. The warm air rises into the raised roof structure creating a comfortable internal climate. Every room in the upper level benefits from a ventilation flap, augmented by individually adjustable air-conditioners set into the niches in front of the windows.

Project Details
Usage: Ambulant and care accommodation with 20 beds
Access: one-sided plan
Internal room height: 2.43 m ground floor
4.32 m first floor
Construction type: reinforced concrete
Total internal volume: 4,083.2 m³
Usable floor area: 1,244 m²
Total site area: 1,425 m²
Covered site area: 834.9 m²
Construction cost: 1.17 million Euros
Date of completion: March 2006

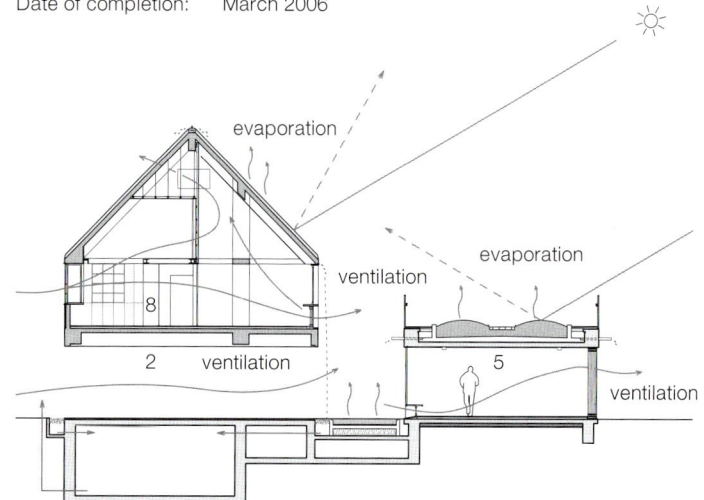

site plan   scale 1:4000
section with ventilation system
scale 1:250
section • floor plans
scale 1:500

1 forecourt
2 garage
3 entrance
4 café
5 dining room
6 kitchen
7 relaxation room
8 single room
9 double room
10 roof terrace

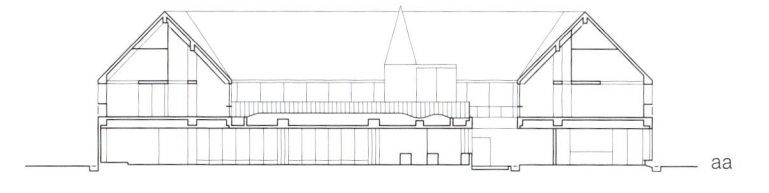

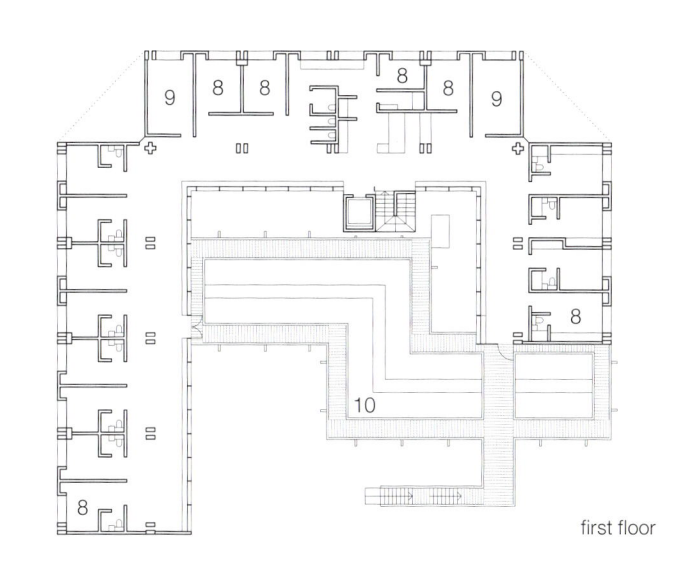

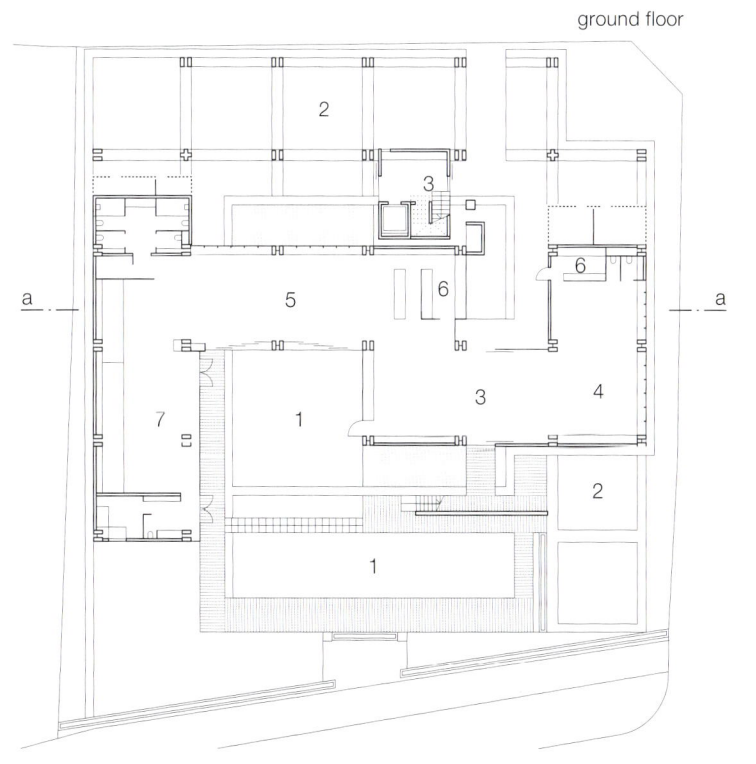

aa

first floor

ground floor

91

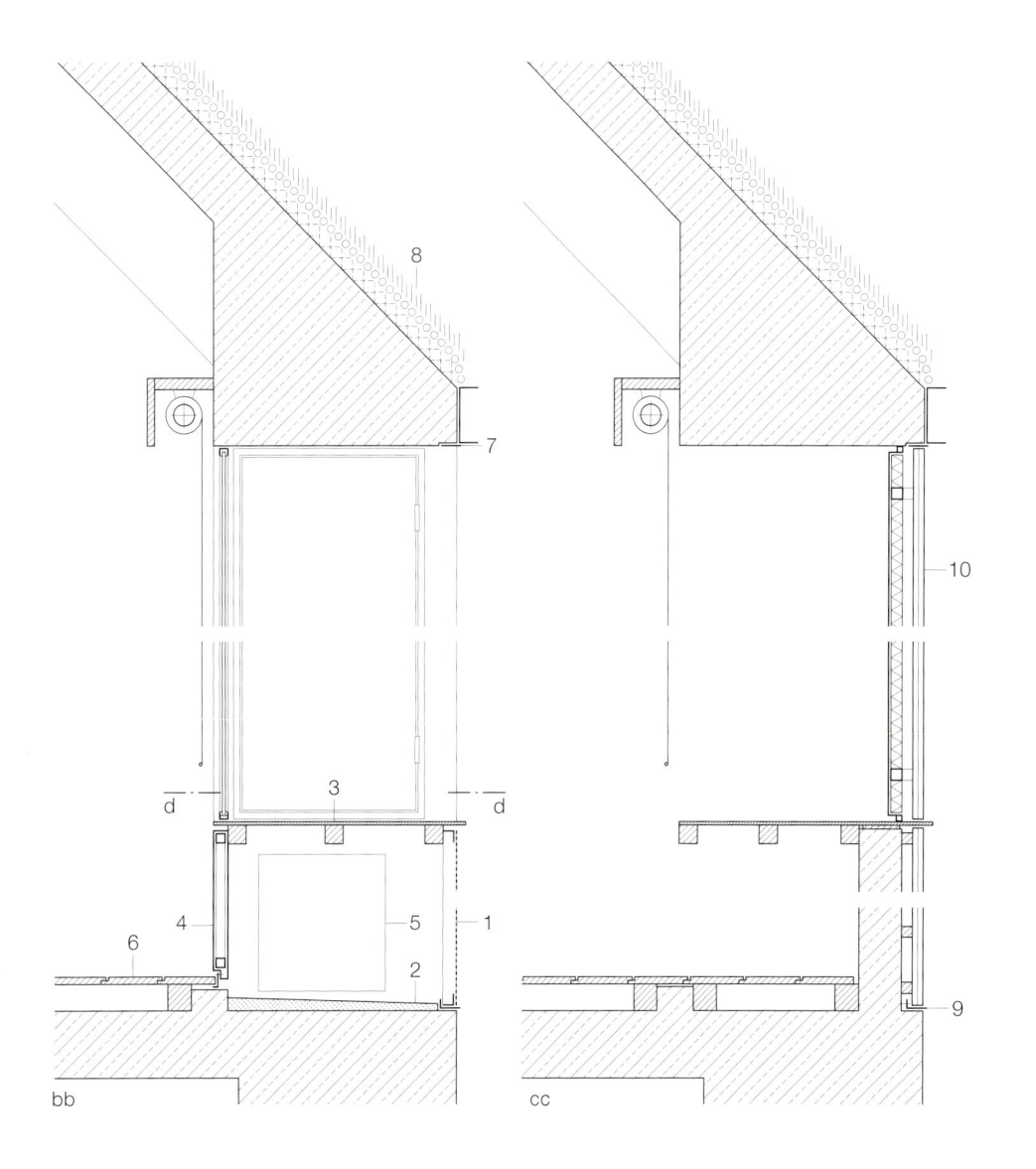

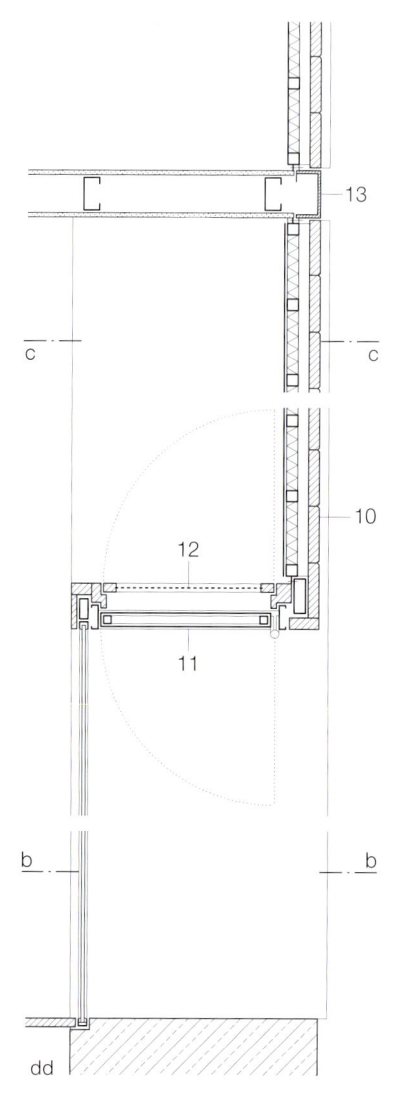

vertical sections · horizontal section
single room facade
scale 1:20

1 expanded mesh
2 waterproof mortar
3 9 mm steel sheet
4 40 mm steel sheet, demountable for maintenance
5 air conditioning
6 floor construction:
   20 mm parquet on
   70 × 60 mm timber framework
   180 mm reinforced concrete slab
7 5 × 80 mm steel flat
8 roof construction:
   extensive greening
   paper underlay, 100 mm cellulose mixed with grass seeds
   wire mesh, reinforced concrete slab
9 0.6 mm galvanised steel sheet
10 wall construction:
   30 mm cedar cladding
   ventilation cavity
   thermal insulation
   0.6 mm steel sheet cladding
11 steel sheet ventilation flap
12 insect screen
13 150 × 75 × 10 mm steel channel

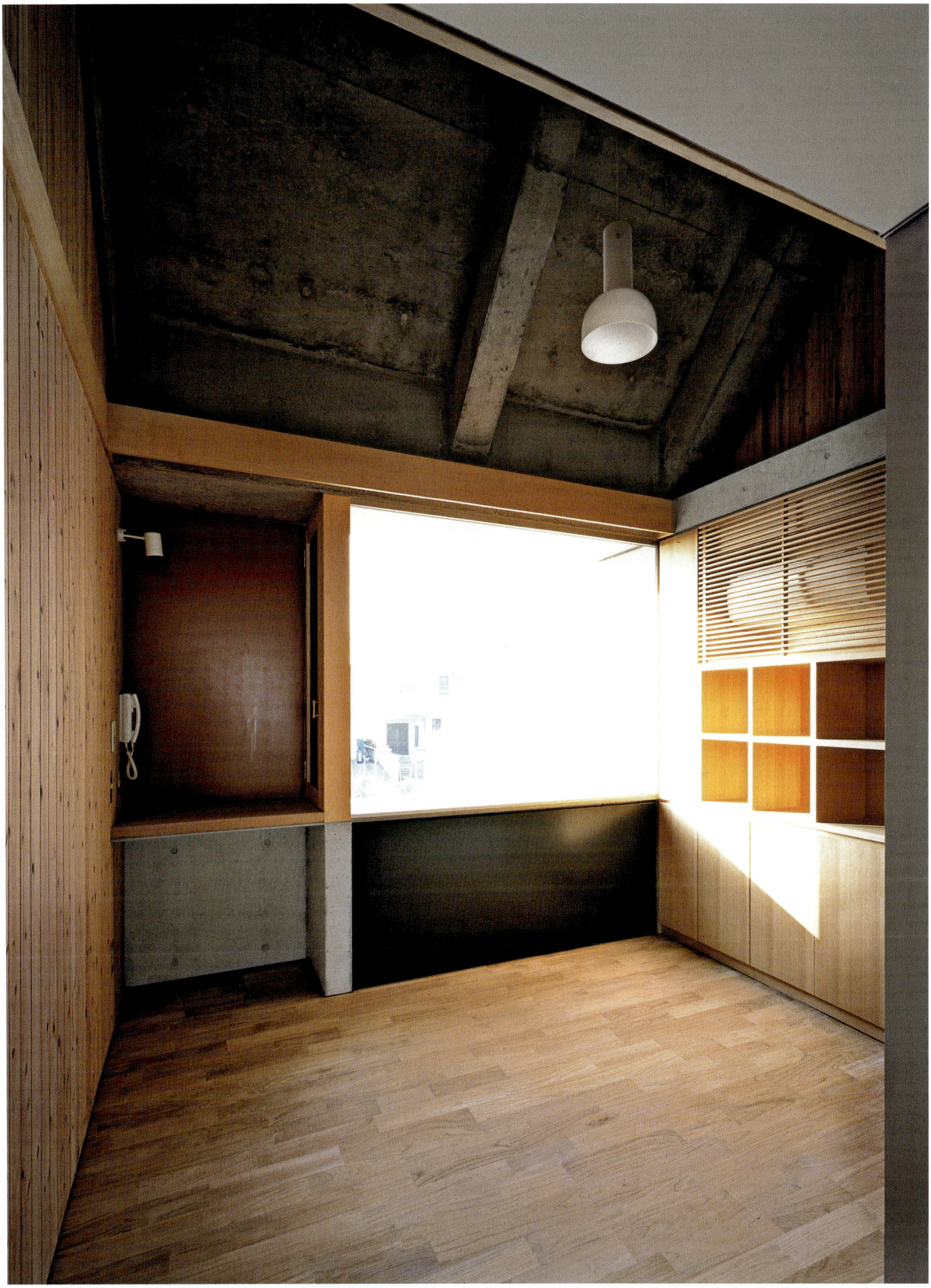

Seniors' Centre in Magdeburg

Architects: löhle neubauer architects, Augsburg

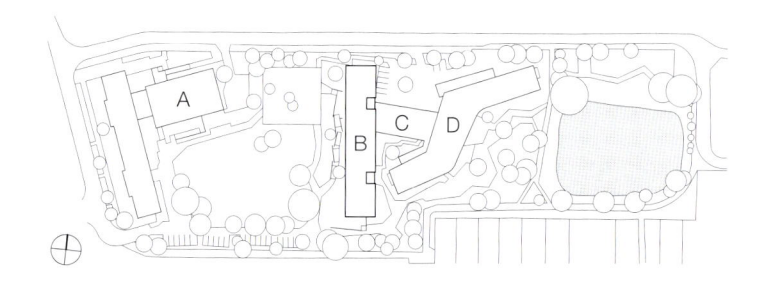

Energy efficient renovation
Technical and design standardisation
Built extension for 80 residents

Sliding perforated metal panels, transparent spandrels and glazed facades – no casual observer would suspect that concealed behind such a facade is a pre-fabricated slab construction dating from the 1970s. But that is exactly the case; this renovated nursing home, which is part of a centre for seniors, was originally built in a large-panel prefabricated construction system. In order to be worthy of this highly attractive location on Neustädter Lake, an all encompassing concept of renovation and extension was developed.

Unification of existing and new constructions

The most western of the four buildings is the six-storey-high seniors' residence, moving eastward the renovated building makes up part of the nursing home after the removal of the original top storey. An interconnecting building, which accommodates administration facilities, links the renovated nursing home to the new nursing home structure. The new construction's irregular form relieves the rigidity of the existing geometry of the scheme and creates an internal courtyard entrance. On the ground floor the dining hall, with open terrace, looks out over the lake. The private rooms are arranged along a "residential street" in the upper levels. The corridors to the north benefit from full-height glazing and widen where the building bends. Semi-private niches articulate the individual entrances to the rooms and are reminiscent of house entrances. Full width glazing in the rooms and low-level window sills allow residents generous views from their rooms.

Renovation

Apart from renovating the building in terms of energy efficiency, the individual rooms in the upper levels have been linked together in pairs, creating new units where the bathroom and change room are shared. The dimensions of the rooms have been enlarged by recessing the wardrobes. By removing certain panels from the facades, the quality of the central corridor has been enhanced and natural illumination increased. Thermally insulated windows, an insulating composite system applied to the external walls, and the new non-vented roof structure all contribute to the reduction of the primary-energy load from 127 to 85 kWh/m^{2}a.

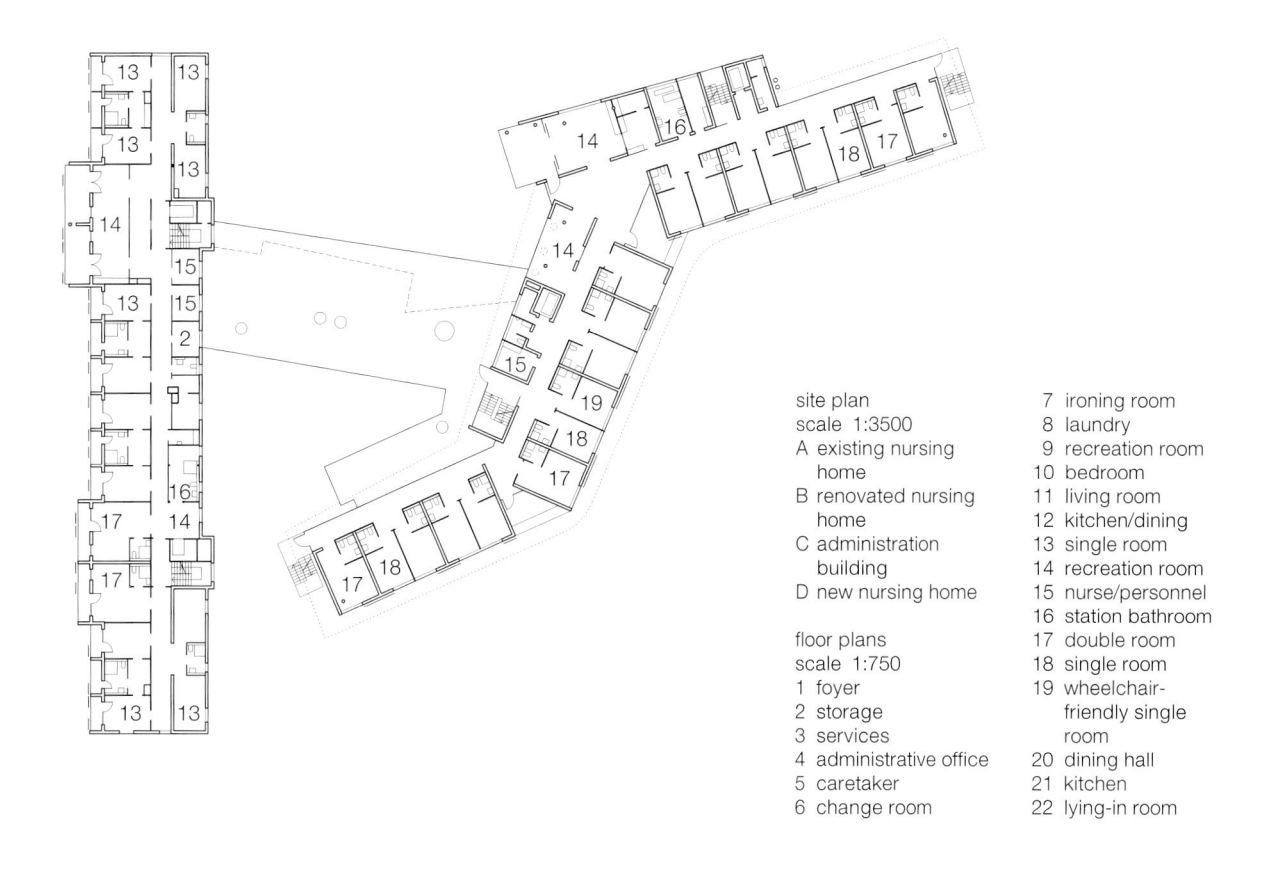

site plan
scale 1:3500
A existing nursing home
B renovated nursing home
C administration building
D new nursing home

floor plans
scale 1:750
1 foyer
2 storage
3 services
4 administrative office
5 caretaker
6 change room
7 ironing room
8 laundry
9 recreation room
10 bedroom
11 living room
12 kitchen/dining
13 single room
14 recreation room
15 nurse/personnel
16 station bathroom
17 double room
18 single room
19 wheelchair-friendly single room
20 dining hall
21 kitchen
22 lying-in room

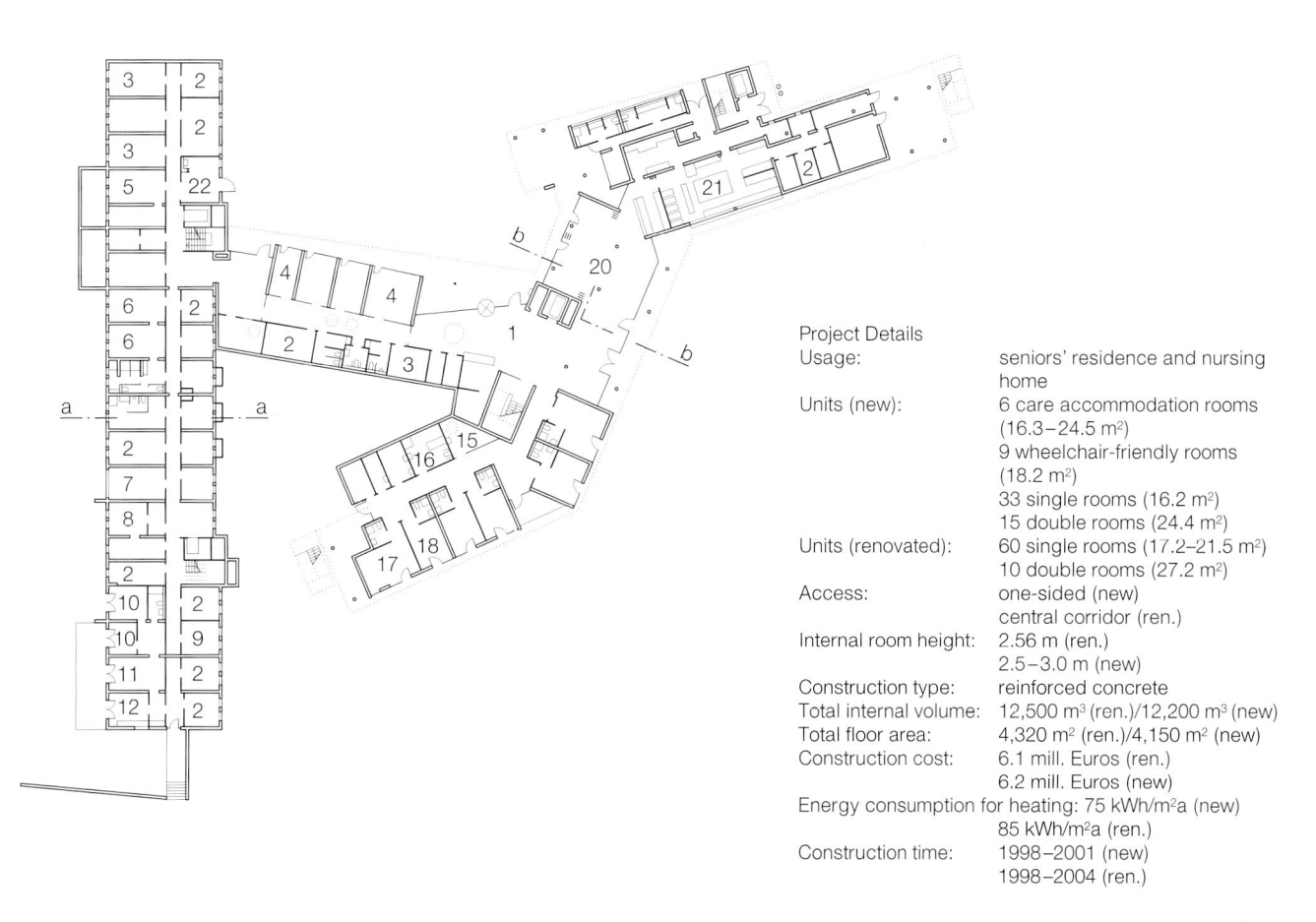

Project Details
Usage: seniors' residence and nursing home
Units (new): 6 care accommodation rooms (16.3–24.5 m^2)
9 wheelchair-friendly rooms (18.2 m^2)
33 single rooms (16.2 m^2)
15 double rooms (24.4 m^2)
Units (renovated): 60 single rooms (17.2–21.5 m^2)
10 double rooms (27.2 m^2)
Access: one-sided (new)
central corridor (ren.)
Internal room height: 2.56 m (ren.)
2.5–3.0 m (new)
Construction type: reinforced concrete
Total internal volume: 12,500 m^3 (ren.)/12,200 m^3 (new)
Total floor area: 4,320 m^2 (ren.)/4,150 m^2 (new)
Construction cost: 6.1 mill. Euros (ren.)
6.2 mill. Euros (new)
Energy consumption for heating: 75 kWh/m^{2}a (new)
85 kWh/m^{2}a (ren.)
Construction time: 1998–2001 (new)
1998–2004 (ren.)

95

floor plan alternatives
scale 1:200
A building B single room (16.4 m^2)
  change room (8.0 m^2)
  shared bathroom (8.3 m^2)
B building D room type
  double room (24.4 m^2)
  bathroom (4.0 m^2)
  wheelchair-friendly single room (18.7 m^2)
  wheelchair-friendly bathroom (5.2 m^2)
  single room (16.2 m^2)

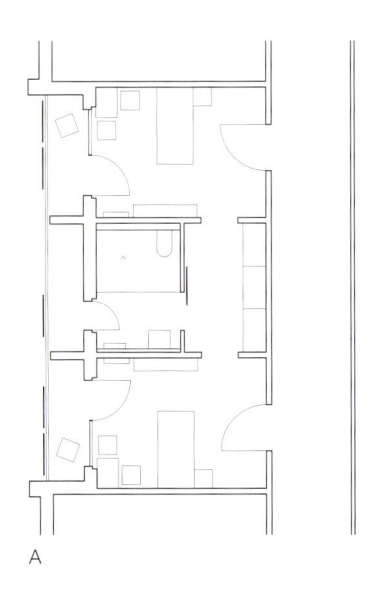

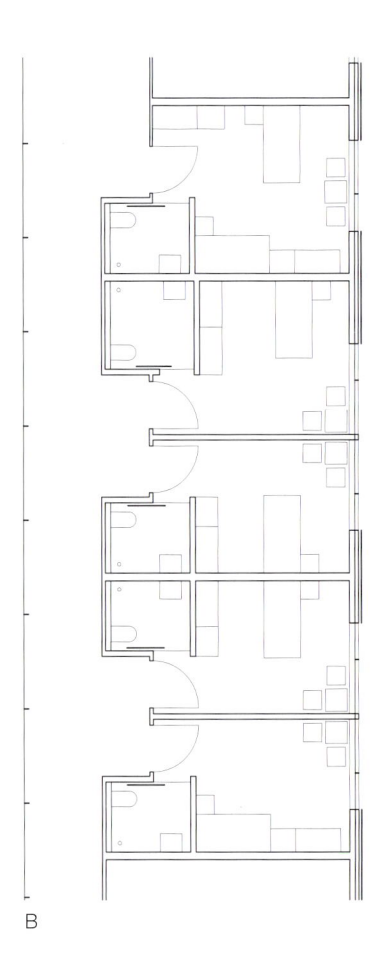

aa

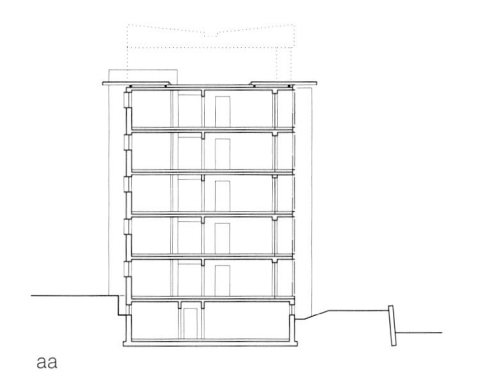

section building B
scale 1:500
section east facade
section west facade
scale 1:20

1 2 mm plastic sealing layer
   4 mm synthetic fibre felt levelling layer
   21 mm timber boarding
   100 × 160 mm timber rafters
   30 × 50 mm battens
   3 mm powder coated aluminium sheeting
2 100 × 180 mm and 160 × 220 mm roof beams
3 roof construction:
   extensive green roof
   50 mm gravel layer, 10 mm protective mat
   2 mm plastic sealing layer
   80–160 mm rigid-foam thermal insulation
   bituminous membrane
   140 mm existing reinforced concrete slab
   15 mm cement-plaster render
4 330 mm steel channel section
5 150 × 30 × 10 mm steel RHS
6 100 × 65 × 10 mm steel angle
7 40 mm and 80 mm rigid-foam thermal
   insulation composite system
8 larch door element with double glazing
9 50 × 10 mm powder-coated galv. steel RHS
10 sliding shutter:
   3 mm perforated aluminium sheeting,
   powder-coated on
   40 mm steel SHS frame
11 balcony floor construction:
   30 mm galvanised metal grating,
   slip-resistant
   40 mm galvanised steel SHS sub-construction
   10 mm protective mat
   2 mm plastic sealing layer
   40 mm rigid-roam thermal insulation
12 single room floor construction:
   3 mm linoleum
   50 mm floating cement screed
   polyethylene membrane
   22 mm impact sound insulation
   30 mm existing bonded cement screed
   140 mm existing reinforced concrete slab
13 3 mm aluminium sheet flashing,
   powder coated and screw fixed to window
14 heavy-weight coated larch window element,
   with insulating glazing
15 30 mm beech wood window sill, oiled
16 240 mm vertically perforated brickwork
   spandrel
17 240 mm existing prefabricated reinforced
   concrete element
18 15 mm single-layer cement-plaster render
19 60 × 80 mm timber scantling
20 22 mm heavy-weight coated lam. timber panel
   15 mm ventilation cavity
   60 mm rigid foam thermal insulation

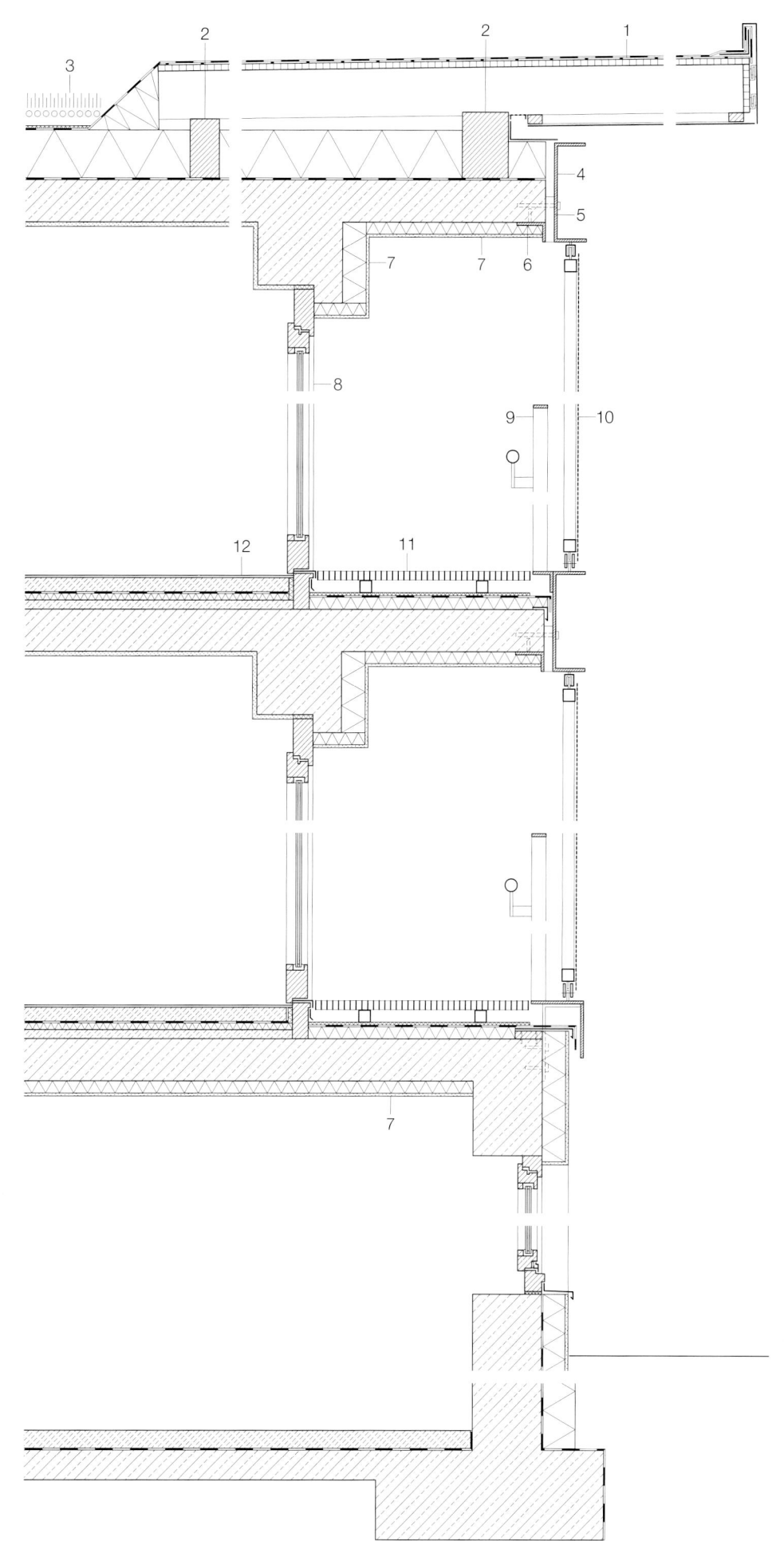

97

bb

section building B   scale 1:500
section north facade
section south facade   scale 1:20

1. 50 mm gravel, 10 mm glass protective mat
   plastic sealing layer
   4 mm synthetic fibre felt levelling layer
   150 mm prefabricated concrete element
2. 175 × 245 mm and 175 × 265 mm lightweight concrete bearer
3. roof construction:
   50 mm gravel, 2 mm plastic sealing layer
   80–160 mm rigid-foam thermal insulation
   bit. membrane, 280 mm r.c. slab
4. 3 mm aluminium sheeting, edged
   50 mm rigid-foam thermal insulation
5. 2 steel flats, 130 × 280 × 5 mm with
   120 × 385 × 10 mm flat steel top plate
6. double glazing in
   50 × 120 mm aluminium frame
7. Ø 45 mm beech hand rail on
   80 × 80 mm steel Z-profile
8. 50 × 50 mm steel angle
9. 2 mm aluminium angle
10. corridor floor construction: 3 mm linoleum
    66 mm screed, polyethylene membrane
    30 mm impact sound insulation
    280 mm reinforced concrete slab
11. 120 × 280 × 10 mm steel angle, welded
12. 110 mm and 140 mm rigid-foam
    thermal insulation composite system
13. double glazing in
    50 × 160 mm laminated beech frame
14. dining hall floor construction:
    25 mm parquet, 50 mm screed
    polyethylene membrane
    22 mm impact sound insulation
    50 mm thermal insulation
    4 mm bituminous membrane
    400 mm reinforced concrete slab
15. 160 mm thermal insulation composite system
16. 75 × 170 × 5 mm steel angle, welded
17. sliding shutter:
    3 mm perforated aluminium sheeting,
    powder coated, on 40 mm steel SHS frame
18. heavy-weight coated larch window element,
    with insulating glazing
19. 30 mm beech wood window sill, oiled
20. sliding shutter: 30 × 60 mm larch louvers
    40 × 60 mm steel RHS frame
21. intensive care station floor construction:
    3 mm linoleum, 50 mm screed
    polyethylene membrane
    22 mm impact sound insulation
    80 mm thermal insulation, bituminous
    membrane, 250 mm r.c. slab

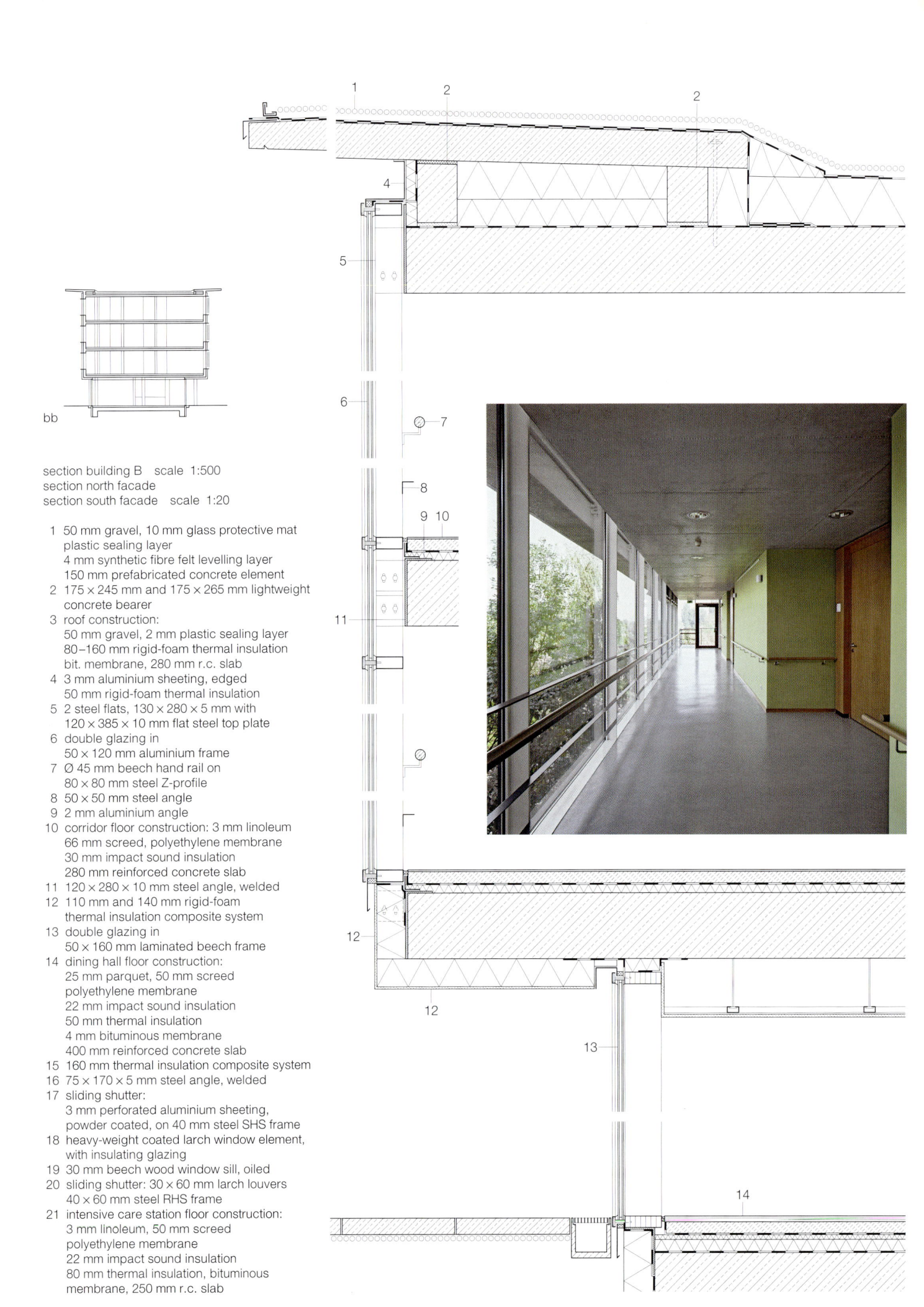

3

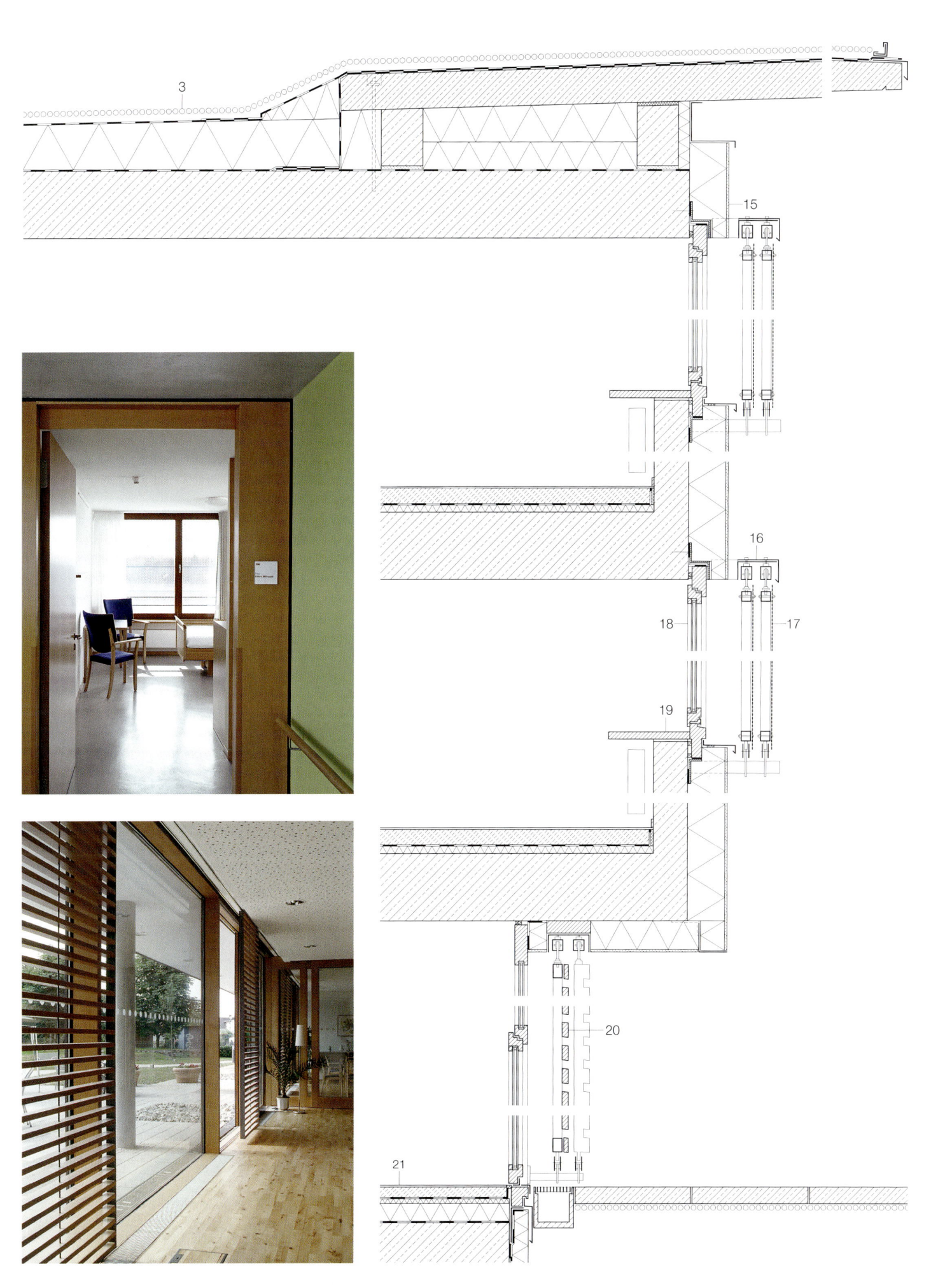

15

16
18 17

19

20

21

99

Residence for Seniors in Neumarkt am Wallersee

Architects: Kada + Wittfeld, Aachen

**58 single rooms with strong external orientation
Access zones with recreational quality
Planted atrium and protected garden zone**

This timber-clad residence for seniors is located adjacent to the church in a small town in the Salzburg lake district. A two storey H-shaped construction, it is orientated east-west and blends well with its surroundings, in terms of scale and material. The residence itself is also structured like a small community. The spatial sequences of courtyards, paths, intermediate zones and residents' rooms offer a whole range of interactive alternatives, from communal to private. The facades are clad with horizontal larch boarding and articulated by the glass and steel of the oriel windows. This wall cladding continues into the interior in the central hall and corridors, creating a warm atmosphere and comfortable internal climate. The ground floor is approached via a wide, paved ramp which leads directly to a double-height hall and intimate planted atrium. In the north-west corner the dining room is located adjacent to a small, private chapel.

The corridors are conceived as residential streets; fully glazed on the outward facing sides, providing views of the opposite wing and enhancing orientation. The internal, semi-private sides of the corridors feature set-back niches which each function as a small entry area to a pair of rooms; furnished with benches they provide seating opportunities next to the individual "front doors". Each private room has its own bathroom and can, when desired, be fitted out with a small kitchen. The oriel windows, with glass sides and tops, project the rooms outward and allow views into the garden, even from the bed. An internal call-system enables residents to contact carers when necessary. Privacy is ensured by the lack of signal lights above the doors and the direct transfer of room number to the carers' station.

sections
floor plans
scale 1:500

A ground floor
B first floor

1 entrance
2 chapel
3 atrium with plants
4 dining room
5 single room
6 carers' station

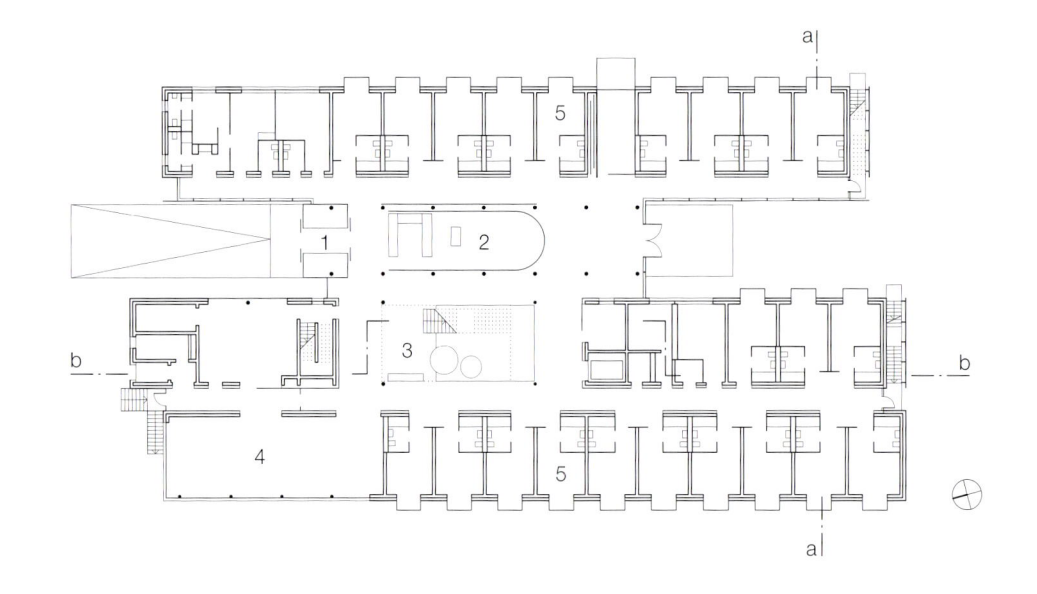

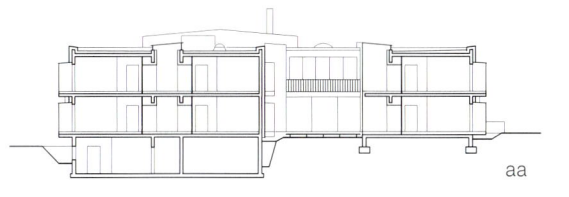

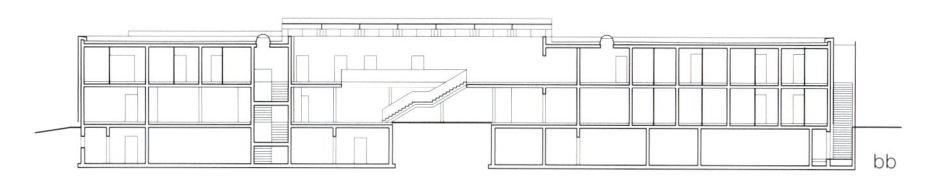

Project Details
Usage: nursing home
Units: 50 single rooms (25 m²)
 5 double rooms (31 m²)
Access: access walkway (glazed)
 central corridor
 (in some sections)
Internal room height: 2,81 m
Construction type: reinforced concrete
Total internal volume: 14,200 m³
Total floor area: 4,300 m²
Usable floor area: 3,900 m²
Total site area: 4,616 m²
Construction cost: 5.3 million Euros
Construction time: 1991–2001

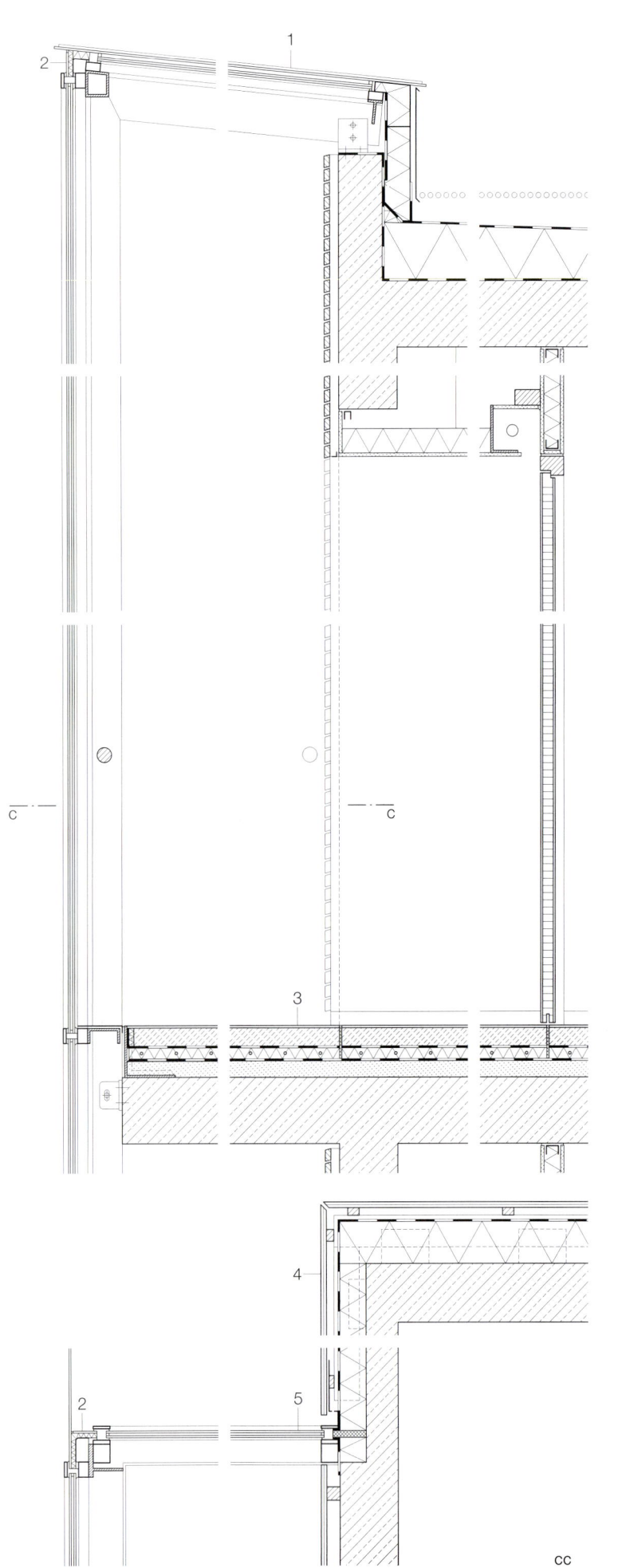

vertical and horizontal sections
glazed corridor/
seating niche/oriel window
scale 1:20

1 overhead glazing:
   8 mm toughened glass +
   12 mm cavity +
   10 mm laminated safety glass with
   screen print UV protection
2 enamelled glass sandwich panel
3 corridor floor construction:
   4 mm rubber
   2 mm grouting
   69 mm screed
   35 mm system board with
   heating pipes
   55 mm gravel
   220 mm reinforced concrete slab
4 wall construction:
   19 × 38 mm larch boarding

pine counter battens
non-combustible black
glass-fibre mat
50 × 80 mm pine scantling in
perforated metal channel
140 mm rock wool insulating board,
hydrophobically treated
150 mm reinforced concrete,
plastered and painted
5 spandrel:
double glazing, 6 mm toughened
glass + 12 mm cavity +
6 mm toughened glass
6 double glazing, 6 mm toughened
glass + 12 mm cavity +
8 mm laminated safety glass in
concealed side/bottom hung sash
7 rail construction:
welded flat steel
8 25 mm stainless steel tubular
column fixed to rail via insert
9 oriel floor construction:
8 mm bonded parquet
66 mm screed
11 mm system board
separation layer
30 mm polyurethane thermal
insulation
120 mm reinforced concrete
50 mm extruded polystyrene
thermal insulation
silicate render

dd

Centre for Seniors in Steinfeld

Architect: Dietger Wissounig, Graz

Nursing home with low-energy standards
Atrium as community centre
Public facilities on ground floor

To the west of the small district of Steinfeld in Carinthia, Austria a new nursing home has been constructed adjacent to the local school and park. The east-west orientation is a direct response to the surroundings; the service facilities provide a buffer zone to the north where a national roadway bypasses the site, while the dwellings and recreational facilities are located on the more peaceful, pastoral side. Externally the compact built form appears simple and monolithic; on the inside the visual orientation is reinforced by internal views and straightforward routes within the building. Flexible, generously-sized rooms enhance interactive communication in the building.

Internal spatial diversity

In addition to technical and administrative services, the ground floor of the complex is given over to the dining and event hall, a library and a chapel. These rooms are available to the residents and the public. Children from after-school-care come here daily for lunch, the library is open to the public and the local church service is occasionally held in the chapel. The two upper levels accommodate both care facilities and independent dwellings. The 34 single and double rooms all benefit from bathrooms designed for disabled users. Ceiling-high windows provide generous views into the surrounding landscape while their deep sills function as shelving for the inhabitants. Large recreational spaces are located between the private rooms, communal kitchens and loggias enhancing the quality of the zones. All rooms are arranged around the internal atrium which acts as both communal conservatory and central access zone with a system of walkways. Barrier-free design and accessibility for hospital beds were fundamental requirements of all rooms in order to remain flexible for possible future changes in function.

Construction

The slightly set-back ground floor is constructed of massive concrete, while the two upper levels are executed in timber framework construction. Laminated timber columns and prefabricated timber-framed walling, with services pre-installed, transfer the loads to the structural concrete slab. The facade is clad with vertical larch panelling. Deep loggias, which occasionally wrap around the corners, and individually adjustable timber shutters animate the image of the building.

Energy concept

The energy efficiency of the compact building form is supported by extensive thermal insulation. The inherent density of the building elements reduces the transmitted heat loss to levels commensurate with low-energy constructions. The ventilation system is supplied through the atrium which is provided with pre-warmed or pre-cooled air from geothermal collectors. Fresh air is supplied individually to each room and heat exchangers extract residual energy from the depleted air. Further active elements like a solar system, district heat, individually regulated heating, utilisation of rainwater and electronic ballast in the lighting system all come together to provide an energy reduction of 30% compared with other similar nursing homes.

Project Details
Usage: library, nursing home
Units: 8 double rooms (28.0 m²)
34 single rooms (19.4 m²)
Access: central corridor
Internal room height: 2.74 m
Construction type: ground floor, reinforced concrete
upper floors, prefabricated timber framing with stacked-board timber ceiling slabs
Total internal volume: 14,903 m³
Total floor area: 3,658 m²
Total site area: 8,100 m²
Construction cost: 4.15 million Euros
Heat consumption: 14 kWh/m²a
Construction time: 2004–2005

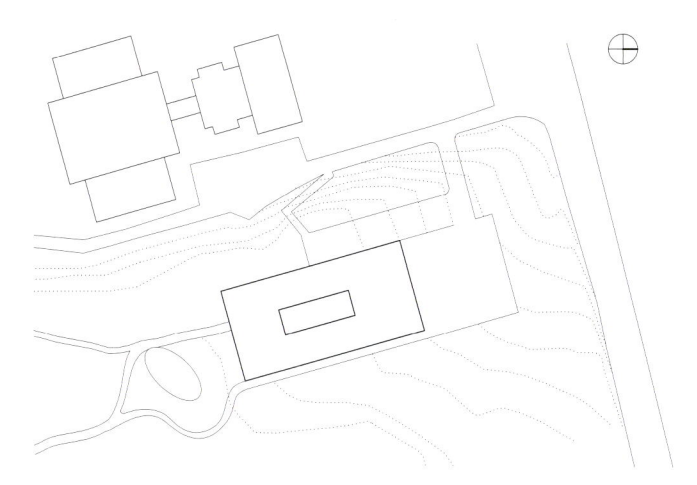

site plan
scale 1:2000

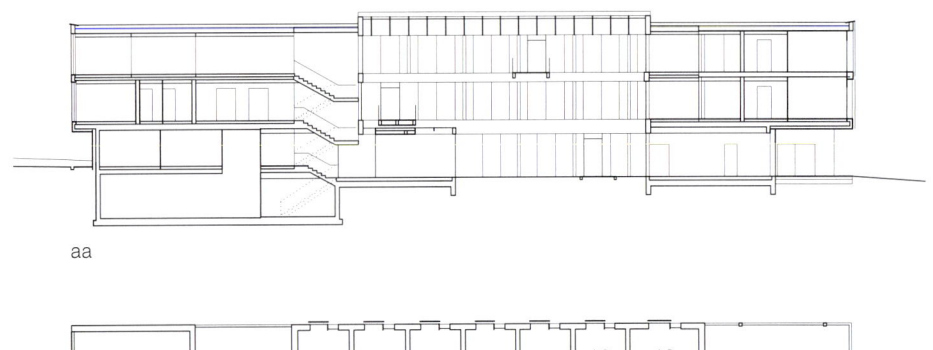

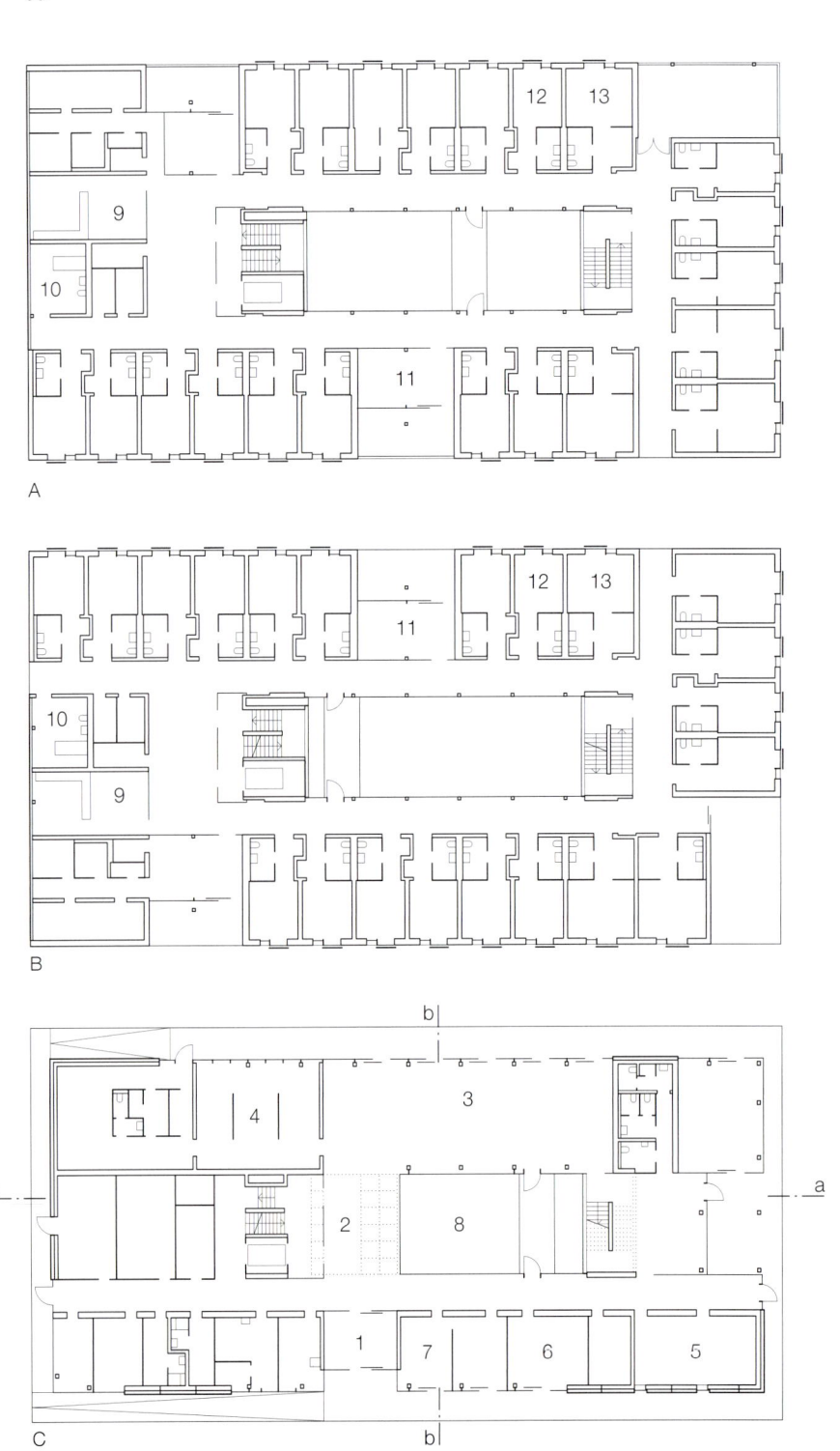

aa

A

B

C

106

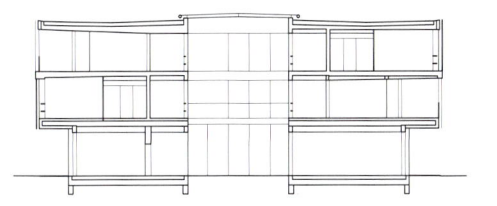

section floor plans
scale 1:500

A second floor
B first floor
C ground floor

1 entrance
2 foyer
3 dining and
  event hall
4 kitchen
5 chapel
6 library

7 administration
8 atrium, conservatory
9 carers' station
10 station bathroom
11 recreational area
12 single room
13 double room

bb

108

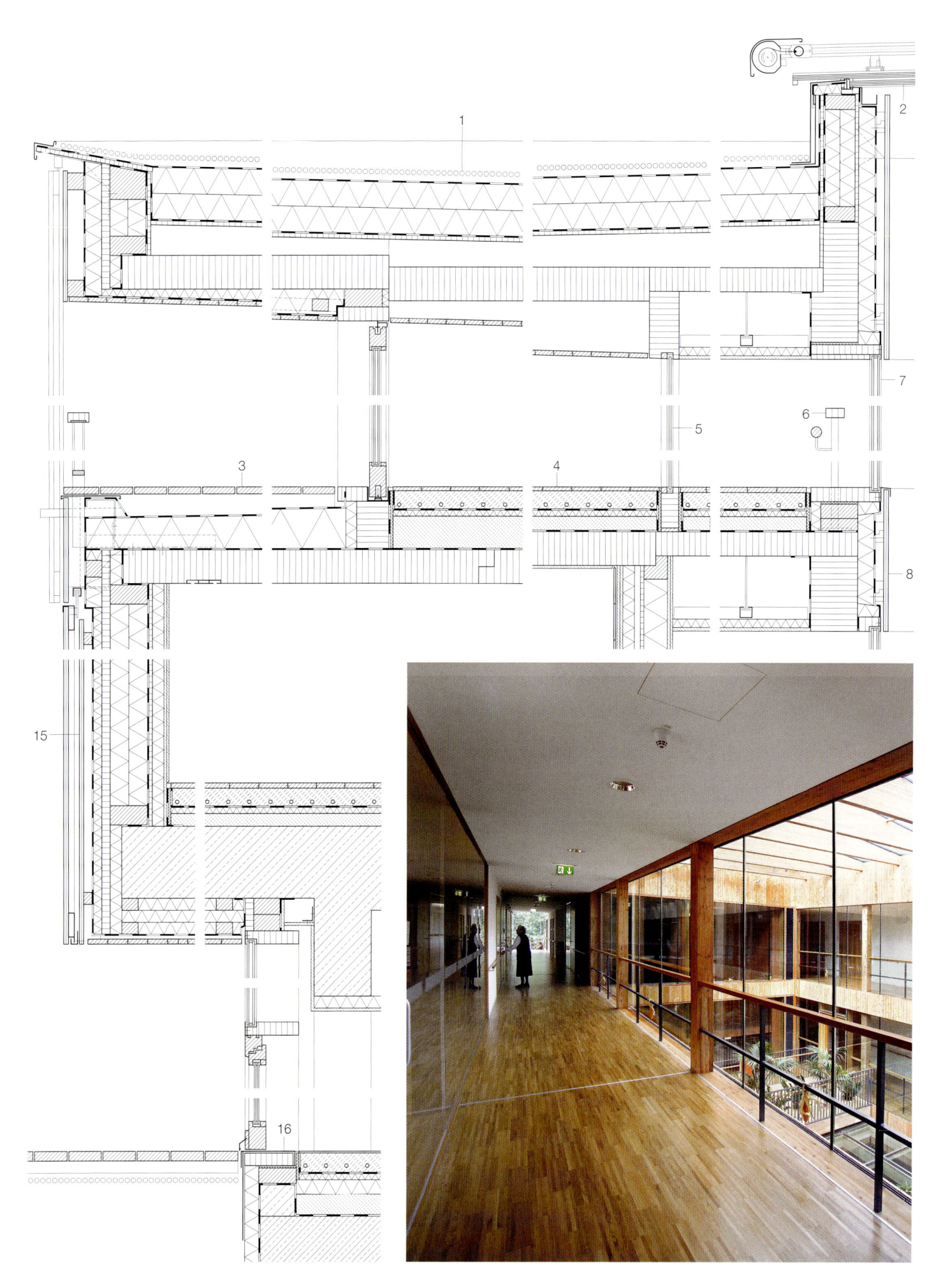

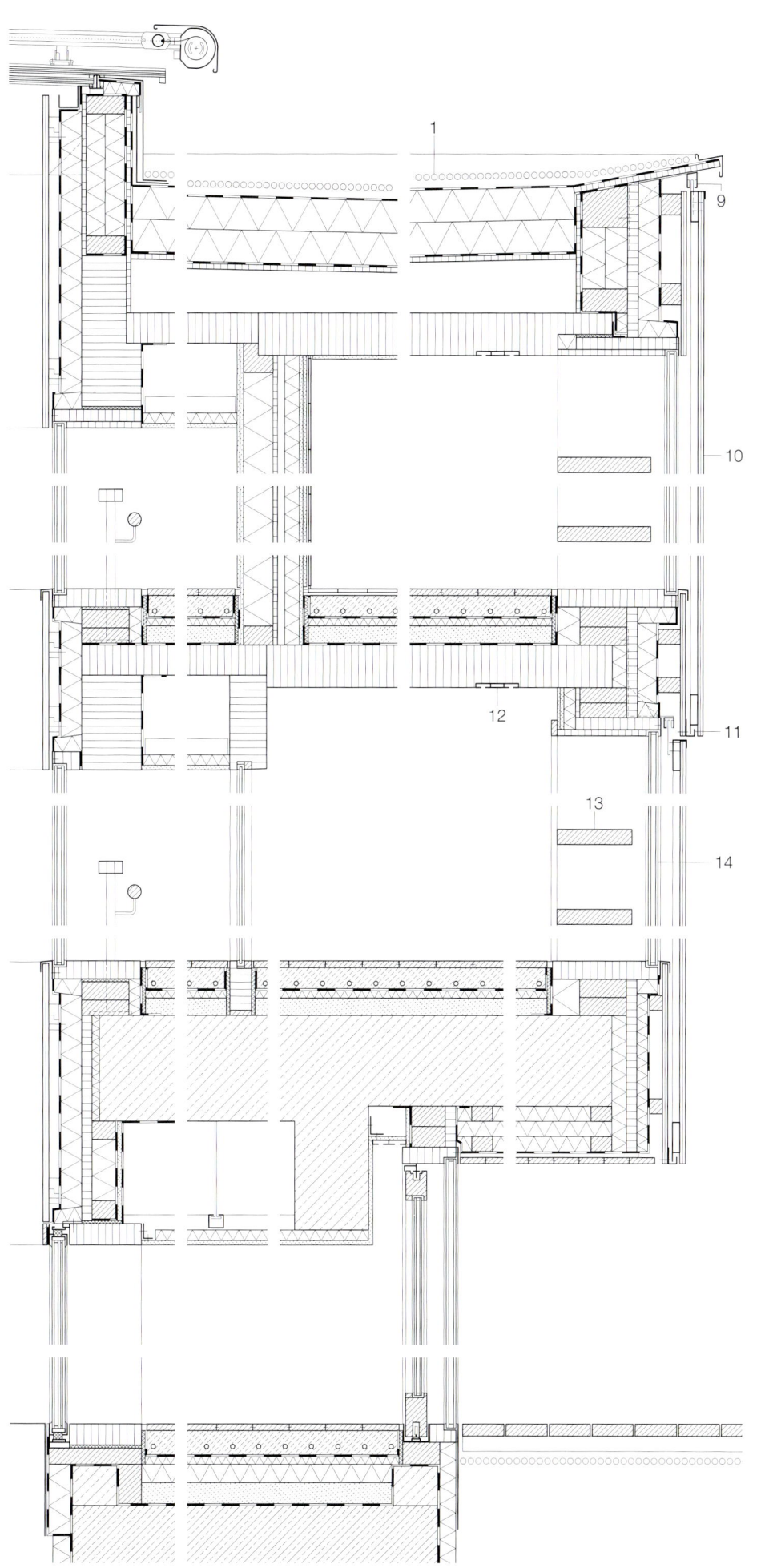

vertical section
scale 1:20

1. roof construction:
   50 mm gravel, 5 mm waterproof membrane
   2× 110 mm thermal insulation, vapour barrier
   18 mm oriented strand board
   20–175 mm varying timber block, for pitch
   140 mm stacked-board timber ceiling
2. sloping glazing 10 mm toughened glass +
   12 mm cavity + 12 mm laminated safety glass
3. terrace floor construction:
   30 mm larch boards, ribbed surface
   50 × 80 mm timber blocks
   waterproof membrane
   160–120 mm insulation with fall, vapour barrier
   140 mm stacked-board timber element
4. single room floor construction:
   22 mm oak parquet
   70 mm screed with underfloor heating
   PE membrane, 25 mm impact sound
   insulation, 63 mm fill, PE membrane
   140 mm stacked-board timber ceiling
5. glass wall: 20 mm toughened glass set in
   75 × 170 mm laminated larch frame
6. 40 × 80 mm laminated timber spandrel
   element with Ø 45 mm timber handrail and
   25 × 25 mm steel SHS post
7. insulating glazing U = 1.1 W/m²K
8. atrium wall construction:
   20 mm vertical larch tongue-and-groove
   boarding
   ventilation cavity, 35 × 50 mm battens
   wind-proof porous membrane
   70 mm thermal insulation between
   70 × 70 mm counter battens
   200 × 320 mm lam. timber beam
9. 30 × 30 mm steel channel guide rail
10. larch sliding shutter
    80 × 20 mm vertical louvers
    80 × 25 mm aluminium RHS
11. 20 × 20 mm steel channel guide rail
12. curtain guide rail
13. 50 × 255 mm laminated timber ledge
14. insulating glazing U = 0.9 W/m²K
15. wall construction:
    80 × 20 mm vertical larch tongue-and-groove
    boarding, 35 × 50 mm battens
    wind-proof porous membrane
    35 mm thermal insulation between
    35 × 50 mm counter battens
    36 mm timber fibreboard
    rock wool thermal insulation
    80 × 160 mm pine rail element
    polyethylene vapour barrier
    15 mm oriented strand board
    stone wool thermal insulation between
    50 × 40 mm battens, 12.5 mm fib. plasterboard
16. stainless steel sheeting fitted to
    50 × 205 laminated timber board

109

Ambulant Care Day Centre in Kamigyo

Architect: Toshiaki Kawai, Kyoto

Communal zones for ambulant care
Tatami room substitutes single room
Ground-level access from courtyard to main room
Ramps and lift establish two barrier-free storeys

Urban planning
Situated in an old quarter of Kyoto in a narrow street with traditional Japanese timber houses, this new day centre for the elderly was inserted into a gap in the existing urban fabric. All that is visible from the street is a narrow, white volume and the small forecourt which is created by its diagonal placement on the site.

Access
This forecourt is approached via a ramp; access is gained to the next internal courtyard via a sliding timber gate which is reminiscent of the formal language of the old tea houses. The entrance courtyard is laid out with large pebbles and is open to the sky. It provides access to the main room of the day centre via another ramp and also takes in a stairway. The main room is connected to the first floor by a lift. The roof terrace alone is reached by a single-storey stair, which is located immediately above a glass strip in the floor, and subdivides the central section of the building between the first and second storeys.

Day care
From the roof level and both main storeys, one has views of the numerous tiled roofs in the neighbourhood. Many old, fragile people are cared for on a daily basis in the main room where a large portion of their routine traditionally takes place on the tatami rice-straw mats placed directly on the timber floor. The patients receive assistance with bathing and meals and take part in rehabilitation exercises. The double-storey glass facade enhances the spatial interaction between the internal rooms and the planted courtyard.

Materials
The immediacy of the old Japanese buildings can be felt in the new construction. Many traditional elements co-exist in contrasting harmony with exposed concrete and glass-and-steel facades. Two rooms for the practice of tea ceremonies are provided on the roof. The rooms are externally clad with metal panels, while internally they have floors laid out with tatami mats and loam-rendered walls. The main rooms are characterized by the solid, exposed concrete wall and the black painted steel stair whereas the suspended ceilings are constructed of bamboo matting and back-lit Japanese paper. The natural materials create a warm, cosy environment in this day centre for the elderly, in contrast to the sterile atmospheres of many European nursing homes.

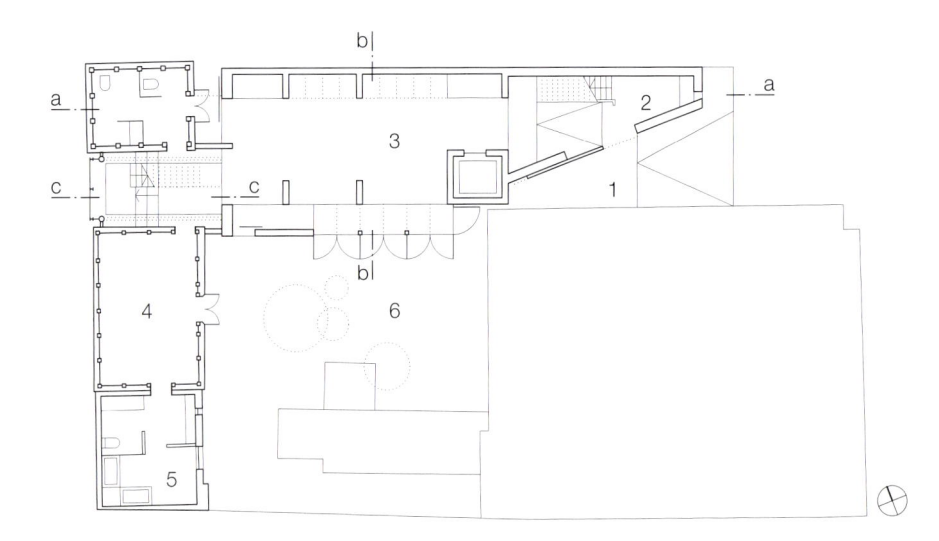

Project Details
Usage: care day centre
Access: multi-purpose room
Internal room height: 2.3 m ground floor
3.12 m first floor
Construction type: reinforced concrete
Total internal volume: 723.9 m³
Total floor area: 187.55 m²
Total site area: 188.44 m²
Total built area: 95.24 m²
Construction cost: 503,144 Euros
Completion date: June 2000

aa   bb

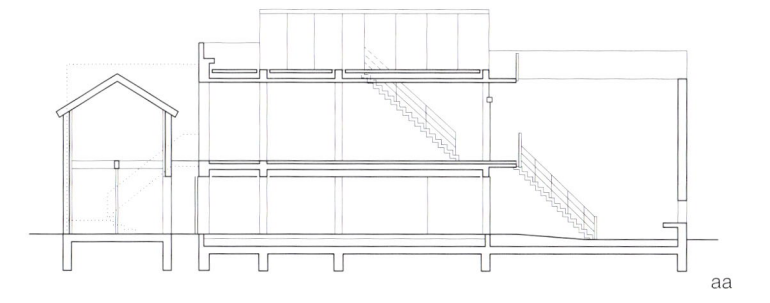

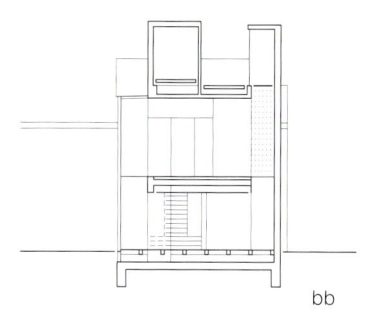

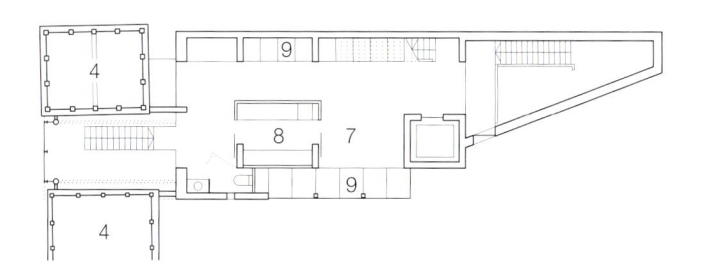

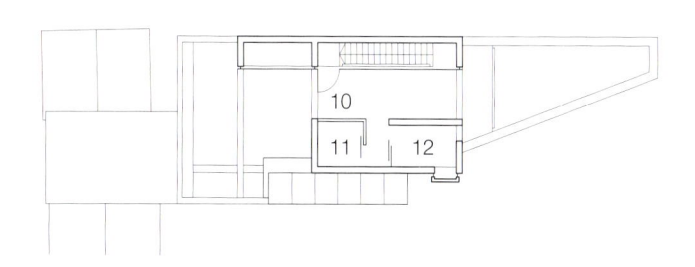

site plan
scale 1:4000
sections · floor plans
scale 1:300

1 forecourt
2 entrance courtyard
3 care facility
4 existing former tea houses

5 bathroom
6 internal courtyard
7 recreation and dining area
8 kitchen

9 glass floor area
10 roof terrace
11 mizuya tea ceremony room
12 tatami room

111

section   scale 1:50
1 roof sealing layer on
  200 mm exposed waterproof concrete
2 laminated safety glass: 2× 8 mm toughened glass
3 60 × 9 mm steel RHS, painted black
4 125 × 60 × 6 × 8 mm steel I-beam
5 20 mm bamboo floor finish
6 100 × 50 mm western red cedar decking
  250 mm waterproof screed
  200 mm reinforced concrete slab
7 sheet steel flashing
8 suspended ceiling system:
  100 mm steel I-beams with woven bamboo matting
9 20 mm cypress boarding on 61 mm plywood
  400 mm substructure
  300 mm reinforced concrete floor slab
10 20 mm cypress treads
11 9 mm sheet steel, painted black
12 38 × 9 mm steel flat, painted black

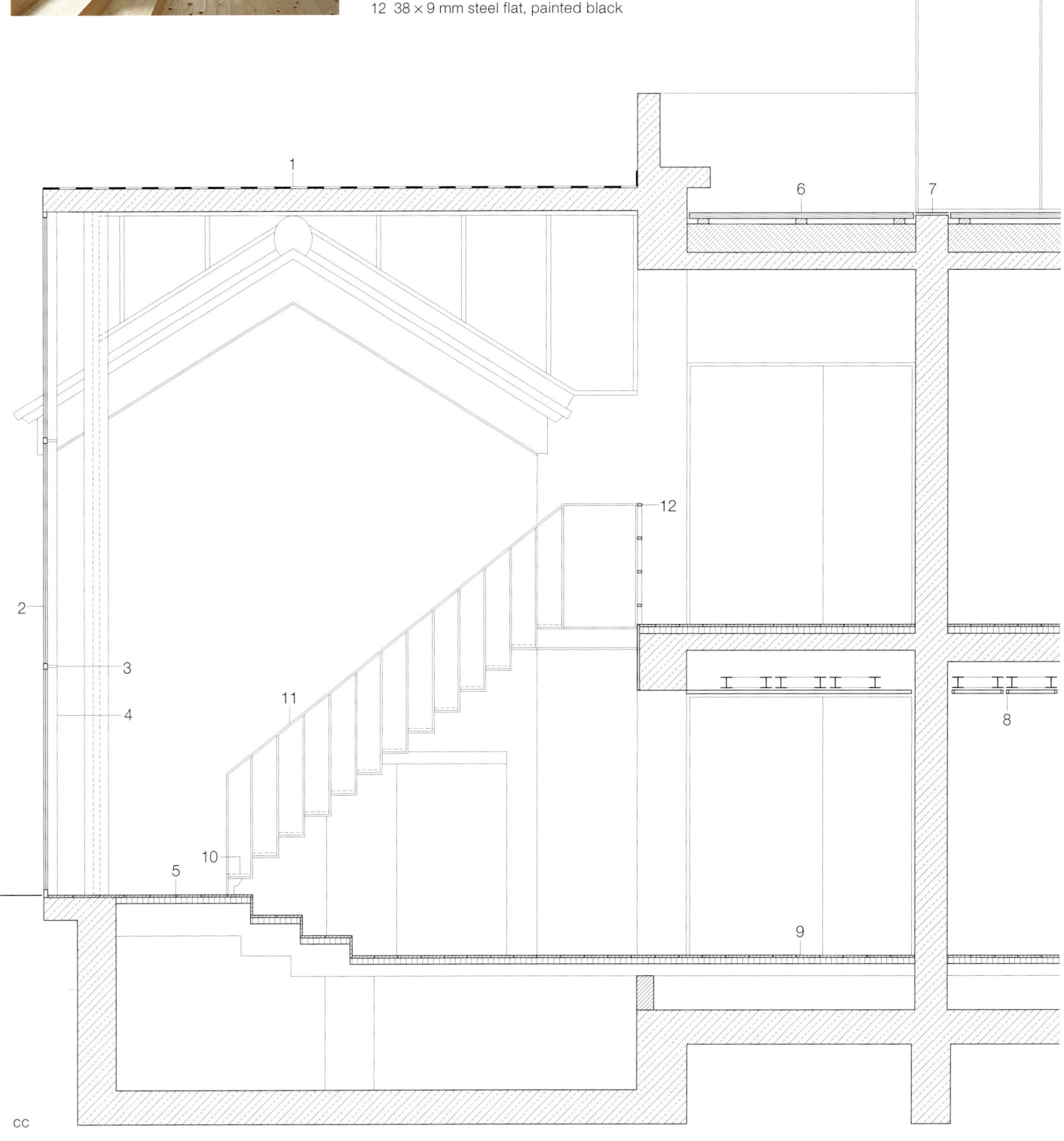

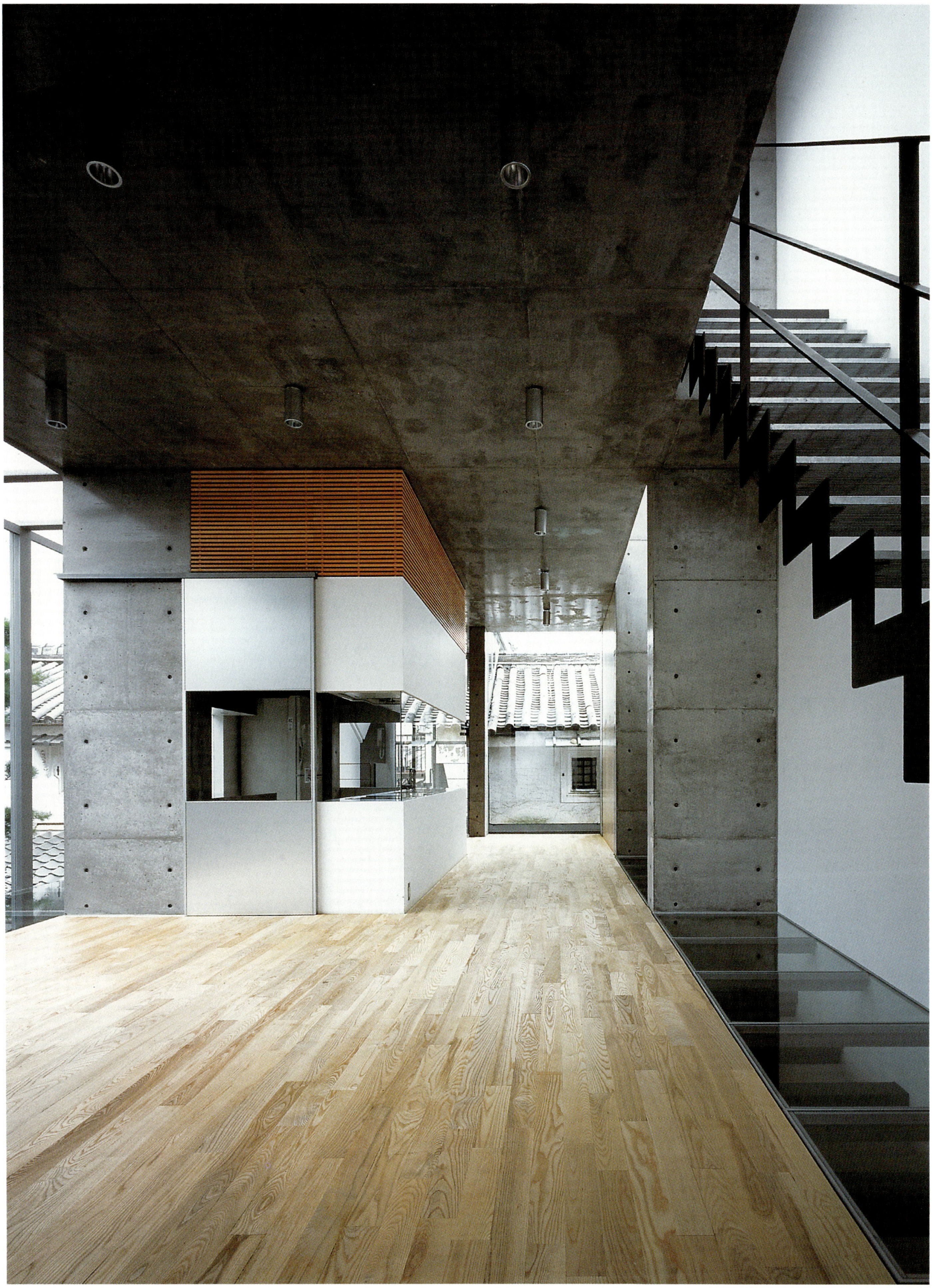

Residence in Gstadt

Architect: Florian Höfer, Oberneuching

Wheelchair-friendly house for a young family
Vertical access via ramp and lift
Open plan layout with wide doorways
Low energy house in timber-frame construction

The image of this single-family house is dominated both inside and out by the ramp. The house is designed around the specific requirements of the owner: confined to a wheelchair since an accident, he and his wife and two small children were no longer satisfied living in an apartment designed for the disabled. Many standard solutions were impractical for the owner, narrow doorways often leading to hand injuries.

Location
This barrier-free house is sited on a small block of land in Gstadt am Chiemsee. The two-storey house with pitched roof and of timber-frame construction blends into the pastoral surroundings. The facade is clad with large format, three-ply larch panels which have been treated with an iron-oxide coating, while the ramp adjacent to the entrance is revealed through a back-lit translucent glass wall on the ground floor. To the west, full-height windows provide generous views of the nearby Alps even when seated. The building is further articulated by the projecting south-west corner, which is clad in untreated larch boarding.

Wheelchair-friendly fit out
Traditional functions have been exchanged in this dwelling; the bedrooms are located on the ground floor adjacent to the garage. The corridor widens and merges into a bathroom suitable for physically disabled users and can be closed off by a translucent sliding glass door. A reinforced concrete ramp leads up to the first floor where the family's daily routine takes place. Together with the double-flight ramp, a lift accessing all levels ensures total freedom of movement for the owner. The upper level is almost entirely given over to the 52 m² living space; incorporating living and dining zones and the open-plan kitchen with wheelchair accessible worktops. A work room and additional barrier-free bathroom are provided on this level. Book shelving is integrated into the elongated ramp balustrade, which simultaneously acts as an informal seating alternative.

Project Details
Usage: single family house
Units: 6-room wheelchair-friendly dwelling (280 m²)
Internal room height: 2.50–4.15 m
Construction type: timber framework
Total internal volume: 1,350 m³
Total floor area: 398 m²
Usable floor area: 432 m²
Total site area: 650 m²
Heat consumption: 50.00 kWh/m²a
Construction cost: 1,728 Euros/m²
Construction time: Nov 2002–Jan 2004

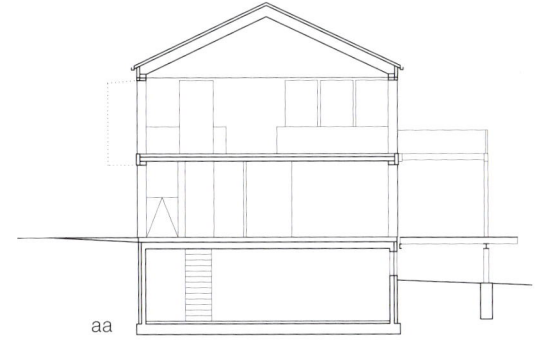

section • floor plan
scale 1:250

A ground floor
B first floor

1 bedroom
2 children's room
3 play corridor
4 bathroom
5 garage

6 10° gradient ramp
7 living/dining
8 kitchen
9 work room
10 pantry

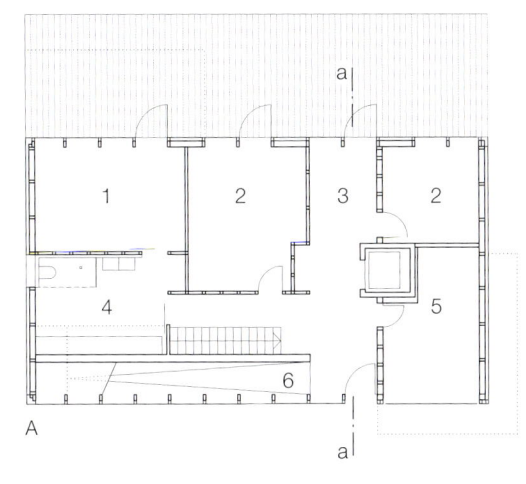

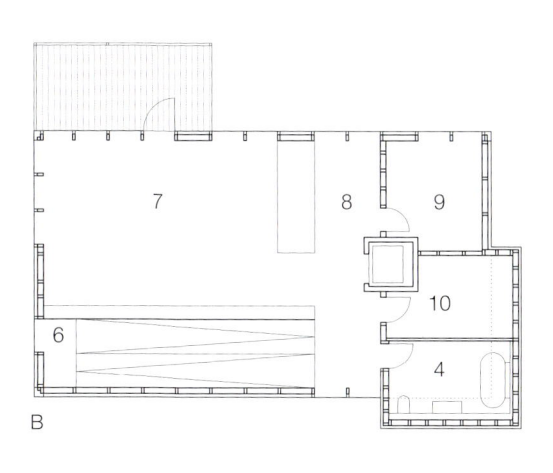

aa

A

B

Multi-generational House in Waldzell

Architect: Helga Flotzinger, Innsbruck

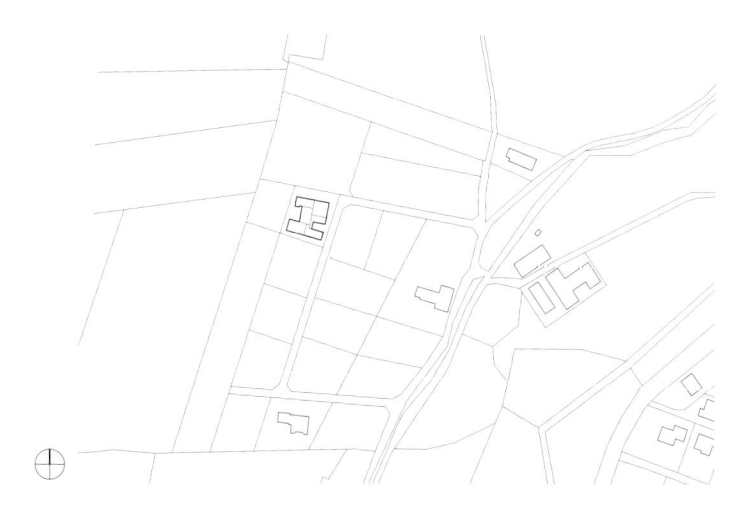

Individual, wheelchair-friendly concept
Self-contained apartment for flexible usage
Diversified spatial composition

Traditionally the courtyard structure of a multi-purpose, multi-generational built ensemble is one of diverse buildings and roof forms, appearing more like a hamlet than a single building. This typology is reinterpreted by a residence in the Innviertel district of upper Austria built for an extended family with a son, a daughter in a wheelchair and a grandmother. The built envelope is of eye-catching, shimmering metal.

Particular layout organisation

Fundamental to the planning of this project were the specific abilities of the wheelchair-bound daughter. As she is unable to use a lift independently, it was necessary for the bungalow to be wholly restricted to the ground floor; seven different built forms of varying heights and contrasting roof directions slot into one another and enclose two semi-internal courtyards. The private, therapeutic and communal zones are spatially separated from one another and emphasised by the two courtyards. Presently being used as a living space, the centrally located swimming hall with integrated therapy pool will be completed at a later date due to funding. The private area for the parents and their son is located in the south-west tract while the grandmother's dwelling is on the eastern side. Her self-contained apartment can be used at a future date by a carer if so desired. The daughter's dwelling to the south-east benefits from a generously dimensioned storage room and specialised therapy zone. Her tract can be converted into an independent apartment by a single partition wall.

Specific barrier-free planning

The daughter's daily routine is predominantly confined within the house. Material selection, the incidence of daylight and stimulating views animate the already interesting spatial composition which nevertheless fulfils all requirements for barrier-free living. All areas comply with the turning circle of a wheelchair; corridors, spaces between furniture and the garage, where particular attention was paid to side and rear boarding space. In addition to which, a bathroom with hydraulically operated bathtub and hand basin and a toilet suitable for the physically disabled was incorporated. All doors open automatically and are operated via hydraulic kickboards, while all light and power switches are mounted at 85 cm above floor level. A threshold-free floor finish flows seamlessly through the entire house and only outside can small differences in levels be found. The landscaping is such that the daughter can enjoy the garden alone and independently, using secure paths which encircle the entire house. The daughter's motor skills have improved due to her increased independence and mobility.

Project Details
Usage: multi-generational house
Units: 1 5-room apartment (parents 197.8 m²)
1 2-room apartment (daughter 59.6 m²)
1 2-room apartment (grandmother 46.9 m²)
swimming hall (62.5 m²)
Access: ground level access
Internal room height: 2.5–4.5 m
Construction type: reinforced concrete
Total internal volume: 2,305 m³
Total floor area: 611.1 m²
Residential floor area: 366.8 m²
Total site area: 1,088 m² built
763 m² landscaped
Construction cost: n. a.
Construction time: 2003–2005

aa bb

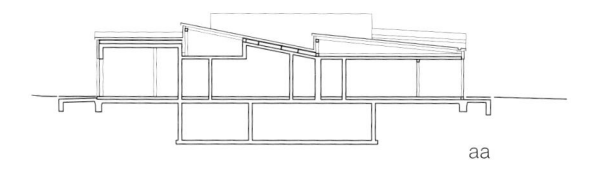

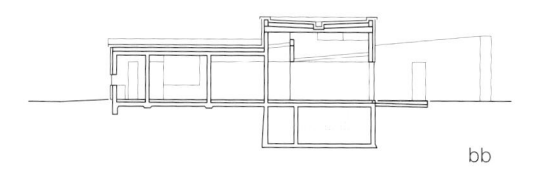

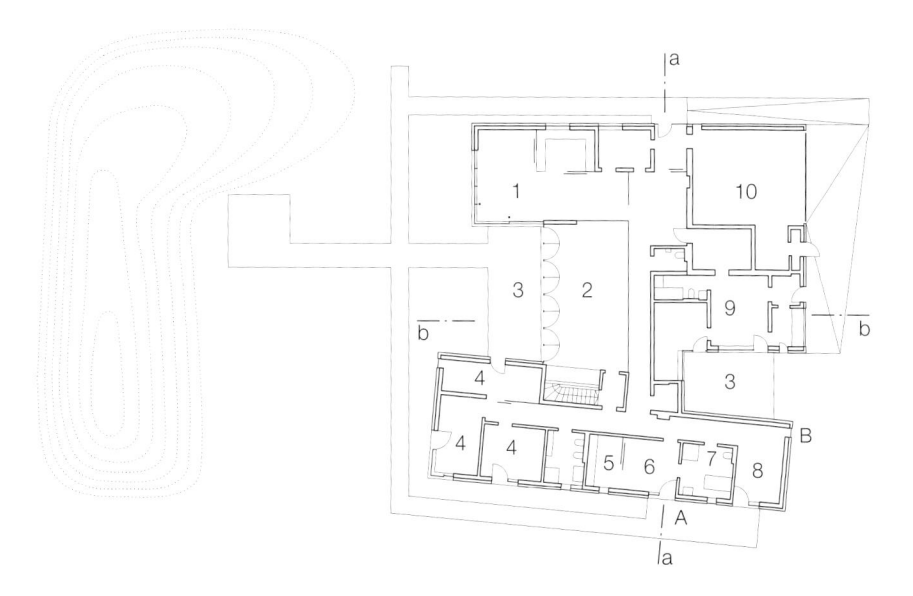

site plan
scale 1:5000
sections • floor plan
scale 1:500

1 kitchen
2 living/swimming hall
  (in planning)
3 terrace
4 room
5 storage room (barrier-free)
6 daughter's room
7 bathroom (barrier-free)
8 therapy
9 self-contained apartment
  (grandmother)
10 garage

117

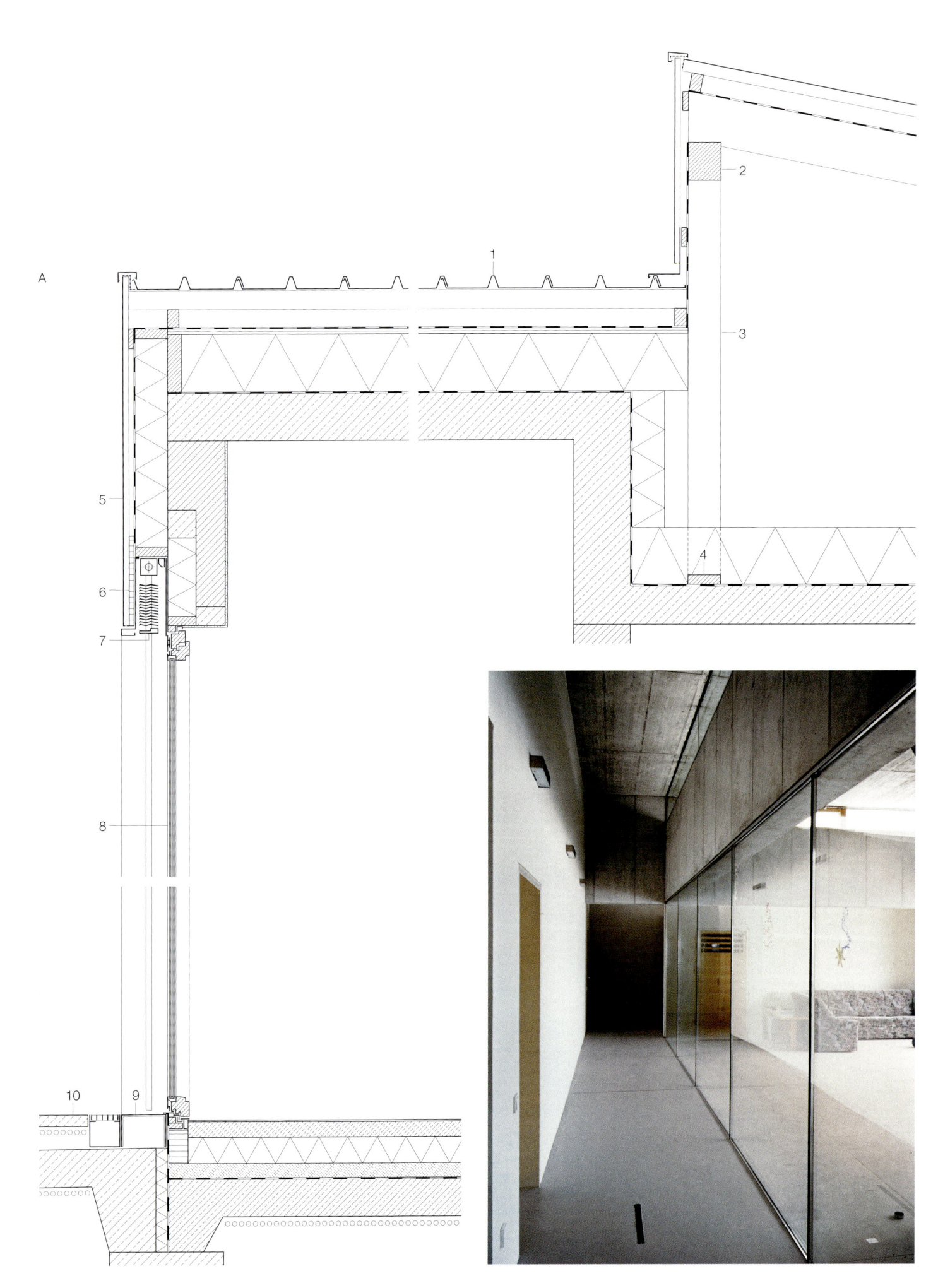

A

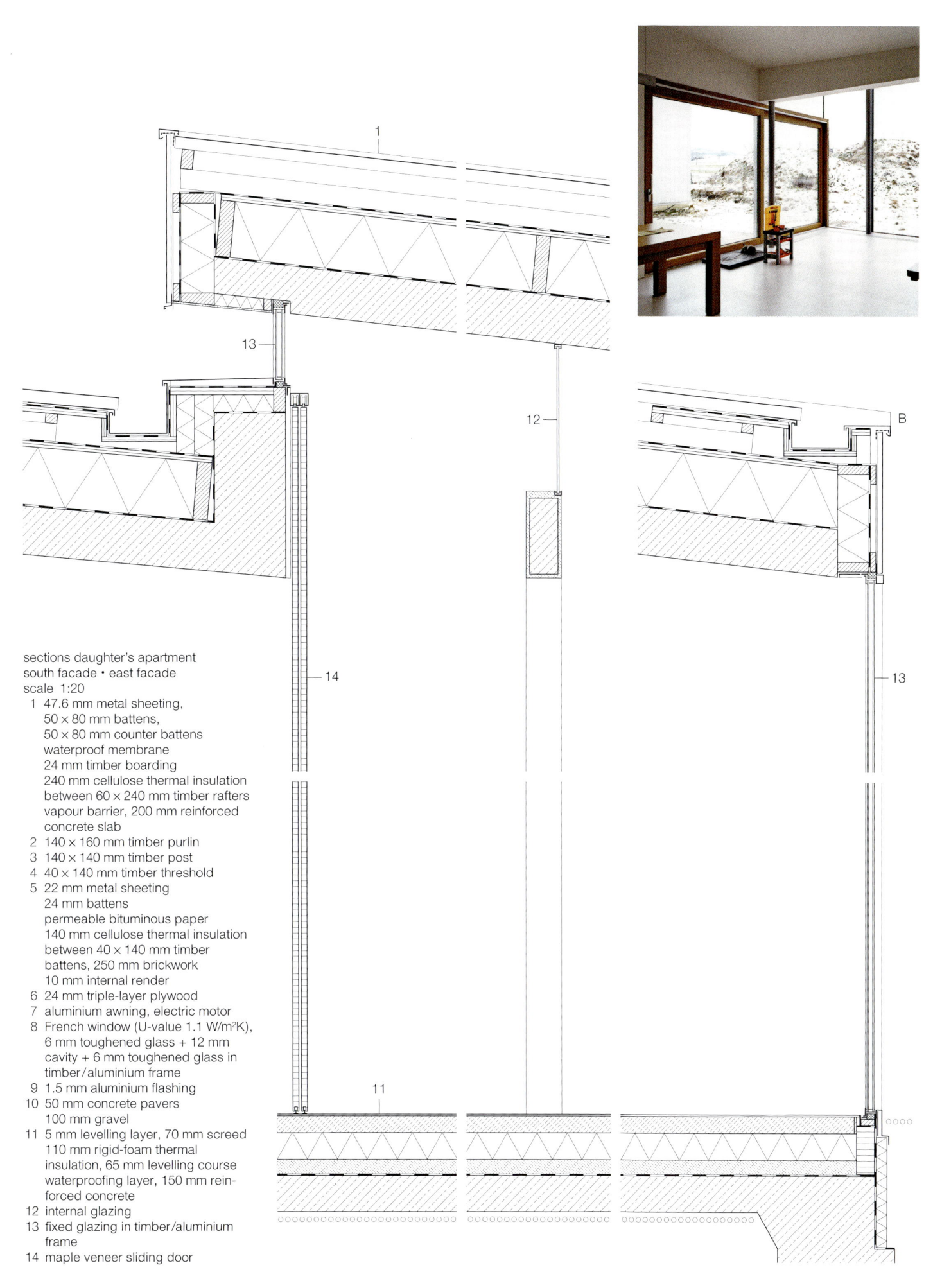

sections daughter's apartment
south facade · east facade
scale 1:20
1 47.6 mm metal sheeting,
   50 × 80 mm battens,
   50 × 80 mm counter battens
   waterproof membrane
   24 mm timber boarding
   240 mm cellulose thermal insulation
   between 60 × 240 mm timber rafters
   vapour barrier, 200 mm reinforced
   concrete slab
2 140 × 160 mm timber purlin
3 140 × 140 mm timber post
4 40 × 140 mm timber threshold
5 22 mm metal sheeting
   24 mm battens
   permeable bituminous paper
   140 mm cellulose thermal insulation
   between 40 × 140 mm timber
   battens, 250 mm brickwork
   10 mm internal render
6 24 mm triple-layer plywood
7 aluminium awning, electric motor
8 French window (U-value 1.1 W/m²K),
   6 mm toughened glass + 12 mm
   cavity + 6 mm toughened glass in
   timber/aluminium frame
9 1.5 mm aluminium flashing
10 50 mm concrete pavers
    100 mm gravel
11 5 mm levelling layer, 70 mm screed
    110 mm rigid-foam thermal
    insulation, 65 mm levelling course
    waterproofing layer, 150 mm reinforced concrete
12 internal glazing
13 fixed glazing in timber/aluminium
    frame
14 maple veneer sliding door

Multi-generational House in Darmstadt

Architects: Kränzle + Fischer-Wasels Architects, Karlsruhe
Klotz + Knecht Architects, Darmstadt

New interpretation of cross-generational living
Flexibility for future changes in family structure
Spatial elements dividing and uniting
Family life and retreat in own home

This cube located on the edge of the city of Darmstadt gives no indication as to what is concealed beneath its clear-cut grey exterior when viewed from the street. To the adjacent parklands, however, the building opens up revealing its internal structure. Three individual dwellings are incorporated into this "family home", providing accommodation for several generations of a single family under one communal roof.
This house is intended to continue beyond more than just one stage of family life and to adapt to potential changes within the family structure.

House in house concept
Flexibility is the fundamental principle when building a multi-generational house capable of reacting to changes within the family. The number and size of the apartments in this project are variable. Communal spaces have been created between the private, independently functioning dwellings. Family-orientated interaction and retreat into the individual private spaces are equally possible for all members of the family. Future changes in the extended family structure; the birth of children, family members moving out or aging, should not cause immense problems to the family home – the three maisonette dwellings can be further sub-divided between storeys to provide a total of six apartments. Another possibility is the absorption of additional rooms into a dwelling from an adjacent dwelling. Room sizes have been so selected to allow their functions to be changed at any time. In addition to the internal access routes within the dwellings, there is also a single-flight stair which connects the basement to the open hall of the ground floor. The communal spaces are characterised by voids, galleries and open spaces which act as puffer zones between the individual dwellings while simultaneously interconnecting them. Externally, the dwellings are linked by the balconies, which run the full width of the building at both levels and can be used by all members of the family.

Material selection
Uniform surface finishes; Solnhofen limestone tiles on the ground floor and oak parquet on the first floor, and continuous, white rendered walls and ceilings enhance the homogeneousness of the composition, allowing the incorporation or separation of individual rooms as desired. All doors are ceiling-high and augment the clarity of the interior. The floor plans are free of thresholds and a lift may be incorporated at a future date if necessary.

Construction and finish
The cube is constructed of reinforced concrete, closed on three sides yet fully glazed to the south. The external walls are triple-layered; 22.5 cm reinforced concrete, 12 cm thermal insulation and 11.5 cm ventilated clinker brickwork. The southern glass facade is fully shaded by the balcony and the roof overhang. Skylights are integrated into the planted roof and protected by individual sun-shading. The solid construction of the internal walls allows them to act as thermal gain elements and underfloor heating has also been fitted.

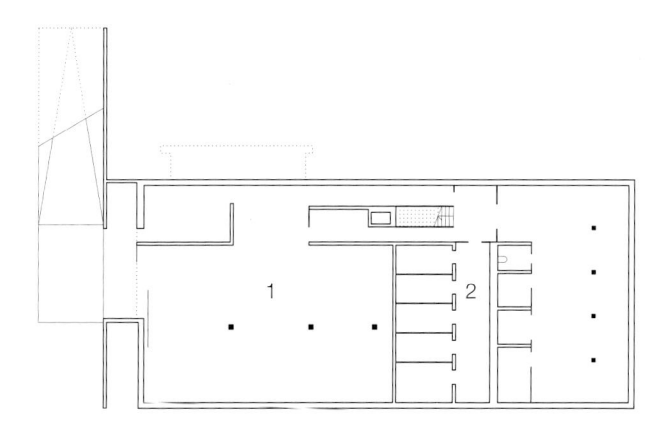

site plan
scale 1:2500
floor plans · sections
scale 1:500

1 garage
2 basement rooms
3 apartment
4 communal area
5 void
6 terrace/balcony

A basement
B ground floor
C first floor

aa   bb   cc

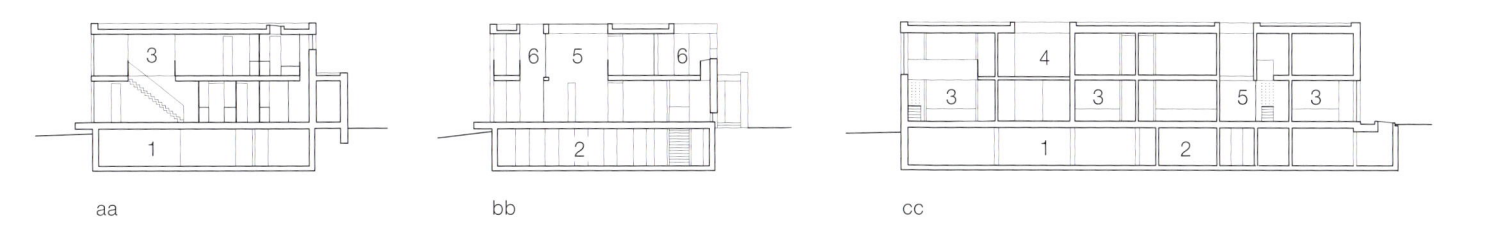

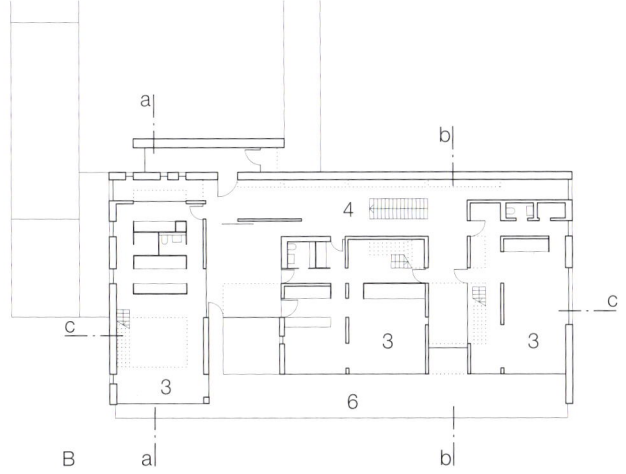

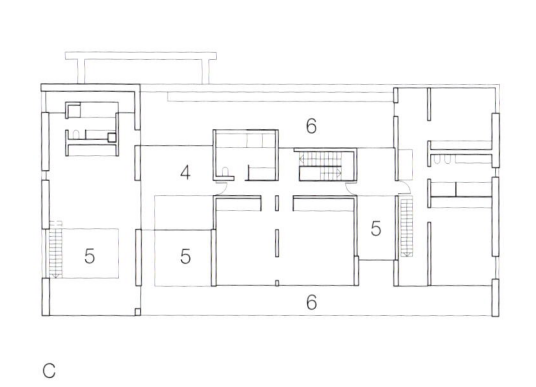

B   C

121

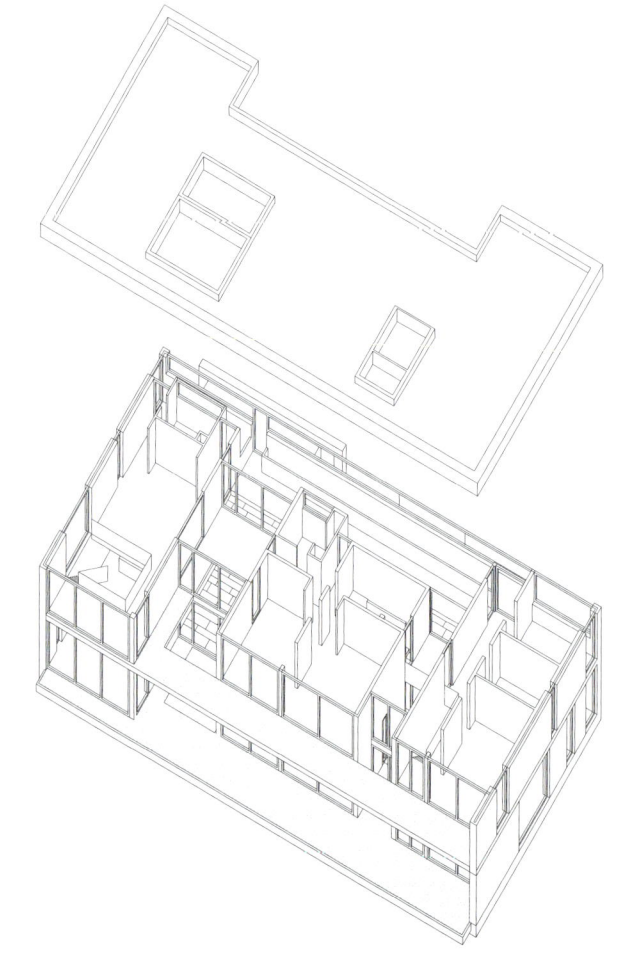

Project Details
Usage: Multi-generational family house
Units: 3 maisonettes
Access: internal stairs
Internal room height: 2.26–3.12 m
Construction type: reinforced concrete
Total internal volume: 4,540 m³
Total floor area: 1,468 m²
Usable floor area: 1,061 m²
Total site area: 1,551 m²
Covered site area: 505 m²
Construction cost: n. a.
Heating consumption 22.26 kWh/m²a
Construction time: 2001–2003

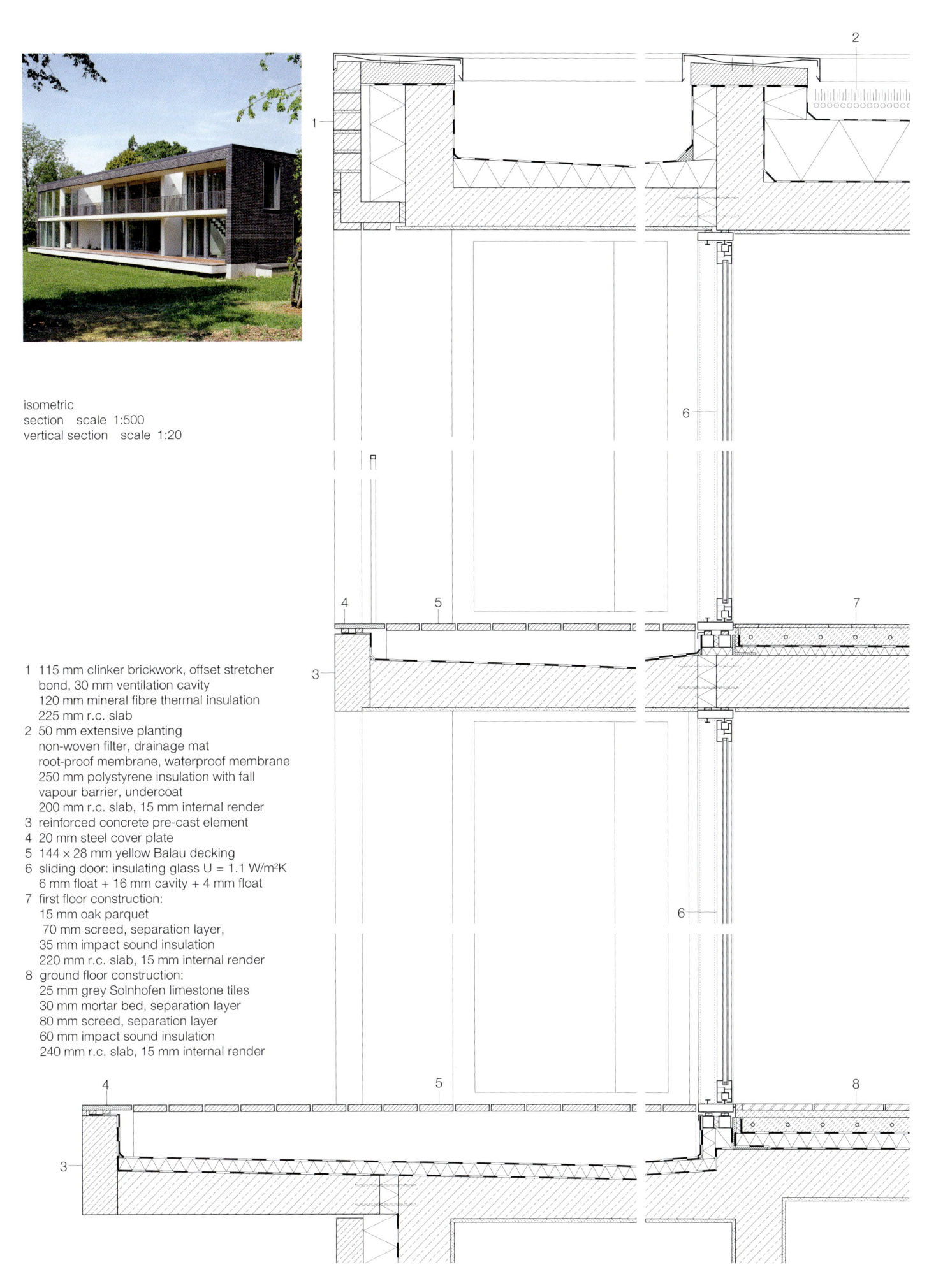

isometric
section   scale 1:500
vertical section   scale 1:20

1 115 mm clinker brickwork, offset stretcher
   bond, 30 mm ventilation cavity
   120 mm mineral fibre thermal insulation
   225 mm r.c. slab
2 50 mm extensive planting
   non-woven filter, drainage mat
   root-proof membrane, waterproof membrane
   250 mm polystyrene insulation with fall
   vapour barrier, undercoat
   200 mm r.c. slab, 15 mm internal render
3 reinforced concrete pre-cast element
4 20 mm steel cover plate
5 144 × 28 mm yellow Balau decking
6 sliding door: insulating glass U = 1.1 W/m²K
   6 mm float + 16 mm cavity + 4 mm float
7 first floor construction:
   15 mm oak parquet
   70 mm screed, separation layer,
   35 mm impact sound insulation
   220 mm r.c. slab, 15 mm internal render
8 ground floor construction:
   25 mm grey Solnhofen limestone tiles
   30 mm mortar bed, separation layer
   80 mm screed, separation layer
   60 mm impact sound insulation
   240 mm r.c. slab, 15 mm internal render

City House in Munich

Architects: Fink + Jocher, Munich

Barrier-free city house with retail units
Two wheelchair-friendly apartments
Maisonettes with roof terraces
Sound insulation against traffic noise

The Westend is an upwardly-mobile inner city suburb of Munich. This new city house replaces five older constructions which were no longer economically viable. As a residential and retail address, this new building contributes greatly to the enhancement of the area by providing spaces commensurate with modern standards of living and working in a city.

Mixed uses

This building accommodates seven shops, diverse communally used spaces and 23 residences of various sizes: 17 single-storey apartments with private loggias and six maisonette apartments with double-storey voids and roof terraces. The load-bearing concept of the building has been pared down to the external walls and the stairwells. By restricting the internal structure to a lightweight system it remains possible to alter plans to meet long-term demands of individual users and adapt to future changes in the real estate market. Communal spaces for all residents have been provided in the forms of generous entry areas adjacent to the stairwells, an internal courtyard with playground and a community room complete with kitchen and direct access to the courtyard.

Accessibility

All routes within the building are threshold-free and each apartment is accessible from a lift. All dwellings are obstacle-free, with the exception of the six maisonette apartments. In addition to which, two apartments are designed to be wheelchair-friendly, while the large entry areas provide sufficient internal parking space.

Energy and ventilation concept

The rooms are heated by an under-floor heating system with a reduced flow temperature and by a controlled ventilation system. Air supply is acquired via the roof due to the close proximity of a heavily used arterial road. Loss of heat is minimised by the application of a heat exchanger. In association with the highly insulated external construction elements, these measures have enabled the architects to surpass the requirements of low energy housing standards.

Sound insulation

The adjacent street is used by 32,000 vehicles and two tram lines daily, leading to sound emissions of up to 75 dB. Noise pollution of this magnitude is not uncommon in inner city locations. In contrast to the popular planning strategy of facing secondary rooms with small opening onto the street frontage, this scheme employs the application of highly insulated, specially constructed windows. The windows are constructed of double glazing on the inside, with an additional single glazing layer applied externally and noise absorbing elements located within the cavity spaces. Thus the apartments remain unrestricted in their layout and can take full advantage of orientation and sunlight, irrelevant of traffic flow and the related noise pollution. The streetscape becomes a public and social, yet controllable aspect of the urban location.

site plan
scale 1:4000
elevation
scale 1:750

Project Details
Usage: residential and retail building
Units: 15 barrier-free apartments with loggias
2 wheelchair-friendly apartments
6 maisonettes with roof terraces
7 shops on ground floor
Development: two and three unit layout
Internal room height: 2.48 m upper floor
2.84 m ground floor
Construction type: reinforced concrete

Total internal volume: 13,206 m³
Total floor area: 3,530 m²
Residential floor area: 2,066 m²
Retail floor area: 616 m²
Total site area: 1,102 m²
Built site area: 783 m²
Construction cost: 3.25 million Euros
Funding: Münchner Gesellschaft für Stadterneuerung mbH
Construction time: 2004–Oct 2005

125

section • floor plans
scale 1:750

A roof level
B 3rd floor
C 1st and 2nd floor
D ground floor

1 retail
2 communal space
3 wheelchair-friendly apartment
4 floor plan with corridor
5 floor plan with loft
6 floor plan with "through" rooms
7 maisonette
8 loggia
9 roof terrace

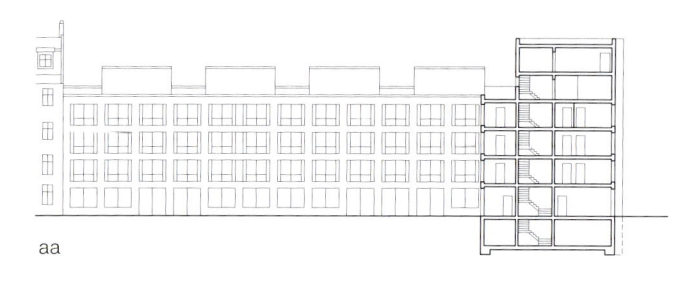

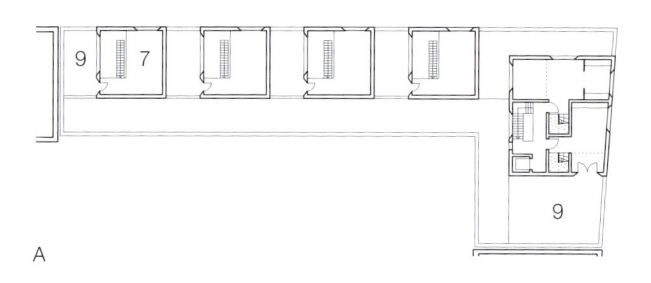

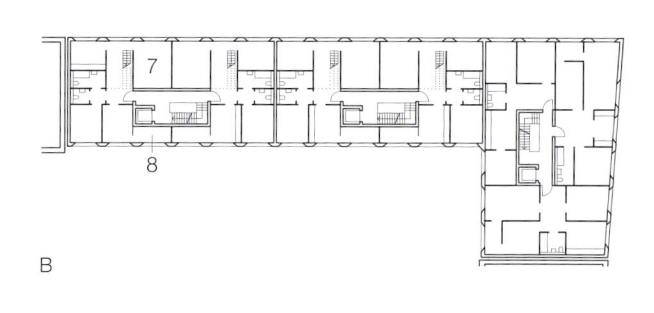

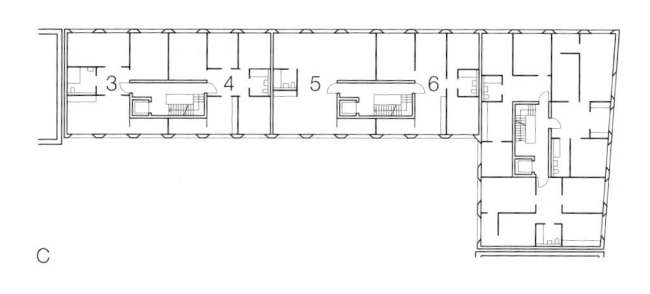

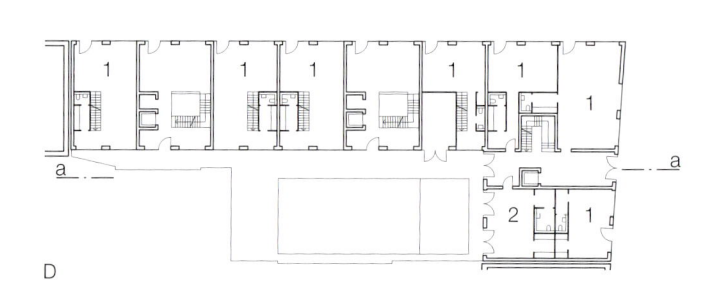

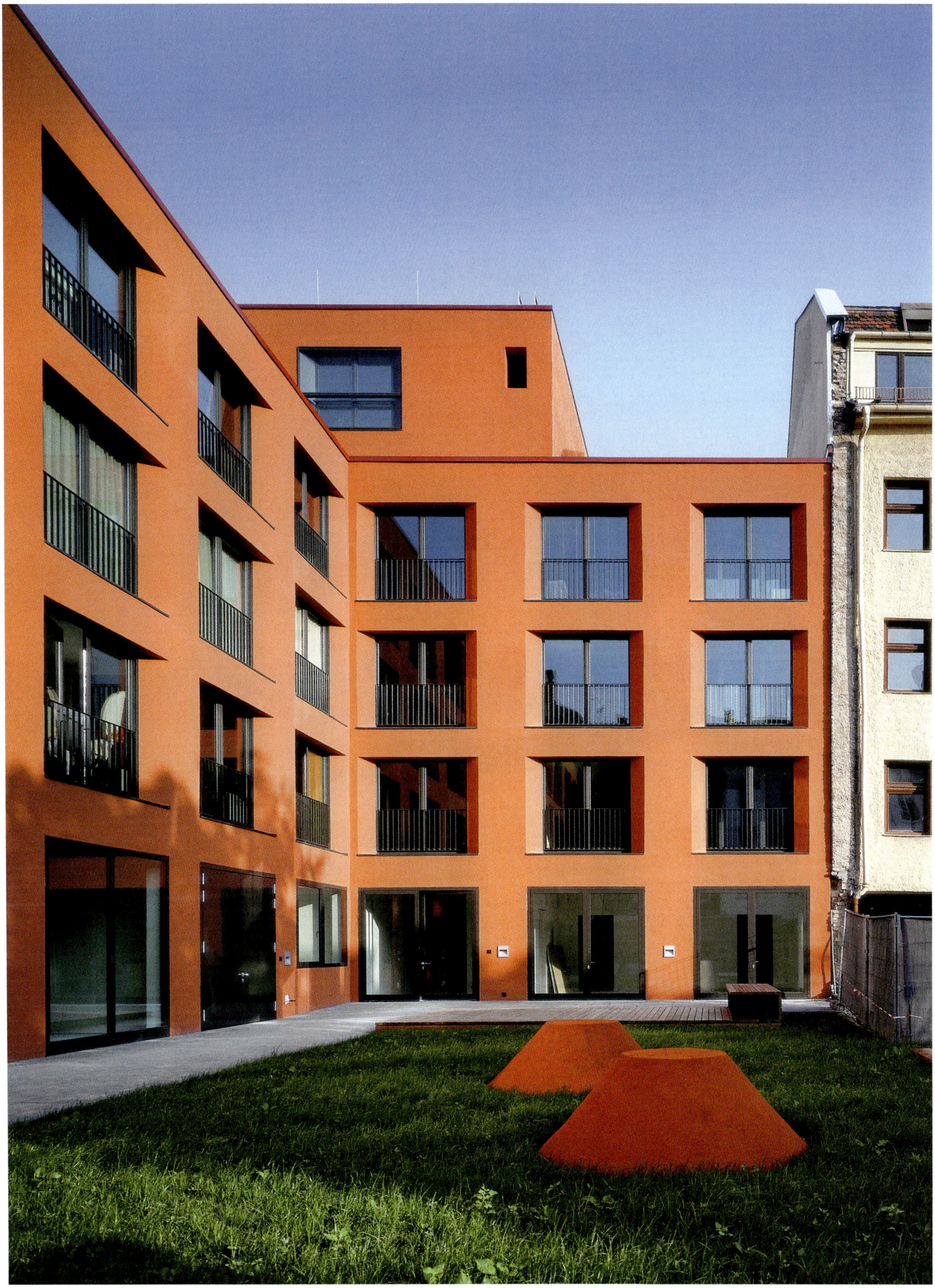

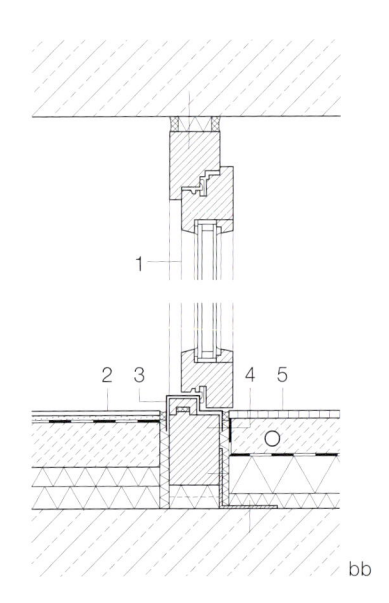

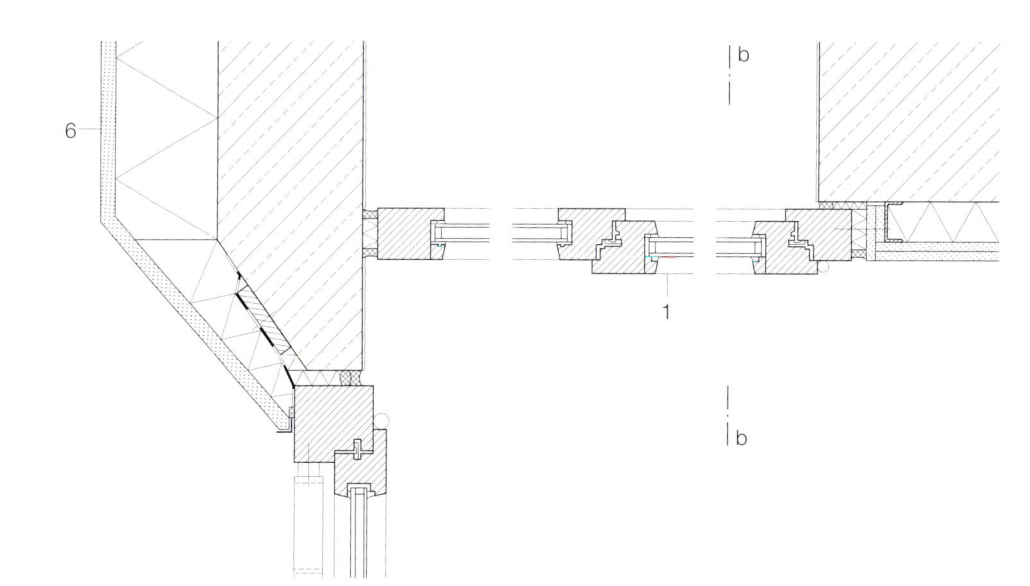

vertical sections
horizontal sections
loggia and casement window
scale 1:10

1 timber door with double glazing, sound insulating glass
2 loggia floor construction:
   12 mm floor tiles in grout waterproofing
   63 mm screed
   25 mm levelling course
   30 mm impact sound insulation
   220 mm reinforced concrete slab
3 2 mm stainless steel threshold
4 115 × 68 mm timber profile
5 living area floor construction:
   10 mm parquet
   50 mm screed for underfloor heating
   50 mm levelling course for ventilation conduit
   20 mm impact sound insulation
   220 mm reinforced concrete slab
6 external wall construction:
   20 mm render, street frontage with glass splitter additive
   140 mm thermal insulation
   200 mm reinforced concrete
7 timber window with double glazing, sound insulating glass
8 50 mm thermal insulation
9 3 mm steel sheet upper and lower reveals, double edged and perforated
10 25 × 10 mm aluminium RHS connection between external and internal window frame
11 25 × 25 × 3 mm aluminium SHS with contact rubber
12 100 × 40 × 4 mm alumuminium RHS
13 160 × 225 × 4 mm steel angle with bracing
14 25 × 25 × 4 mm alum. angle
15 70 × 30 × 5 mm alumuninium angle
16 8 mm toughened glass
17 laminated safety glass fixed balustrade:
   2× 8 mm float glass + 1.5 mm PVB membrane
18 2 mm alumuminium sheet side reveals, single edged and perforated
19 30 mm acoustic insulating screed panel
20 40 mm thermal insulation
21 110 × 90 × 4 mm steel angle with bracing

cc

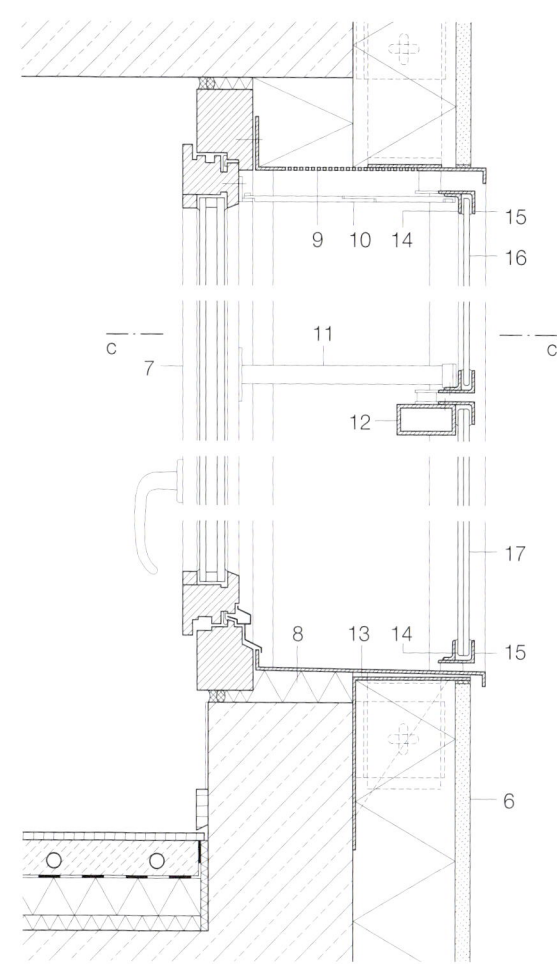

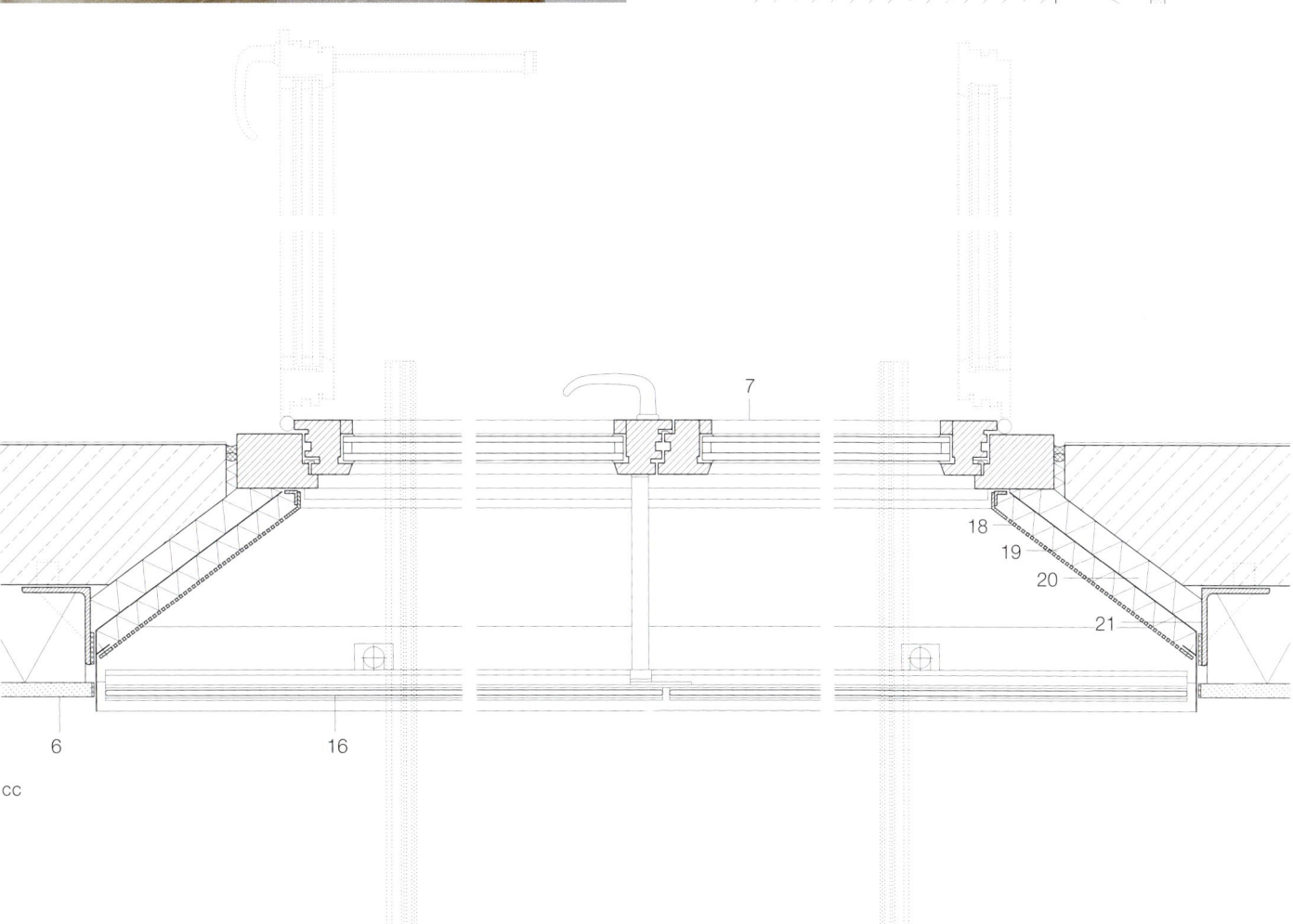

129

Multi-generational Housing Development in Freiburg

Architects: Pfeifer Roser Kuhn, Freiburg

Project Details
Usage: single storey apartments
Units: 30 apartments (53.4 m² – 117.2 m²) which include
3 2-room apartments for disabled (56.1 m²)
6 1-room apartments for seniors (47.4 m²)
3 2-room apartments for seniors (56.1 m²)
Development type: three and four unit constructions
Internal room height: 2.4 m
Construction type: sand-lime brickwork and reinforced concrete slabs
Total internal volume: 8,476 m³
Total floor area: 2,376 m²
Residential area: 1,929 m²
Total site area: 6,214 m²
Construction cost: 3.3 million Euros
Funding: sponsored housing development
Heat consumption: 65 kWh/m²a
Planning/construction: 1999 – 2004

**In-fill development in established residential area
Solitaire houses for all generations
Splayed window reveals for increased daylight**

A casual observer would never expect these five storey solitaire houses to contain apartments for seniors behind their facades. This integrative housing development provides accommodation for seniors, handicapped residents, young families, single parents and singles. The buildings are located north-west of the Freiburg city centre at the edge of an established residential area. Apartment buildings of single-storey apartments and terraced houses dominate the local urban structure. By rotating the various building forms by 90° to each other the architects reacted to the complex existing urban landscape, redefining the streetscape and simultaneously creating new semi-public green zones.
30 residences of various sizes can be found within the apartment blocks; ranging from compact one-room apartments for seniors to family-friendly five-room dwellings. The block to the south-east houses twelve barrier-free apartments; nine are for seniors and three for disable residents.
In-house access is provided by internally located stairwells which benefit from natural daylight and supplemented by lifts. Almost all apartments are able to take advantage of corner situations. Within each dwelling the individual rooms are organised around the central living space which is enhanced by a loggia. The internal walls are of lightweight construction to allow future adaptations to be simply executed. Variations in depth of the facade at the loggias and the setting back of the roof-storey alleviate the otherwise rigid geometry of the cuboid structures. Splayed window reveals soften the effect of the facades and enhance the incidence of daylight within the dwellings.
The rendered buildings are constructed of sand-lime brickwork and reinforced concrete slabs with only the set-back roof storey being constructed of timber framework construction. The compact forms are insulated with 18 cm thick thermal insulation and furnished with a controlled ventilation system.

section · floor plans   scale 1:500
A roof level
B standard floor
C ground floor

aa

1 entrance
2 owner-occupied apartment
3 apartment for seniors
4 apartment for disabled
5 roof terrace

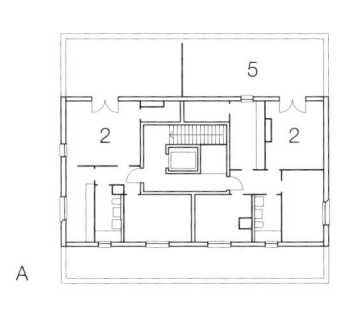

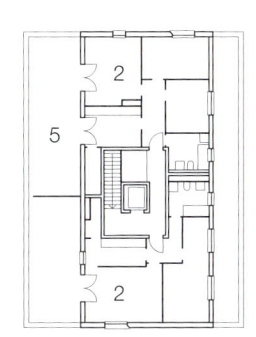

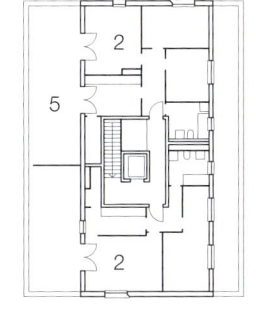

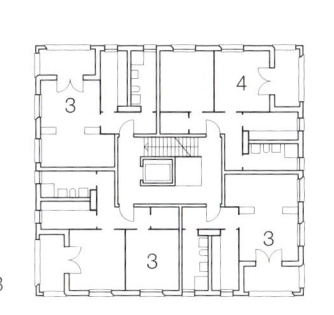

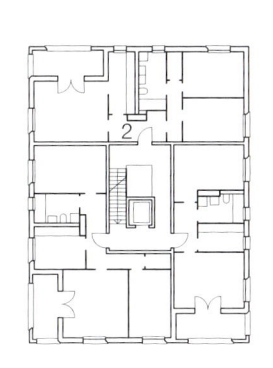

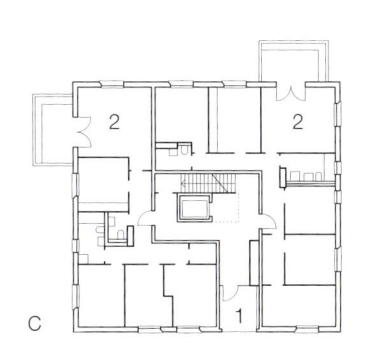

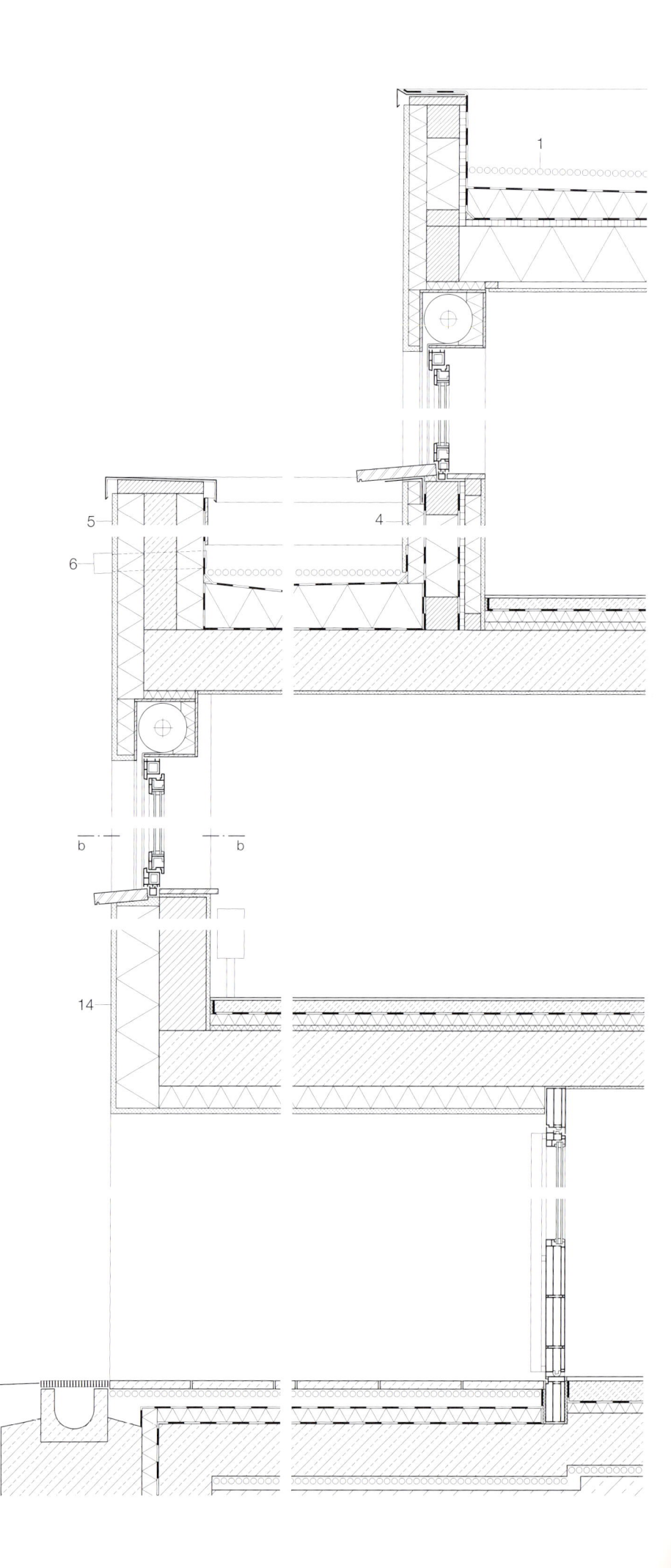

vertical section
horizontal section
scale 1:20

132

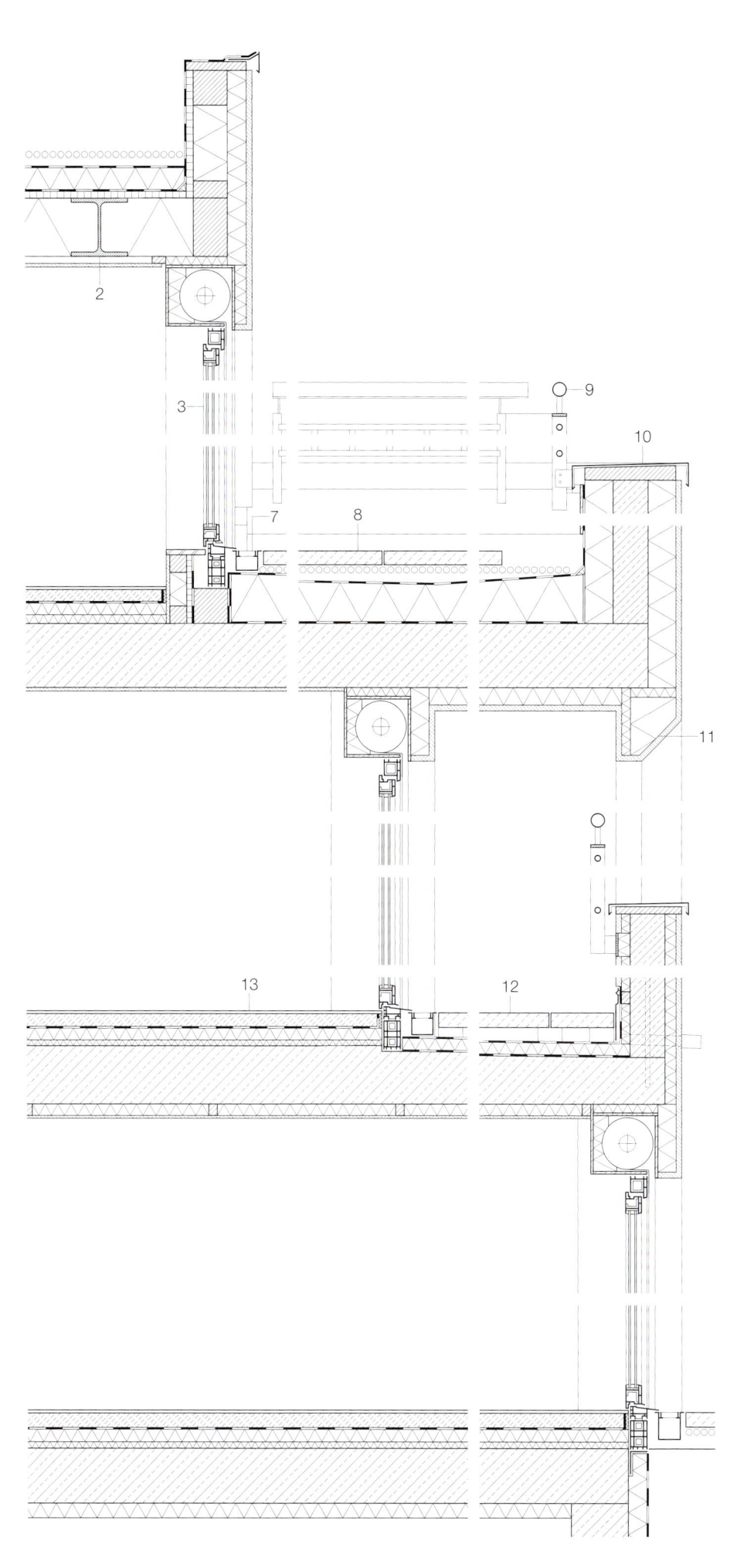

1 roof construction:
  50 mm gravel, impermeable membrane
  200–280 mm thermal insulation with fall
  vapour barrier, 24 mm triple-ply board
  200 mm thermal insulation between
  100 × 300 mm rafters
  24 × 48 mm counter battens
  12.5 mm plasterboard
2 200 mm steel I-beam
3 insulating glass in synthetic frame
4 roof level wall construction:
  20 mm render, 60 mm thermal insulation
  diffusion open separation layer
  120 × 80 mm timber-framing
  120 mm thermal insulation, vapour barrier
  19 mm oriented-strand-board
  60 mm thermal insulation
  40 × 60 mm battens, 12.5 mm plasterboard
5 spandrel:
  20 mm render, 100 mm insulation
  120 mm prefab. reinforced concrete element
  100 mm insulation with sub-construction
  10 mm cement fibreboard
6 Ø 35 mm steel pipe overflow
7 100 mm gutter
8 400 × 400 × 50 mm concrete slab
  30 mm gravel bed, separation layer
  thermal insulation with fall, 170 mm max.
  vapour barrier
  220 mm reinforced concrete slab
9 25 mm steel pipe balustrade post
10 1 mm galvanised zinc sheeting
11 insulating wedge
12 loggia floor construction
  400 × 400 × 50 mm concrete pavers,
  height adjustable
  impermeable membrane
  40 mm impact sound insul., vapour barrier
  reinforced concrete slab,
  with fall, max. 160 mm
13 floor construction:
  10 mm linoleum, 40 mm screed
  polyethylene separation layer
  40 mm thermal insulation
  30 mm impact sound insulation
  200 mm reinforced concrete slab
14 wall construction:
  20 mm render, 160 mm insulation
  175 mm sand-lime brickwork
  15 mm internal render

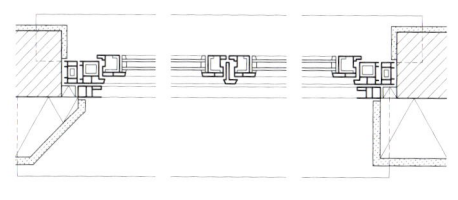

bb

Housing Development in Wiesbaden

Architects: Dietz Joppien, Frankfurt am Main

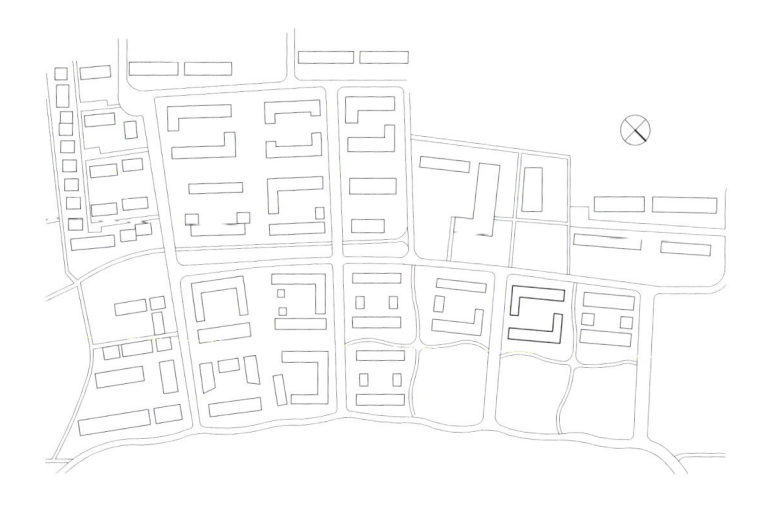

Urban development model
Flexible layouts for different lifestyles
Apartments for disabled users on ground floor

These housing blocks to the south-west of Wiesbaden are the result of a community housing programme, designed to provide affordable rental and owner-occupied accommodation for families and young couples. The architects won the competition with a proposal demonstrating highly flexible, yet economical layouts and an efficient usage of space. Adjustable dwelling units, capable of adapting to the requirements of the users, rather than rigidly structured floor plans are the basis of the project.

Neutral spaces

The project includes six housing blocks with a total of 400 dwellings; the three pairs of L-shaped buildings each encompass a semi-public courtyard with a children's playground. The southern buildings are entered from the courtyards, while the northern buildings are approached from the roadway. Almost identical, the five-storey buildings accommodate 66 dwellings each, which range in size from two to five room layouts. There are three staircases per storey; two access only two dwellings each, while the third also provides additional access to the external walkways along the narrow elevation. The floor plans are notable for their flexibility. Neutral spaces, which can be interconnected or divided by ceiling-high sliding walls, allow numerous floor plan alternatives. It is possible for the living spaces to be orientated to the street frontage, the courtyard side, or both, thus providing an open volume from facade to facade. Ceiling-high glazing opens the internal spaces out to the balconies and the outside. All ground floor dwellings and external spaces were planned to be barrier-free and unrestricted.

Construction and facades

The buildings have been constructed of a mixture of light-weight masonry and reinforced concrete slabs.
The appearances of the northern facades are determined by vertical and horizontal windows which are off-set from each other in strict rhythms, while the plasticity of the east and west-facing facades is enhanced by deep, cantilevered balconies. The elevations facing the internal courtyards are strongly influenced by the individually adjustable sun-shades constructed of sailcloth stretched over light-weight metal frames. In order to separate the individual dwellings, the continuous balconies are interrupted by fixed storage cuboards. By limiting material selection and employing vibrant colours, the architects have produced a unified and cohesive appearance.

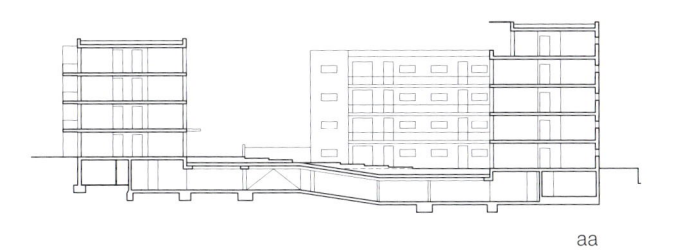

Project Details
Usage: apartment block
Units: 70 apartments (55–100.5 m²)
Access: two apartments per stair per storey and access walkways
Internal room height: 2.5 m
Construction type: reinforced concrete
Total internal volume: 28,591 m³
Total floor area: 5,766 m²
Usable floor area: 4,715 m²
Total site area: 4,878 m²
Construction cost: 5.78 million Euros
Funding: publicly funded housing
Construction time: 1999–2000

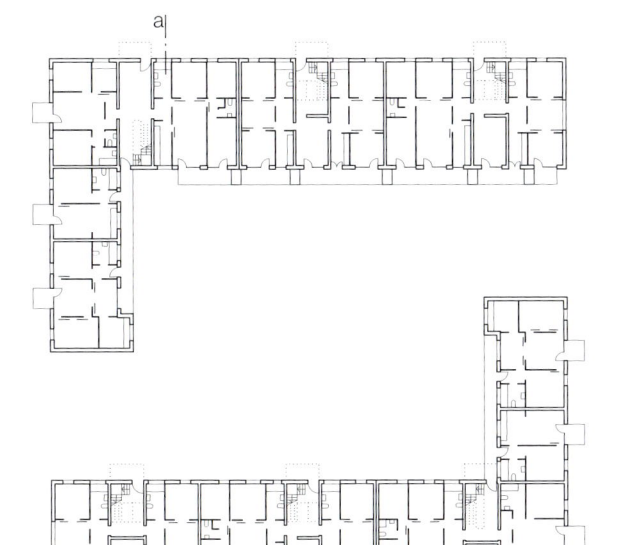

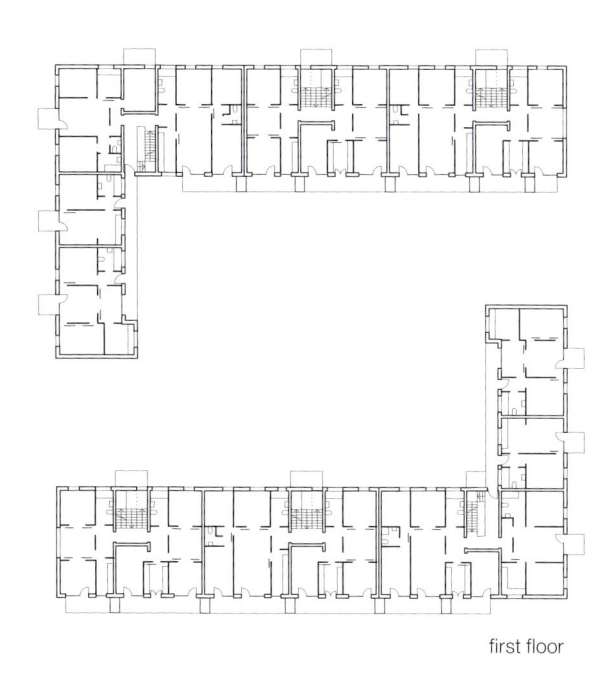

aa

ground floor

first floor

site plan
scale 1:7500
section • floor plans
scale 1:750

floor plans
scale 1:400

A Adaptation to changing generations
B Spatial flexibility according to daily routine
C Adaptation to various lifestyles

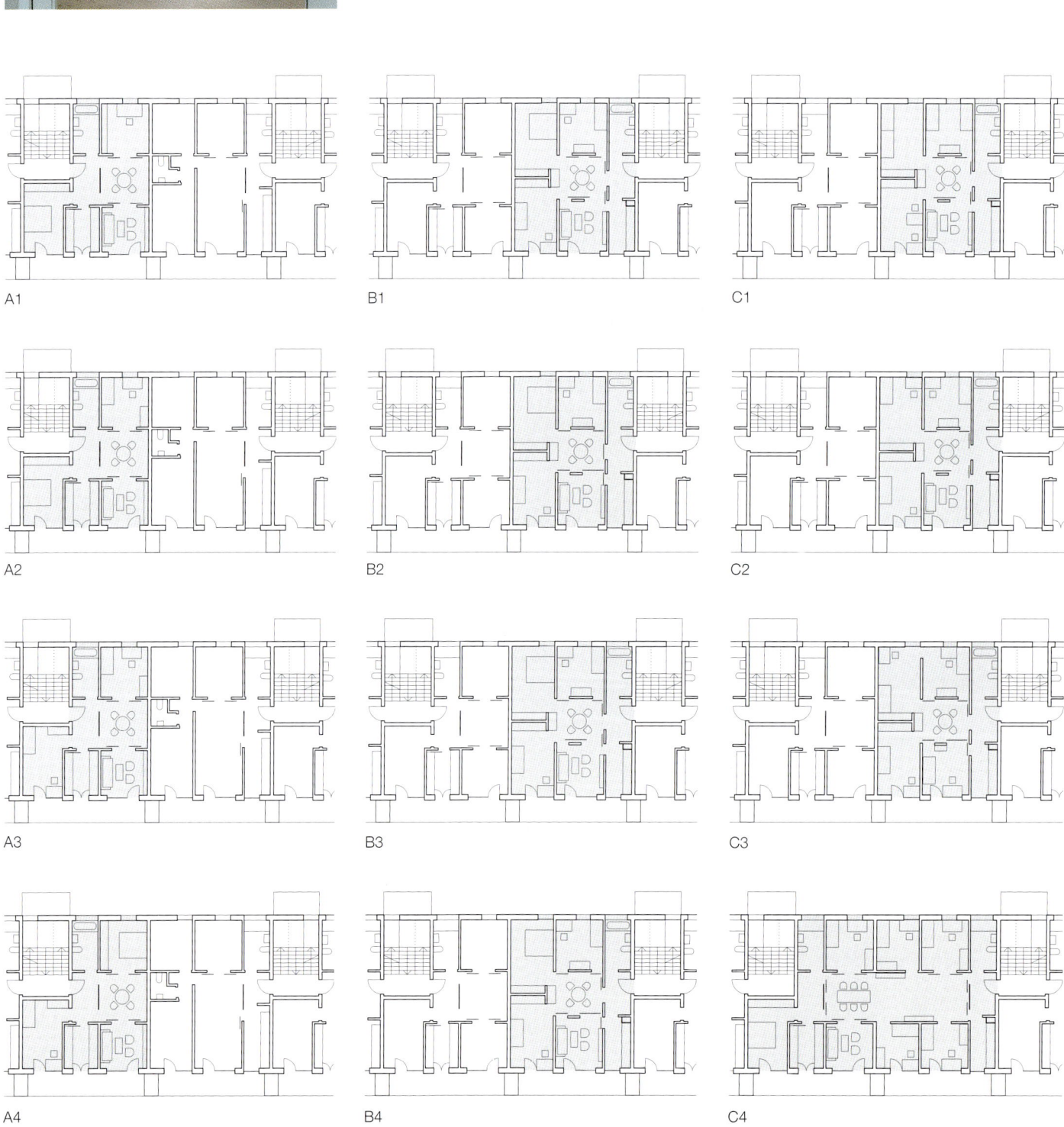

A1

B1

C1

A2

B2

C2

A3

B3

C3

A4

B4

C4

A1 Baby sleeps in master bedroom; living, working and dining space extends from one facade through to the opposite facade.
A2 Child becomes older and has own bedroom, extended play space in dining area with the possibility of separation.
A3 Child is grown and moves out, two individual rooms for the parents become available.
A4 Grandmother in need of care moves into an independent, south-facing room, north-facing room becomes a bedroom.

B1 11 a.m.: older child at school, younger child plays at home. Open living space simplifies child care while working. Play zone easily extended by connection of adjacent rooms.
B2 3 p.m.: neighbours visit for afternoon tea, living space is extended by the use of the balcony. Child withdraws into own room for homework.
B3 9 p.m.: parents watch television, children asleep, dining and living areas connected, individual rooms separated.
B4 10 p.m.: friend visits, withdrawal into living area, those sleeping in bedrooms remain undisturbed.

C1 Central room with seating; spatial connections with internal and external zones are available.
C2 Small family unit with grandmother; individual rooms for child, grandmother and parents, flexible communal living and dining space can include balcony as desired.
C3 Two single parents with one child each; interconnected two-room units are provided with shared kitchen, dining room and bathroom facilities.
C4 Shared accommodation for five residents: central dining space with associated private rooms which can be interconnected as desired. Balcony as extended living space.

Housing Development in Ypenburg

Architects: van den Oever, Zaaijer & Partners
with John Bosch, Amsterdam

Conceptual urban
planning sketches
site plan
scale 1:2500

1 Block A
 20 terrace houses
2 Block B
 12 terrace houses
3 Block C
 18 terrace houses
4 Block D
 4 residential groups

Development model for disabled residents and families
Large scale urban planning
Courtyards as centres of communication

A collection of nine large buildings creates an autonomous built environment which lies to the east of Ypenburg. The housing development, providing accommodation for about 120 families and disabled, is based upon a master plan by MVRDV and is also a fundamental element in the urban development scheme of The Hague.

Homogenous housing structure

Surrounded by water and off-set from one another, the houses of varying sizes are distributed along three elongated embankments. The housing blocks, which vary from one to three storeys in height, contain either 12 or 20 single family houses or four residential groups under one roof. They are arranged around communal courtyards. Atrium spaces provide internal access and large open areas for interaction between residents. The sloping roofs, orientated to optimise the levels of natural daylight, create a polygonal geometry which varies according to the location of the observer. Parking spaces are incorporated between the courtyard buildings.
Dark reddish-brown clinker brickwork determines the appearance of the external facades, walkways and parking spaces. The internal facades orientated towards the courtyards are clad in large format green timber panels which will eventually be covered in ivy.

Various organisational layouts

The two externally located blocks to the north of the development provide accommodation for eight groups of mentally and physically challenged residents. Each residential group is organised on a single level and their internal layouts are in accordance with the limited mobility of many of the users. The private rooms are linked directly to the communal space, the middle point of which is the centrally located, free-standing kitchen. The upper levels benefit from the sloping roofs with ceiling heights of up to seven metres while the internal spaces vary in their colour treatment.
The remaining seven housing blocks accommodate compact dwellings which penetrate the depth of the buildings. While offering young families an alternative to the traditional terrace house with garden, the development still provides affordable residential space with sheltered play zones for children.

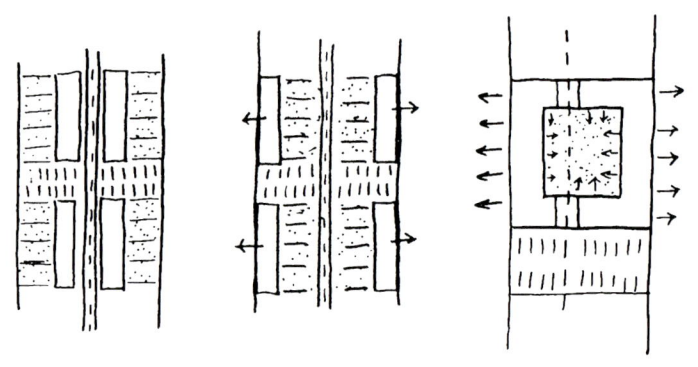

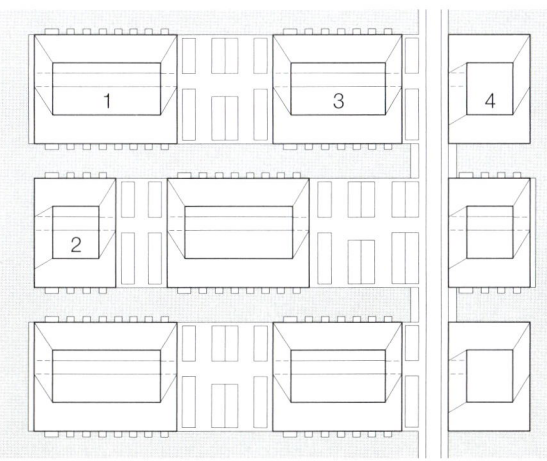

Project Details
Usage: terrace houses, residential groups
Units: 120 2-room apartments (90–170 m²)
2 residential groups (3,000 m²) of
48 rooms (14 m²)
Access: communal space (groups)
terrace houses
Internal room height: 2.5–4.0 m
Construction type: reinforced concrete
Total internal volume: 55,600 m³
Usable floor area: 19,850 m²
Total site area: 22,700 m²
Construction cost: 2.8 million Euros
Construction time: 2002

140

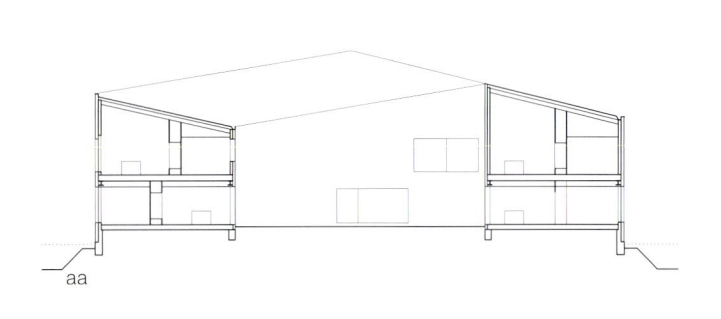

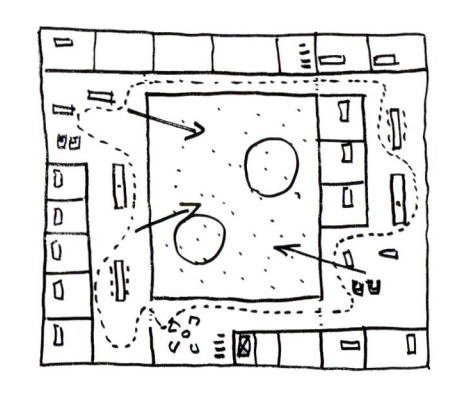

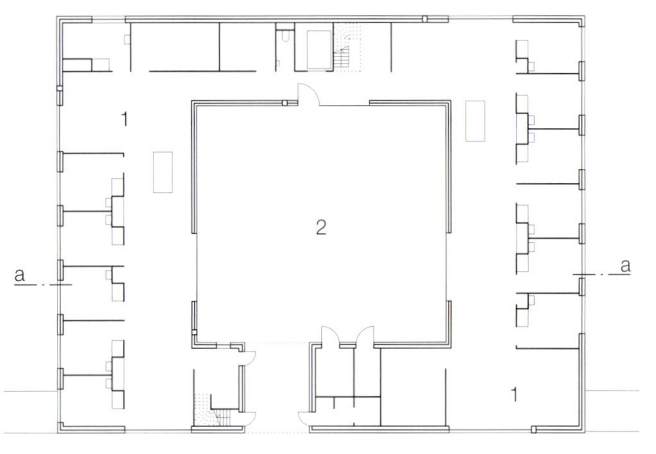

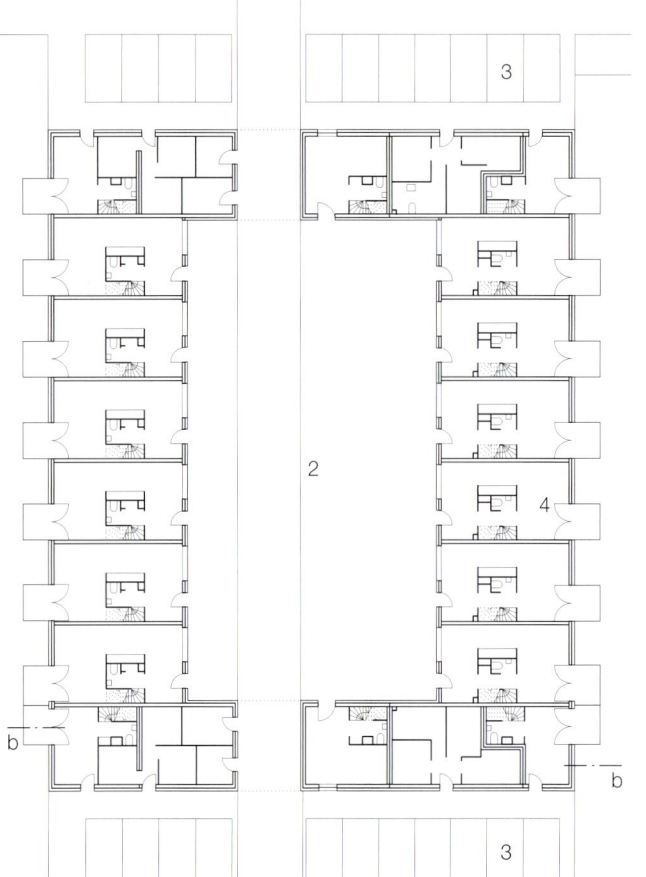

Conceptual sketches residential group
sections • floor plans
ground and first floor
scale 1:500

1 residential group
2 planted internal courtyard
3 parking space
4 terrace house

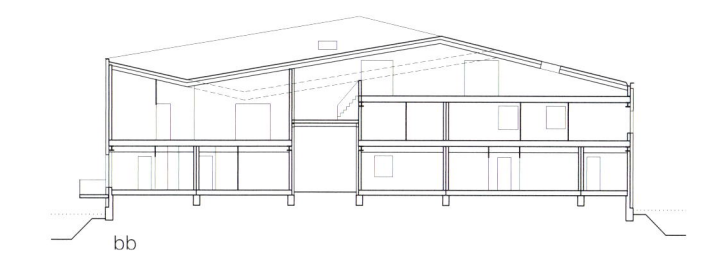

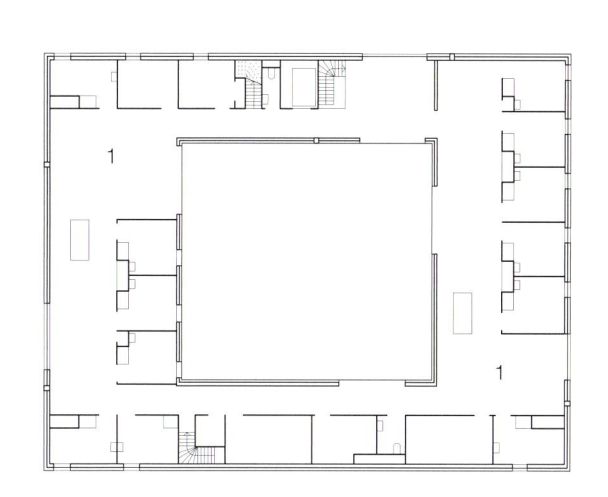

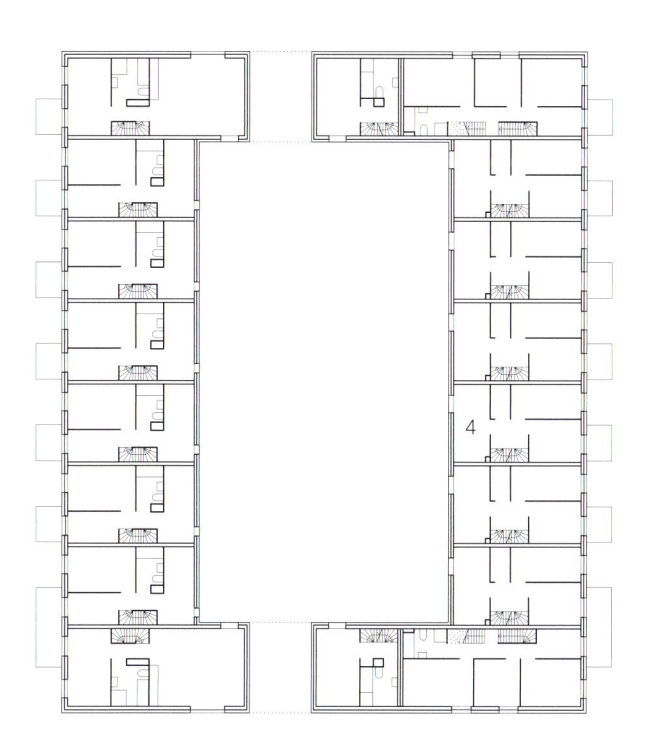

bb

141

142

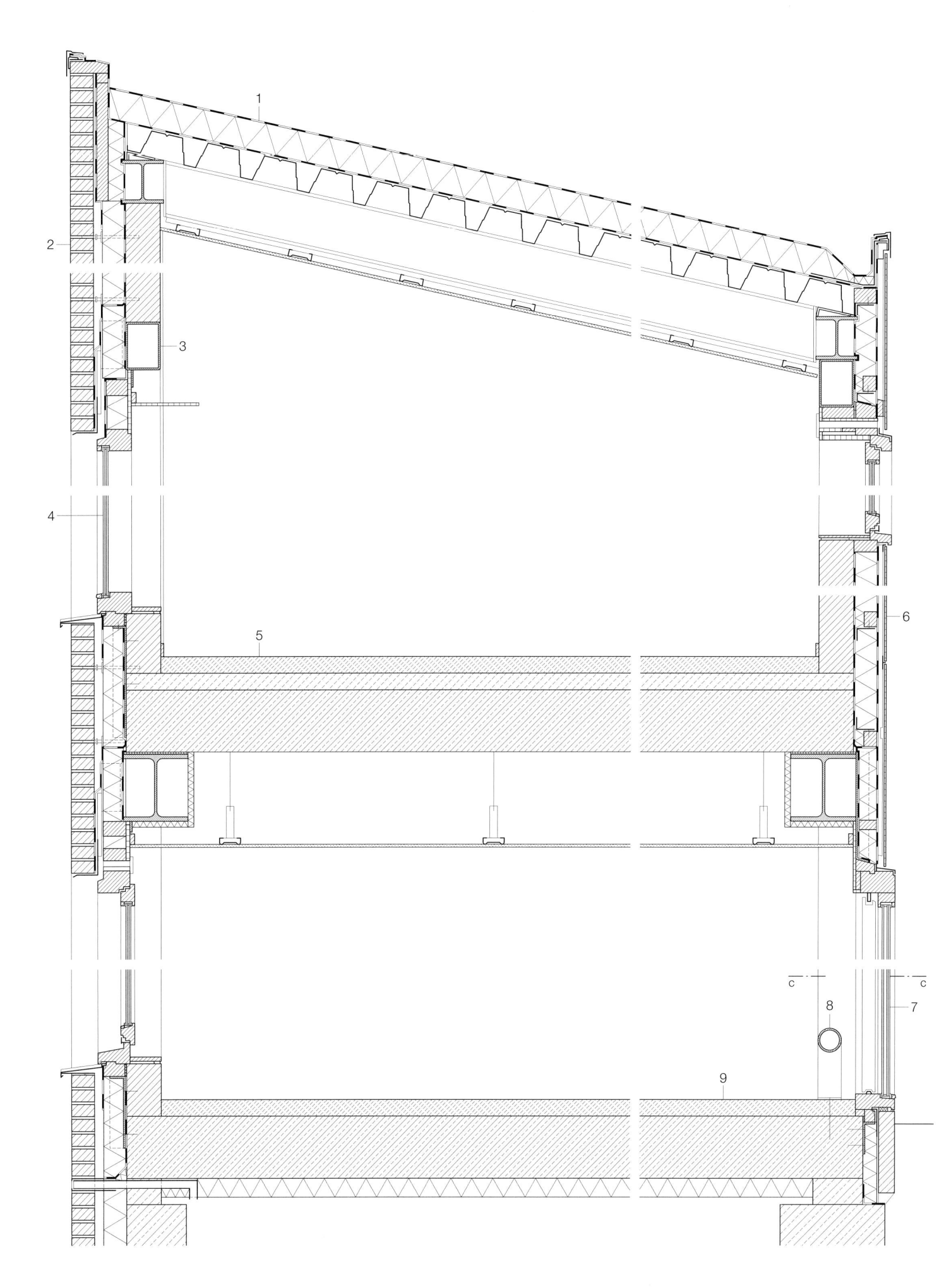

sections   scale 1:20

1. roof construction:
   single layer bituminous membrane
   120 mm rigid foam thermal insulation
   vapour barrier
   110 mm trapezoidal metal sheeting
   230 mm steel I-beam
   12.5 mm plasterboard on sub-construction
2. wall construction:
   100 mm face brickwork
   40 mm ventilation cavity
   100 mm thermal insulation
   vapour barrier
   150 mm sand-lime brickwork
3. 200 × 150 × 6 mm hollow steel profile
4. insulating glass in timber frame
5. upper floor construction:
   70 mm screed
   70 mm concrete
   260 mm prefabricated concrete slab
   280 mm steel I-beam
   12.5 mm suspended plasterboard ceiling
6. wall construction:
   8 mm timber construction board, green
   40 mm sub-construction with ventilation cavity
   45 mm thermal insulation
   vapour barrier
   150 mm sand-lime brickwork
7. sliding door, insulating glass in timber frame
8. Ø 100 mm steel pipe stopper at 250 mm above floor level
9. ground floor construction:
   70 mm screed
   260 mm prefabricated concrete slab
   80 mm thermal insulation

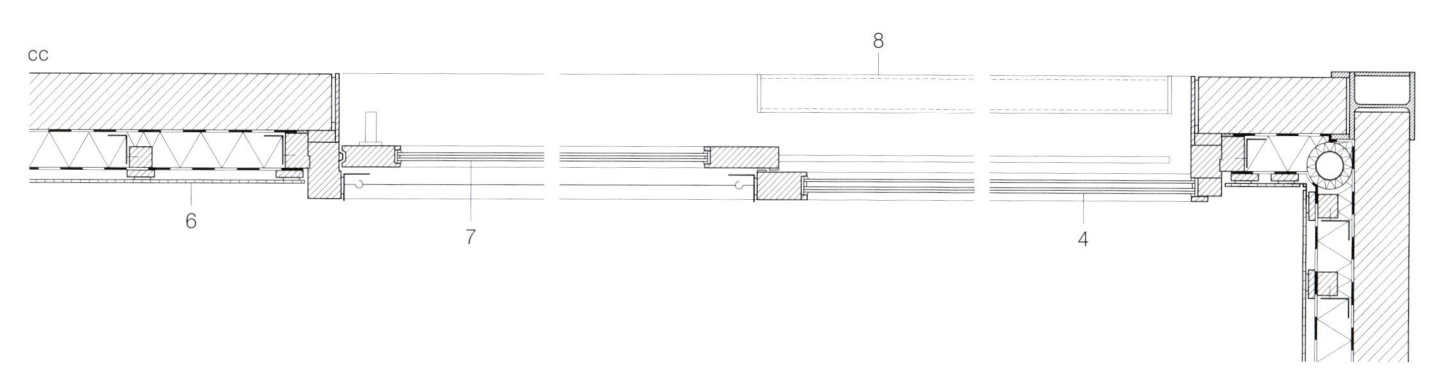

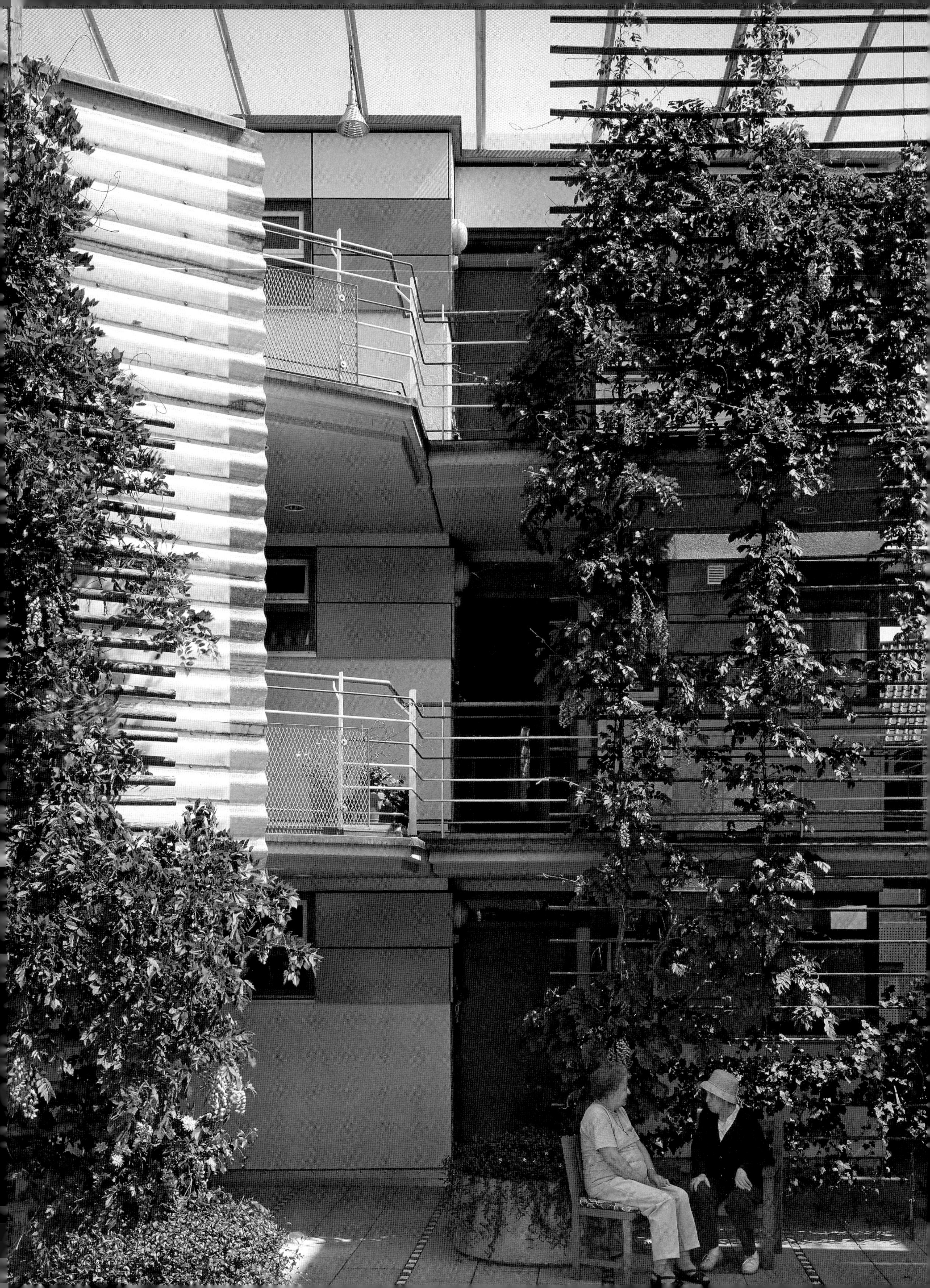

Building in Accordance with the Needs of the Elderly

by Joachim F. Giessler

Analogue to the demographic development in our country, the home increasingly will become the centre of everyday, independent life for around 94 % of the population over 60 years of age.
Because the life expectancy is rising, residents will spend ever longer periods of their life in the home. This development will generate new needs and thus place demands on both the existing dwellings of such residents and on any newly constructed housing that is purchased or traded. Judging from current developments, the expectation is that tomorrow's care increasingly will take place in the domestic arena.
Yet considerations about housing that does justice to the needs of the elderly make sense only if the necessary furnishings are available for the rooms and the functions they are supposed to perform. Unfortunately, the German DIN 18025 standard, and presumably the new DIN 18030 as well, provide too few useful specifications. They specify merely that "Furnishings are the parts required for the room to fulfil its intended function, e.g. sanitary accessories, appliances and furniture; these can be introduced by the builder or by the user of the dwelling."
It is not enough to merely fulfil construction specification norms like wider doors, sufficient space to manoeuvre a wheelchair or crutches, and accessibility for the wheelchair-bound and disabled. Increasingly, additional demands must be addressed and fulfilled relating to the psychology of dwelling and social integration.

After the children leave home, a typical German apartment is converted for an elderly couple, undergoing a sensible and foresighted renovation (ill. 3.2):
This conversion did more than just provide for freedom of manoeuvre, a barrier-free bathroom and wider doors in accordance with DIN:
- Each of the two residents could be given his or her own bedroom, if a change to different sleeping habits were to necessitate such a measure. The living room becomes a shared living area.

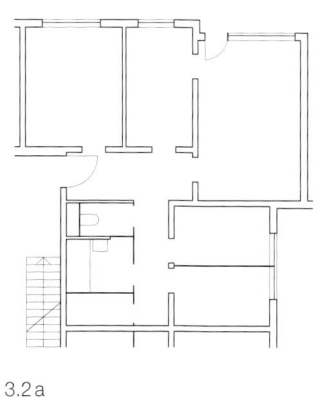

3.2 a 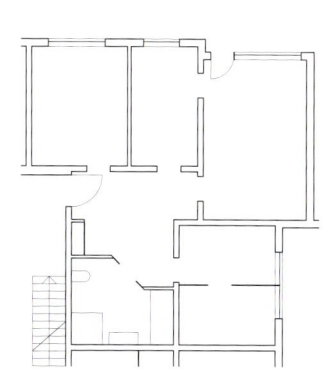   b

3.3 a   b

3.1 Seniors' Centre in Stuttgart, 1995; Kauffmann Theilig & Partner
3.2 Adaptation of an old apartment
   a Floor plan before conversion
   b Floor plan after conversion
3.3 Barrier-free bathrooms
   a Senior Dwellings in Domat/Ems, 2004
      Architect: Dietrich Schwarz
   b Centre for Seniors in Lich, 2003
      Architects: Pfeifer Roser Kuhn

3.4

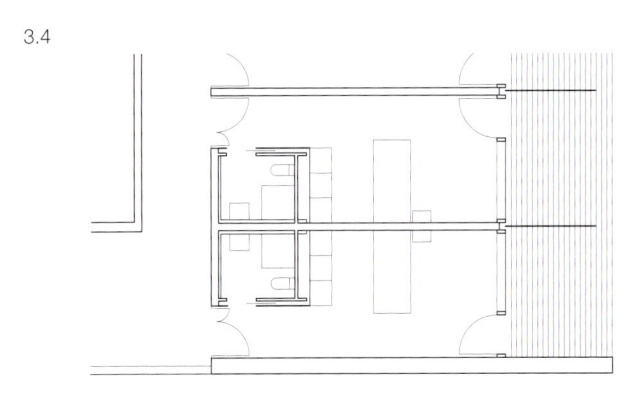

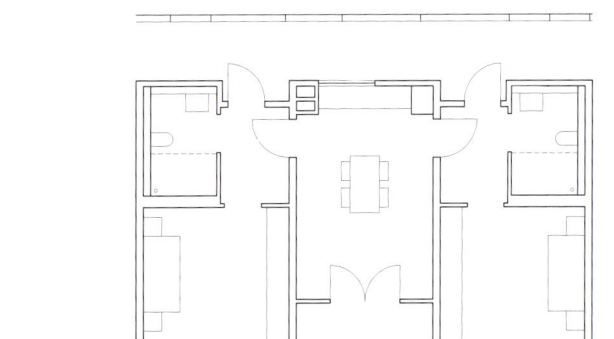

3.5

3.6

- If either of the residents should require care, direct and closer access from the room of the patient to the bathroom could be provided by removing the bathtub.
- The entry door to the apartment has been burglar-proofed and monitoring installed – in keeping with the increased need for security perceived by the parents now living alone. However, the cost of this conversion would run to somewhere between 40,000 and 50,000 euros.

The primary problems of the future as regards building in accordance with the needs of the elderly are thus: Adapting existing housing to needs economically, planning and building new dwellings with particular regard for the later years of life, and, finally, considering residential forms in which young people can live with seniors, or seniors with each other. Some examples are familiar by now:
- the senior flat-share (ill. 3.4)
- multi-generation housing structures
- units for assisted living (ill. 3.5, 3.6)
- "smart-home" developments in which only elderly residents live together

All of these different residential possibilities entail a number of considerations about the future floor plan so that the given conditions can be fulfilled (ill. 3.7):
- Functional connections between bedroom, sanitary areas and stowage space must be considered very carefully to make barrier-free care possible in the home.
- It should be possible to combine rooms that become free after the children move out, to set up a rental unit to supplement a less than opulent pension, or to provide accommodation for a care worker.
- The most elementary wishes for privacy, intimacy, and a feeling of security must be addressed. This includes the need for a dwelling to be self-contained, as well as blinds, design with suitable materials and also appropriate burglary protection.

On the secondary tier, but also important, is the question of the kind of surroundings suited to the needs of the elderly:
- Public transport connections should be located nearby and/or private means of transport conveniently accessible.
- Services for the elderly, day hospitals, day care or rehabilitation centres should be in the vicinity.

And it also means that a café, a supermarket, doctors' offices, hotel, post office and banks in the area should also be designed barrier-free.

But on to the demands for alternative and supplementary furnishings:
The market must be trawled through for usable articles and products. Since there is not much to be found here yet, once again – and above all, immediately – manufacturers should turn to the determination of design tasks and their implementation in finished products.
At present few declarations from the German furniture industry promise any success; at most, rudiments can be identified. Most recently a prototype of a "voice-controlled" bed was introduced at the IMM Furniture Fair in Cologne, equipped with a slatted frame whose head and foot ends can be raised and lowered by means of spoken commands.
Further glimmers of hope: A few rest and massage armchairs are on offer, equipped with electronic raising aids and con-

trols to adjust the footrest and seat back; and some bedroom catalogues now even include night tables equipped with a pill drawer.

Because most people do not like talking about old age, and a vocabulary around the concepts of wheelchair and disability has certainly raised many a threshold in recent years, it is clear that the industry will not designate products as "for seniors", "meets the needs of the disabled", or "wheelchair accessible", for they would find no takers for such items.

Whether the elderly will adopt special furniture like that described above, whatever it is called, has yet to be seen. Several luxury manufacturers even raise doubts that seniors require any special furniture for old age. They believe that because every good piece of furniture is conceived according to ergonomic and haptic criteria, all quality pieces must fulfil the needs that are important for the elderly.

However, doubts are certainly justified on this score: If one looks for suitable pieces in furniture stores, soon it becomes apparent that there is little available. A couple of half-hearted approaches in bedroom catalogues, the attempt to offer assistance in the form of height-adjustable sinks, desks, and cabinets using newly developed furniture fittings, plus a few good developments in scattered individual pieces, all of which are still quite unaffordable.

Because industry only manufactures products when it can sell sufficient numbers, the goal stated above can be achieved only by thinking about multi-generation products. That is, products that are needed and can be used by different generations at the same time: for instance, a small kitchen unit for cooking in a seated position, which the elderly lady uses because she can no longer stand very well – but also the young cashier who spent the whole day on her feet and is happy that she can sit down to prepare her dinner in the evening.

In the area of sanitary and cooking facilities a number of products are already on the market: Bathroom catalogues include a well-sorted selection of furnishing objects, and the corresponding sales consultants are increasingly welltrained and educated. Yet grip holds and shower seats to simplify the personal hygiene of the elderly are not enough. Clearly, it is more difficult to find the tiler who is able to produce level, tiled bathrooms that are watertight. Affordable, height-adjustable toilet bowls in a design fit for human beings are hard to find, and in this country bathtubs are still cemented fast to the building with the disadvantage that their removal requires disproportionate cost and effort.
There are accessible, height-adjustable kitchens, but the electrical systems used to adjust them drive up their cost. This also raises the question as to whether such devices need be controlled mechanically at all, and how large or small such a kitchen must be for an older couple that does not want to do without. At this time, not a single reasonable analysis has been submitted of how many dishes and appliances a one-person or two-person elderly household needs.

Perhaps the kitchen industry still orients its production too closely on conventional kitchen sizes. Whatever the reason, when converting a dwelling, which often occurs sometime around the time the resident is 55 years of age, builders still buy traditional kitchens, even though it is not possible to convert them later into kitchens where the residents can work while seated. The consciousness for looking ahead with regard to dwellings and furnishings simply has yet to develop.

Today it is possible to find a few good beds that can also serve as hospital beds should stationary care become necessary as the resident ages. But these are not beds from a normal bedroom catalogue.

But what about the surroundings of a bed the resident has to spend more time in, whose occupant still wants to take part in the life around him?
- Can the occupant of the bed see who is at the front door when the doorbell rings?
- Is it possible to turn on a pivot-screen television screen whilst lying in the bed? Can a laptop also be used there comfortably?
- Can the window be opened or closed when the occupant is about to fall asleep and does not wish to get up again?
- Is it possible to eat comfortably in bed, without feeling like one is in hospital?
- Can the light be adapted to the occupant's reading habits, and more generally: Are there studies about light and colour for the elderly? What light is right and which colours are preferred or rejected as people become older?

These are all questions designers urgently need to ask if the answers to these questions are to become more than a mere scenario for the future.

New considerations must also be made about how to make it easier, and above all, more humane, for people to get out of the bed and to the bathroom. Transfer aids or new means of transport must be developed that do not smack of high-tech gadgetry, hospitals or welfare centres. Mobile wash stands would also be a great help. Although all of these approaches have been seen before in competitions or at trade fair events, they can not be found as purchasable products.

Our 60-cm-deep wardrobes, in which the socks are difficult to find behind the stack of shirts in everyday operation, also have rotating doors that get in our way when we open them. Further, there is no real need for the wardrobe to have a foot, as eliminating this feature would make it possible to walk or push a wheelchair inside it (ill. 3.8).

Stowage spaces, be they bedroom or bathroom cabinets, and furniture in hallways, are still built up to 2.50 metres high, with the consequence that things located at a height of over two metres can only be taken out by standing on a footstool or stepladder. But maybe this is something the owner can no longer do – to say nothing of the risk of accidents!
This is also true for bookshelves, from which the years' long collection of art books on the upper shelves can no longer be lifted out, because they are too heavy and the upper arm musculature has become too weak.

3.4 Seniors' Residence Multengut in Muri near Bern, 2004
   Care accommodation
   Architects: Burkhalter Sumi
3.5, 3.6 Multi-generational House in Stuttgart, 2001
   Shared accommodation for seniors with communal kitchen
   Architects: Kohlhoff & Kohlhoff

3.7 a b

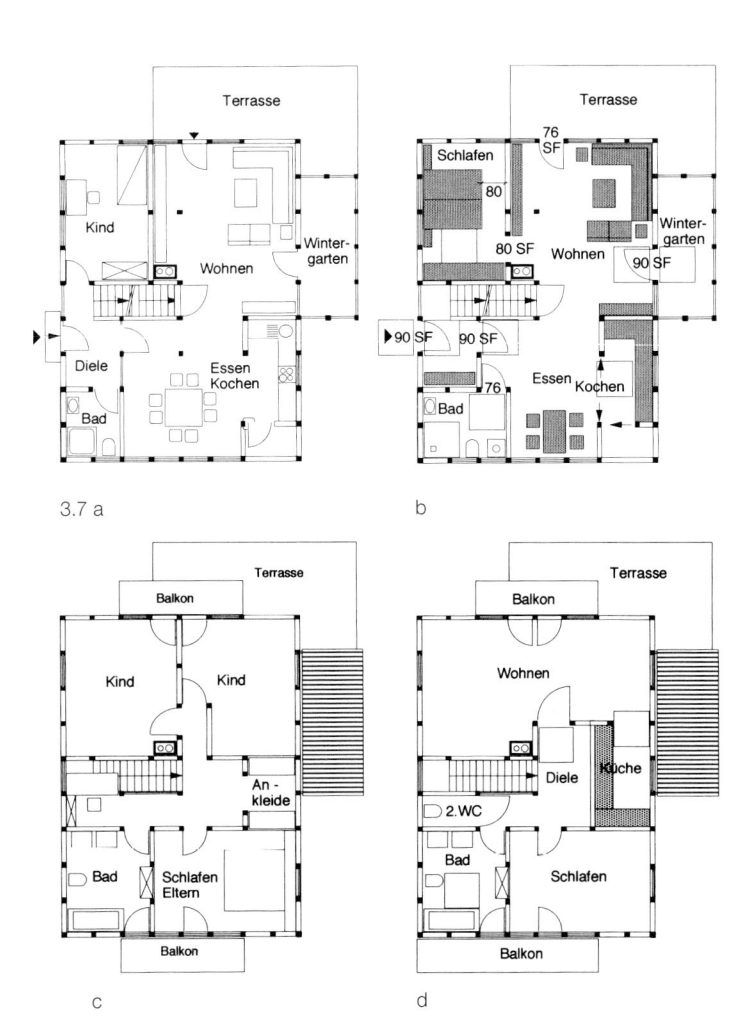

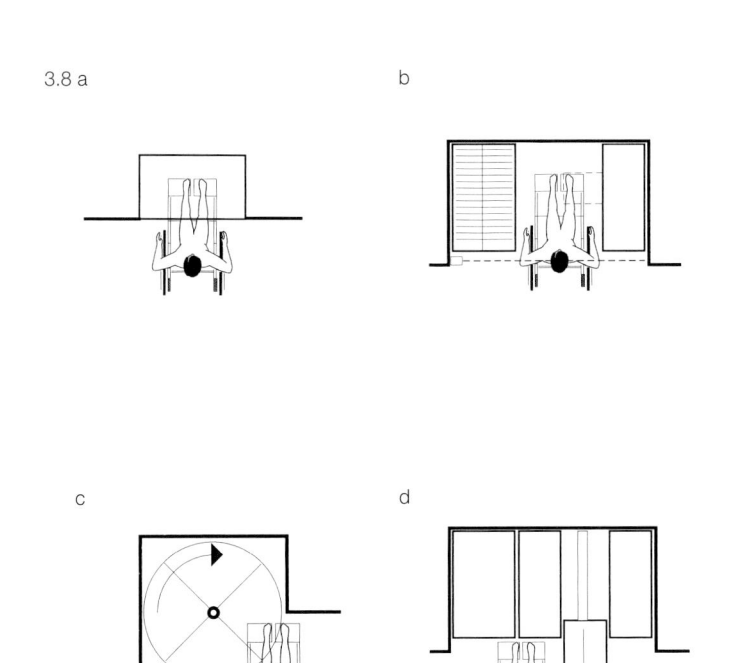

c d

3.8 a b

c d

Alternatives to these stowage spaces are being sought. The paternoster lift solutions attempted so far have been anything but affordable. And the list of the furnishings that are missing or should be reconsidered continues. The search includes suitable chairs with slanted backs that make standing up easier, and are spacious enough to allow someone to sit down even with a blanket wrapped around his or her shoulders. Also: an armchair equipped with a truly effective raising aid, which lifts the body a couple of centimetres before the seat tilts forward.

Summary:
Disabilities due to age are not diseases. When sight fails, hearing, memory, and mobility become reduced; when the directions and distances a person can reach change, or muscle strength ebbs; when reaction times and the sense of touch diminish; this need not mean that an independent, safe and comfortable life in one's own home is no longer possible. With interdisciplinary collaboration among architects, interior designers and industrial designers, each of whom see their own task in solving the situation thus defined, it will be possible to develop a consciousness for building in accordance with the needs of the elderly, among the population and in industry.

This points toward the development of different floor plans and furnishings for dwellings, which would have to look slightly different than most of what is on offer so far.
A few examples of such developments:

- An open addition of rooms, without any nesting and with fewer doors, all of them without thresholds. Thus mobility for the resident can be guaranteed, no matter what the resident's disability.
- Room for walk-in or wheel-in closets, in which not only clothes and linens could be stored, but also a resident's other devices and means of mobile communication, for instance, those required when family members come to visit.
- Overlapping spaces to manoeuvre a wheelchair, as ascertained by questioning and evaluating the everyday practice of the wheelchair-bound. Is an area of 1.50 × 1.50 m really needed, or would 1.20 × 1.20 m be enough?
- Flexible, light, dividing walls of suitable materials, which make it possible to adjust rooms to new needs such as changes In sleeping behaviour.
- Innovatively designed sanitary stalls with short, barrier-free routes from the sleeping area in case independent mobility should become restricted.
- Room colour schemes with preferences and utility ascertained in a scientific manner. Colour contrasts used in a meaningful way can assist in improving orientation should sight become impaired. One criterion is high recognizability: Where is the door to the adjacent room, and where is the edge of the kitchen counter?
- The use of suitable and mobile lighting, which can be adjusted to failing eyesight and which obeys the needs of the resident, and not the other way round.
- When hearing begins to fail, acoustic signals can be supplemented with optical ones.
- Newly developed furniture and fittings that can be used by different generations and produced industrially. Here electronics can be of assistance when perception or memory is impaired: for instance, controls can monitor the stove and automatically shut it off if the resident forgets to.
- The placement and form of metal fittings, corresponding to

the degrees of human growth, are integrated into development and also oriented toward the probability of reduced muscle strength or restricted motor co-ordination.
- Household appliances that can be operated easily and safely with the disabilities listed above and used just as easily by persons without disabilities.

Recognizing and accepting imminent, irreversible societal change, alternative thinking, preventative planning and building, situation-oriented development and design of suitable products are more than expedient today. Only if everyone involved works on the task at hand with commitment will we be able to make major advances in the future.

3.7 Single family house in timber-frame construction,
☐ mobility space 120 × 120 cm
a ground floor prior to conversion
b ground floor after conversion
c first floor prior to conversion
d first floor after conversion
3.8 Storage concept
a wheel-in cupboard
b cupboard sections can be rolled out of the nich
c carousel cupboard
d wheel-in niche cupboard
3.9 Therapy chair
Design: Udo Feldotto
3.10 Transfer aid
Design: Christina Finger, Dominik Tesseraux
3.11 Mobile washstand "Hydrix"
Design: Michael Strobel

3.9

3.10

3.11

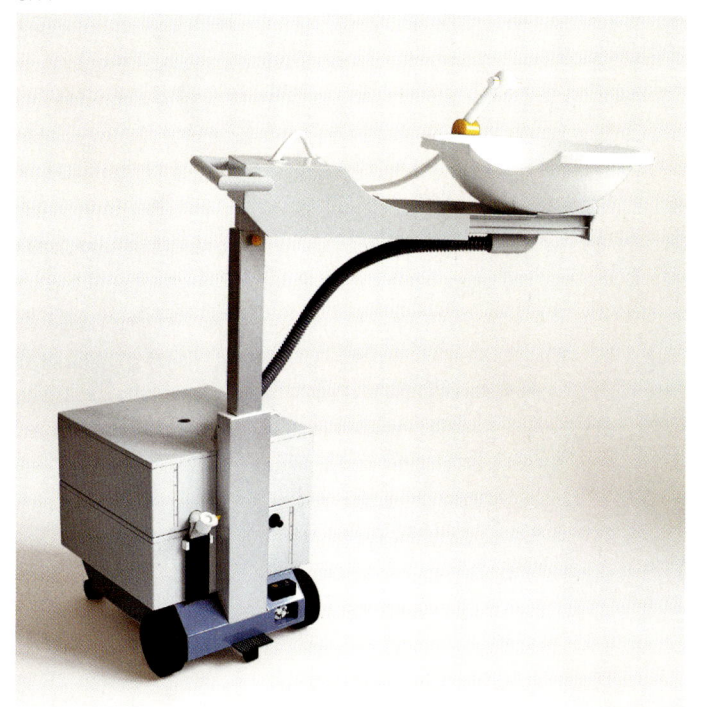

149

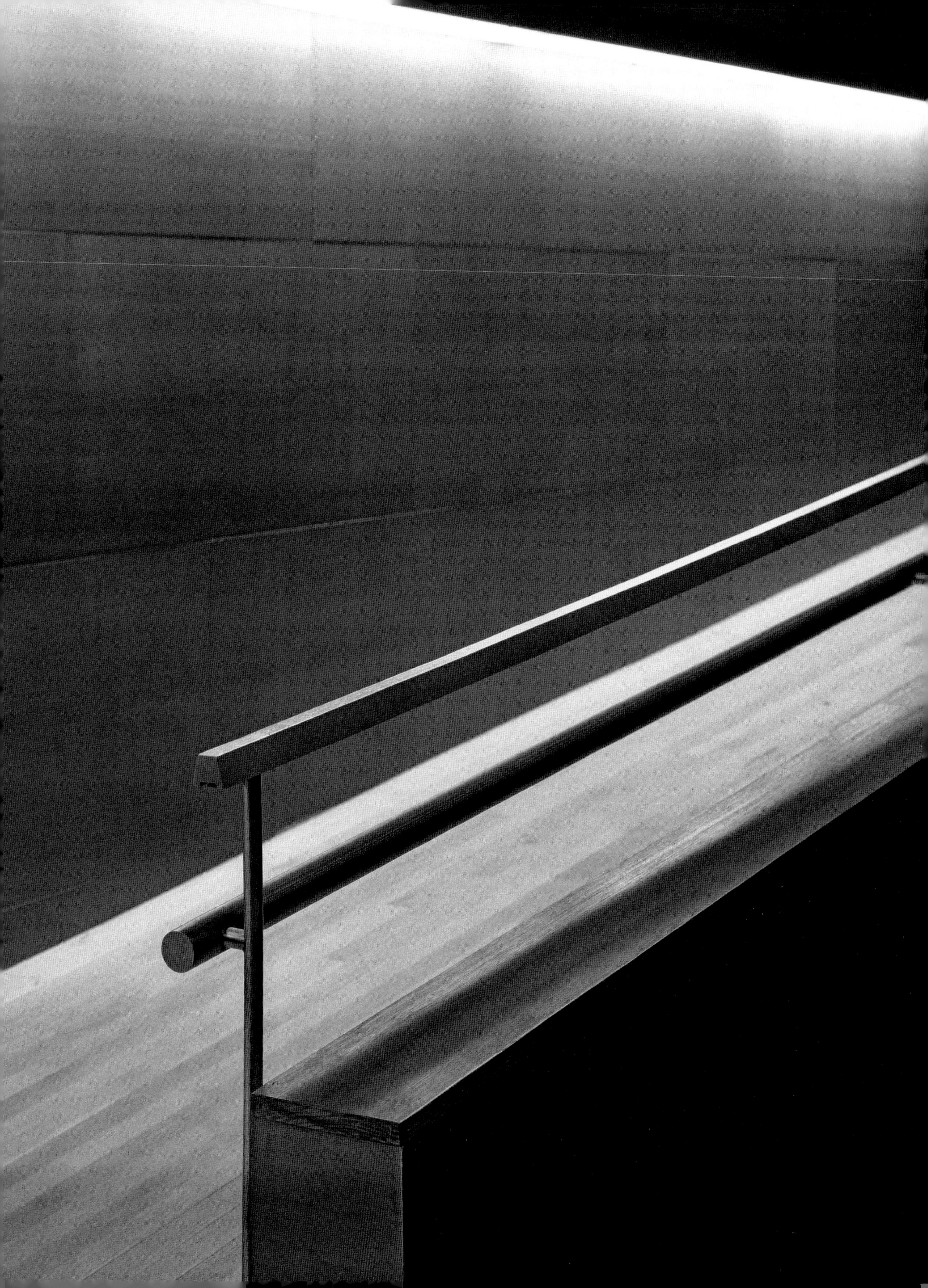

Barrier-Free Design and Construction for New and Existing Buildings

by Lothar Marx

Introduction

People change as they age. Biological changes are accompanied by a reduction in their sensory and mobile capabilities: Physical activities take place more slowly, less often and more cautiously, necessitating an attendant process of adjusting to the environment. To some extent, capabilities that have been lost can be compensated for by utilizing appropriate aids (e.g. glasses, hearing aid, cane, walking frame), yet fundamental planning for housing in old age is a must. It goes without saying that the edificial structures of the environment and homes of the elderly must fulfil numerous demands. A person should not be forced to adapt himself to the dwelling and its surroundings, rather, structural adjustments for the given life conditions should be made before they become urgently necessary. The needs to be expected later in life can also be provided for in advance through the specifications of a global construction standard.

Such a construction standard should be based on the planning recommendations of part 1 of the German DIN 18025 norm for common areas in a housing development and part 2 of DIN 18025, "Barrier-Free Housing", for the private, individual sphere. In drafting their designs, planners require and rely on their knowledge of human nature as well as their expertise in implementation.

Applying the DIN 18025 Standard to New Buildings
If the planning project does not pertain to the concerns of the wheelchair-bound, simple and economical implementation is possible. Where dwellings must also be wheelchair-accessible, the project costs will increase by approximately 6 to 8 percent. The goal of barrier-free design can be achieved in part by implementing the planning recommendations of the DIN norms; however, in some cases technical aids can replace the data of the norm. An example: The norm stipulates that a level surface must be located at the end of every ramp. If the passage between the subterranean garage and the stairwell/elevator ends at a T 90 door, which can only be opened by applying more strength than anyone with a walking disability can muster, installing a photo sensor to open the door before the person enters the swing area of the door would make passage possible for everyone. It would not be necessary to install a level platform. In this case the costs for this level platform per cubic meter of gross cubic volume must be compared with the cost of the sensor – with a clear result. It would be great if the norm allowed for such creative impulses in implementation, but the planner's expertise can make up for its deficits.

Applying the DIN 18025 Standard to Existing Buildings
Implementing the planning recommendations of the DIN norm in existing housing (for renovation or conversion) often founders on the local circumstances. Yet in order to make it possible to deal with existing housing without becoming liable for planning mistakes, the section "Application Area and Purpose" stipulates:
It is valid in principle – corresponding to the individual need – for the planning, execution and furnishings of (Part 1: wheelchair accessible) (Part 2: barrier-free) new construction, expansion, conversion, and modernizations of condominiums, owner-occupied housing estates and owner-occupied homes.
Therefore deviation from the specifications of the DIN norm is permitted.

Sensors

Planning projects for people with sensory disabilities (hearing, sight, smell, taste, and touch) have been critically neglected in the past. The necessity for such projects is apparent in the constantly growing number of people with sensory disabilities.

In Germany, 660,000 people suffer from moderately to seriously impaired vision or blindness, seventy percent of whom are over sixty years of age (source: Deutscher Blinden-Bund). Similarly, it can be established that every fifth person in Germany has below-normal hearing (source: Deutscher Schwerhörigen-Bund).

If reduced abilities can no longer be compensated using appropriate aids such that one sense is lost completely, another sense must take over compensatory functions (in the blind, the sense of hearing or touch; in the deaf, the sense of sight or touch). This is known as the "two-senses principle". The signals and information people have to receive are of varying importance.

- Alarm and warning signals in situations that endanger life and limb have the highest objective priority (Mind the step!),

4.1　Ramp in Community Hall in San Sebastian, 1999; Rafael Moneo

4.2

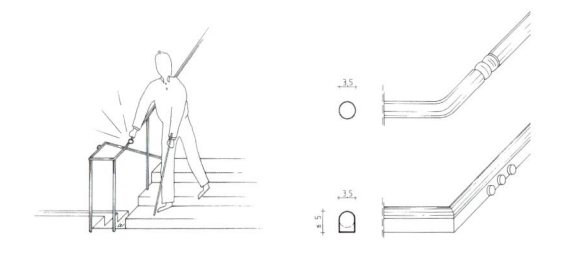

4.3

- information needed for decision-making is weighted with moderate importance (elevator button up/down) and
- signals that provide auxiliary information have the lowest priority.

Sufficient and sensible lighting is very important for visual orientation. Especially in the surroundings of the elderly, a higher intensity of illumination is generally recommended. How intense the illumination in a space should be depends on the the colour scheme of the surfaces in the given space. Perception can be improved significantly through such measures, and fear and accidents as a consequence of insufficient lighting avoided. The quality of light also can be improved significantly by changing its colour and reducing glare. Last but not least, a high-contrast design co-ordinated with the colour scheme and the specially selected materials are needed, especially in danger spots (e.g. glass surfaces, stairs, etc.). Living spaces should be designed to support people who need tactile and haptic orientation aids: for example, tactile orientation aids should be highlighted through the use of different textures and materials in the adjacent areas.

Mobility

The interplay among the skeletal, ligamental and musculoskeletal systems, connected with the neuronal system, is the prerequisite for mobility. Missing limbs, paralysis, or impairments as a consequence of illness may be compensated for or replaced by suitable aids. Yet these can only be effective if the entire environment is also designed in accordance with DIN 18025. The specified room for manoeuvre is a fundamental condition to ensure that the paths of motion and activities can actually be performed.
In this context special consideration is required for fine motor skills. The hand, a versatile part of the body, with the help of which a wide variety of actions are performed, must determine the design of such elements as handrails and grip holds.

Circulation Systems

The accessibility of the residential building must be ensured by a solution with neither stairs nor thresholds. This fundamental assertion is also valid for developing all other circulation areas within the building. In multiple-storey buildings an elevator accessible without stairs, as a means of vertical access, is an imperative requirement to ensure that all residents (be they singles weighted down with shopping bags, families with baby carriages or seniors) can use it with equal ease.

Stairs
In order to guarantee safe and convenient use, vertical accessibility should be designed according to the ideal gradient ratio (17-cm step riser/28-cm step tread). Handrails installed on both sides, ergonomically adapted to the hand (round or oval with a diameter of three to four centimetres) facilitate their use (ill. 4.3). They are not only a must for people with a walking disability, but also a good guidance system for the sight-impaired. For better recognition at least the first and last steps of the staircase must be marked. They should be distinguished using high-contrast markings in a

different colour and material, with a strip four to five centimetres wide attached to the step tread, and two centimetres high on the step riser. It is better to mark every step of the stairway, however. The light in the stairwell must be glare-free and must not throw any drop-shadows.

Ramp
Ramps are suitable for surmounting smaller height differences. In a new development ramps are limited to a six percent gradient; at a height of 36 centimetres or greater a platform must be installed, for the physical possibilities of many users are quickly exhausted. The extreme spatial demands of ramps limit their utilization within buildings (ill. 4.2).

Lift
New Building
The elevator car must be 110 cm wide and 140 cm deep. The elevator doors must provide an unobstructed passage 90 cm wide. The control panel and call button must be installed at a height of 85 cm above the floor to grant easy accessibility for all persons. For the blind and visually impaired, the information on the control panel must use tactile markings and a high-contrast design. Touch keys are not suitable for the blind.

Existing Building
If the elevator is to be installed in an existing building, there is often not enough space available to comply with the dimensions specified in the DIN norm. A car 90 cm wide and 120 cm deep, with a door width of 80 cm, can be a suitable compromise and should be regarded as the absolute minimum (ill. 4.7).

Stair Lift
These lifting devices[1] have different means of lifting loads: the person to be transported can be lifted either in a standing or a seated position. An additional means of lifting is the wheelchair platform: in this case the person is transported along with the baby carriage, the walking frame or the wheelchair. Stair lifts can be installed with a demand switch for remote-controlled operation. After use, the lift moves into a parking position where the platform folds up. The parking position is also used to reload the battery.
Stair lifts must be adapted to the given stairway. It is advisable to check at the beginning of the planning phase whether this technical aid can be installed, as under certain circumstances overlap with escape routes can occur. Therefore this aid should be used in multi-family housing only for minor height differences. In new buildings the required space should be planned for; in existing structures it may be necessary to change the floor plan to install a stair lift (ill. 4.4).

Lifting Platform
Lifting platforms are also categorized as special lifts. They are permitted up to a lifting height of 1.80 m and are usually used to access ground-floor dwellings located half a storey

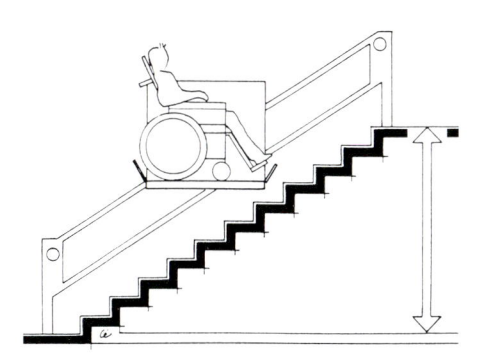

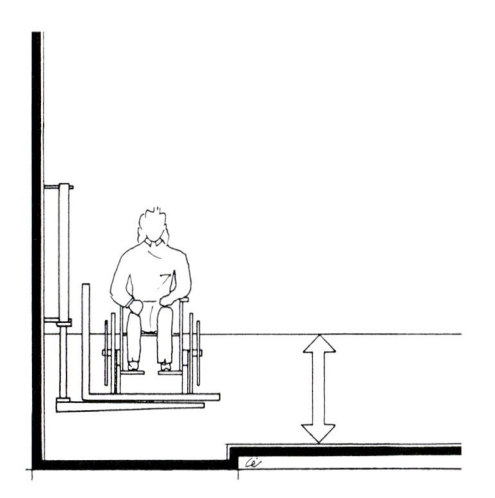

4.2   Ramp for barrier-free access
4.3   Details of a barrier-free stair
4.4   Lifting platform
4.5   Stair-lift
4.6   Lifting platform for barrier-free access
4.7   Mathildenstift in Munich, lift for
      barrier-free access; architects: Marx, Rössel, Franke

4.4

4.5

4.6

4.7

higher than the building's entryway. The space created underneath the platform when the lift is raised must be enclosed. The space needed for this solution must also be calculated for in building plans (ills. 4.5, 4.6).

Doors

Doors must have a minimum passage width. In general an unobstructed passage of 80 cm is sufficient. For wheelchairs to be able to use these doors, the average width must be 90 cm, to ensure that a wheelchair user does not injure his arms and hands while pushing the hand wheels. All swing doors to bathrooms must open to the outside so that the room for manoeuvre inside the bathroom remains unrestricted. Alternative to this solution, sliding doors can be used.

Building Entrance Doors/Patio Doors without a Threshold in Accordance with the DIN Norm[2]
In accordance with DIN 18195 part 5 numeral 8.1.5, junctions at building entrances and patio doors can be built without thresholds if certain measures are planned like sufficiently large projecting roofs, and gutters with gratings to prevent water from getting in the door or behind the waterproofing. Steps must be taken during planning to prevent any slack flow on the surface of the paving and toward the building. This means that water on the surface and façade must be conducted away as quickly as possible. For building entrances, patios, balconies and loggias, gutters with gratings are favoured. This guarantees that any precipitation is "collected" to prevent water from splashing on the surface of the doors or glass surfaces. The grating should be laid with the longer mesh width perpendicular to the direction of motion to prevent objects such as the wheel of a wheelchair from getting caught. Similarly, no gutter covers should be utilized whose drainage slits are cut in the direction of motion. Weatherboarding guarantees that water (e.g. driving rain) is conducted to the gutter via the grating.

For new buildings quite simple solutions can be planned and implemented in practice (ill. 4.10). Thresholds are eliminated using a combination of a gutter with a grating located in front of the door and waterproofing using a magnetic strip. The function of the magnetic strip can be described as follows: The doorframe integrates a U-shaped aluminium track containing two moulding seals. A magnetic strip is attached to the bottom of the door leaf. When the doors are opened, the moulding seals are pulled up away from the magnetic strip; when the doors are closed the mouldings shear off, fall back into the U-shaped aluminium track and seal the crack between the door and the floor. The aluminium track contains openings through which any water that penetrates the seal is conducted to the outside.

The Patio, Balcony, or Loggia

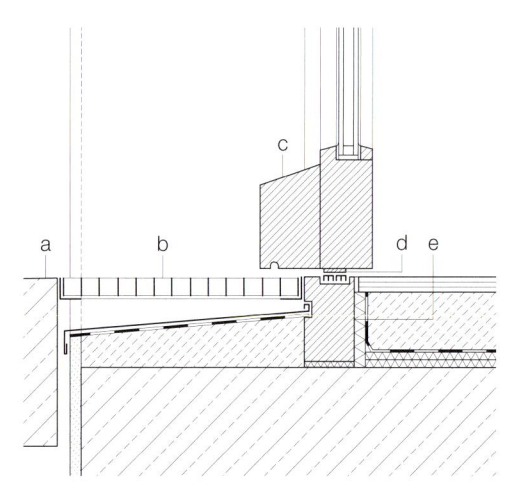

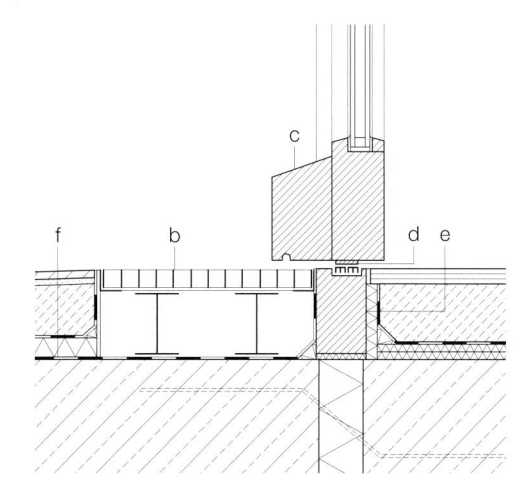

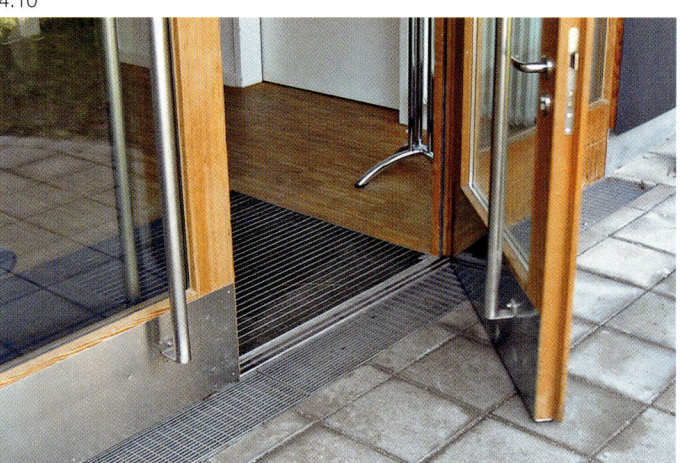

The exit door from the living room or bedroom to the patio, balcony or loggia generally has been designed as a raised swing door, the construction of which necessitated a threshold. A raised swing door requires only one sliding track (threshold) of approximately 1 cm, yet because of the stipulations in the roofing directives and part 5 of the DIN 18195 norm, both solutions require that the surface of the balcony or patio floor, because it can conduct water, be located fifteen centimetres lower than the floor of the dwelling, unless solutions like the installation of projecting roofs and gutters with gratings have been implemented, as described under "Building Entrance Doors/Patio Doors".

Patios
The exit to the patio requires a construction solution similar to the building entrance. Possible measures including roofing, inclining the patio paving, and installing a wide gutter with a grating, as well as waterproofing, comply with part 5 of the DIN 18195 norm and the roofing directives (ill. 4.12).

The Balcony
Balcony, New Building
The junction between the living area and the balcony can be solved using a separate construction in front of the balcony. Similar approaches are also possible for existing dwellings, as described in the following example.
For the Neues Mathildenstift in Munich, part of the conversion project involved hanging balconies into a steel construction in front of the façade. One window of each dwelling was converted into a balcony door. The lower edge of the door opening was shaped like a window sill. A grating attached in the embrasure over the window sill allows the residents barrier-free exit. The steel construction bears a prefabricated reinforced concrete slab, the balcony. Thus there is no layer that could conduct water, because any water that runs through the grating is conducted away from the building via the "window sill". Drainage of the balcony slab takes place via a surface gradient. The waterproofing of the bottom edge of the doors is provided by the magnetic strip. This design could also be a convenient solution for a new building, as no extra waterproofing measures would be necessary, yielding additional savings (ills. 4.8, 4.11).

Balcony, Old Building/Renovation
For existing raised swing doors and their corresponding threshold to the balcony, the following simple conversions could be performed as dwelling adaptation measures:
The doorframe remains intact. The paving of the balcony is raised to the height of the doorframe, and the guardrail must be adjusted accordingly. A grating is installed in front of the door. This preserves the water-bearing layer and the drainage of the balcony. From the interior of the dwelling a wooden wedge (it is advisable to use hardwood) is laid at the threshold to allow a wheelchair to surmount it (ill. 4.13). This solution is a compromise, however, as getting over the threshold is always a risk for a resident with a walking disability and involves increased effort for the wheelchair user. As a result of the elevation the balustrade must be raised.

Should a major conversion be undertaken, the following solution can be offered:
A new door is installed as a swinging door. During conversion the lower mortise is removed and the magnetic strip installed; the paving must be adjusted for a swinging door (ill. 4.14).

Loggia
Loggia, New Building
For a loggia it is important to ensure that the reinforced concrete slab is sufficiently lower than the living area (thermal insulation using Isokorb). The drainage of the gutter can take place via a draining mat, but the author has had better expe-

4.12

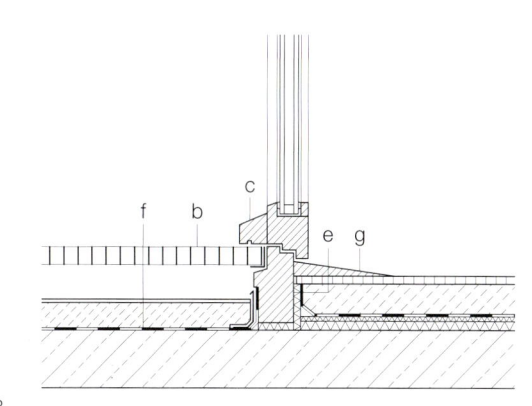

4.13

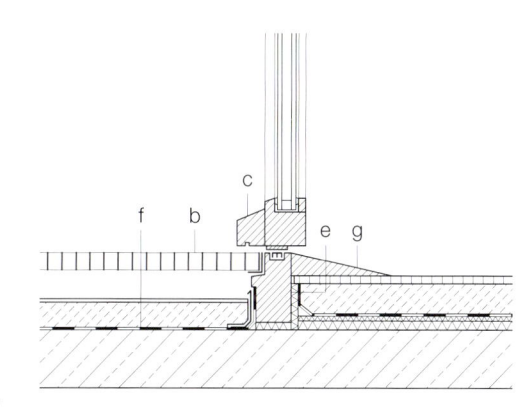

4.14

a   prefabricated balcony slab
b   grating 10 × 30 cm
c   weatherboarding
d   alumat magnetic seal
e   doorframe
f   concrete cantilever slab at gradient to raised floor
g   wooden wedge

4.8   Detail of balcony at Mathildenstift (old building) in Munich, scale 1:10, architects: Marx, Rössel, Franke
4.9   Detail of loggia in new building, scale 1:10
4.10 House entrance without threshold; architect: Lothar Marx
4.11 Door to balcony; architects: Marx, Rössel, Franke
4.12 Patio entrance; architect: Lothar Marx
4.13 Detail of balcony, old building/renovation
4.14 Detail of balcony, old building/renovation

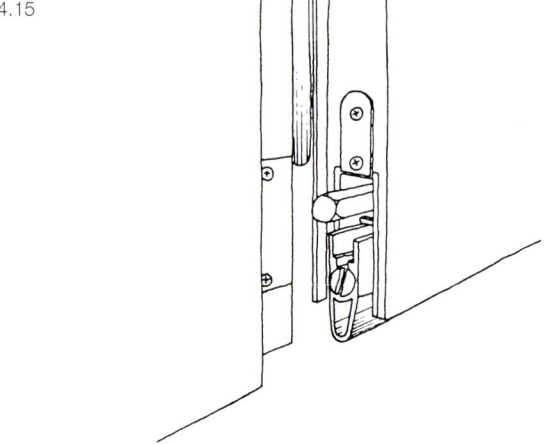

rience using a separate drain for the gutter. The water-bearing layer is the level that has been waterproofed. The surface (e.g., floor paving with an R 10 anti-skid rating) should be laid at a gradient of one to two percent (ill. 4.9).

Loggia, Old Building/Renovation
The construction adjustments can be carried out in a manner similar to that described under "Balcony, New Building and Balcony, Old Building".

Entrance Doors to Dwellings
Generally thresholds in the entrance area of doors to dwellings used to be treated to prevent the transmission of sound (ill. 4.17). Constructive solutions have been found in the mean time, including Alumat magnetic strips and Schallex, which make sound isolation possible without a threshold (ills. 4.15, 4.16).
The magnetic strip is installed and fixed in position before the screed is poured. In practice this process turns out to be difficult sometimes, as damage through other craftsmen or contaminations by flowing screed can not be ruled out. In connection with poured asphalt screed, keep in mind that this material shrinks considerably upon cooling, causing gaps along the edges of the magnetic strip. Such gaps can be sealed with epoxy resin.
Schallex isolation is installed in the lower area of the door leaf. Closing the door triggers a mechanism that causes the door's isolation moulding to descend. When the door is opened, the isolation moulding is raised by means of a spring.

The Bathroom

In recent years it has become apparent that the trend is moving toward replacing the bathtub with a shower. Especially if the shower is built barrier-free, use is much simpler and the risk of accident considerably reduced. The DIN 18025 norm stipulates that the shower should be accessible on foot or by wheelchair. A threshold is required for technical reasons, but care must be taken that its border not take the form of an edge (risk of stumbling). Instead, tiles are laid at an angle to ensure a smooth transition.
By now industry has also developed shower basins with thresholds no greater than two centimetres high, which thus also comply with the DIN 18025 norm.

Bathroom, New Building
The screed area of the shower is lowered to one to two centimetres below the rest of the bathroom. The shower area is enclosed with a row of tiles laid at an angle (there are specially shaped tiles for such constructions), to compensate for the height difference and form a basin (ill. 4.18). In accordance with DIN 1986 Section 5.2, the tiles of the interior area of this basin must be laid so that no puddles form (ill. 4.19). Stability must be ensured through corresponding anti-skid tiles or other surfaces with an R 10 rating.

Another example demonstrates that comfort can dictate construction to a significant degree (ills. 4.21–4.23). Before installing the floor and wall coverings, a stainless steel gutter for drainage was set, and then the screed work performed. As a consequence of the different screed thicknesses and the associated risk of cracking, 30-cm long slits were cut at 15-cm intervals along the transition from the bathroom to the

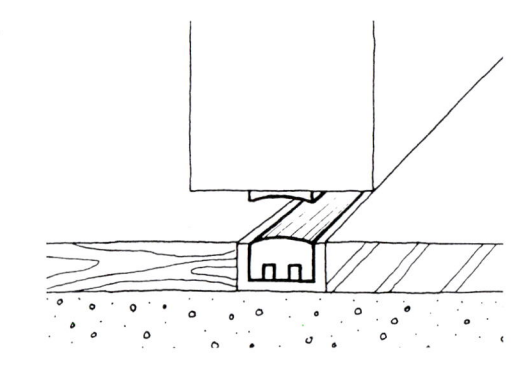

4.15 Retractable floor seal
4.16 Magnetic seal
4.17 Threshold
4.18 Shower contour tiles
4.19 Detail of shower seal, scale 1:10
 a row of angled tiles
 b sheeting
 c compensating wedge around circumference
 d reinforced and gummed expansion joint
 e reinforced cement screed
4.20 Detail of bathroom in natural stone, drain, scale 1:5
 f natural stone, 3 cm
 g stainless steel drain
 h sheeting
 i gradient on screed 0–1.5 cm
 j screed
 k reinforced flat joint, cemented with epoxy resin
4.21 Bathroom in natural stone;
 planning: Studi Interni, Linda Ossola, Munich
4.22 Screed reinforcement with flat joints and grouting with epoxy resin;
 Studi Interni, Linda Ossola, Munich
4.23 Seal in accordance with Part 5 of DIN 18195;
 Studi Interni, Linda Ossola, Munich

shower area. The slits were reinforced and sealed with epoxy resin. After these preliminary tasks, the surface was isolated against moisture in accordance with the DIN 18195 norm. In front of and behind the gutter, strips of the floor surface were laid at an incline to the floor slab and gutter to prevent water from collecting in the corner where the wall meets the floor. The floor slab of the shower was lowered to 0.5 cm below the level of the bathroom floor and laid at a gradient of 1.5 % to the gutter (ill. 4.20).

Bathroom, Old Building / Renovation
For conversion and renovation projects, solutions like the ones shown below can make it possible to install a shower retroactively or convert a bathtub into a shower. Often the existing floor foundation is not high enough.
In older buildings the difference in height between the bathroom and the corridor usually takes the shape of a threshold in the area of the door. For a barrier-free solution, the direction in which the swing doors open to the bathroom must be changed, or sliding doors must be installed to guarantee enough room for manoeuvre in the bathroom. The height thus obtained is often required for installation of a floor drain. If this height is not sufficient, an inclined surface can be installed in the area of the door.
The floor of the shower area remains at the same height as that of the bathroom. The demarcation is provided by tiles laid at an angle to constitute a threshold edge.

Bibliography:
Lothar Marx: Barrierefreies Planen und
Bauen für Senioren und behinderte Menschen.
Karl Krämer Verlag, Stuttgart 1994.

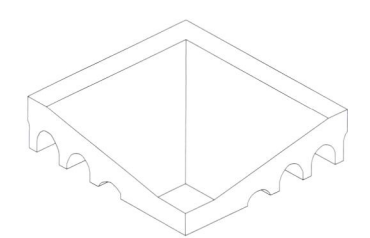

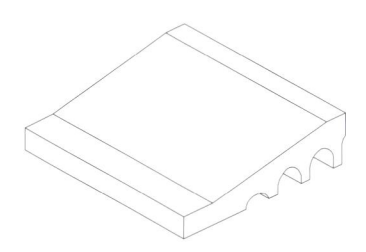

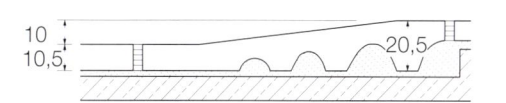

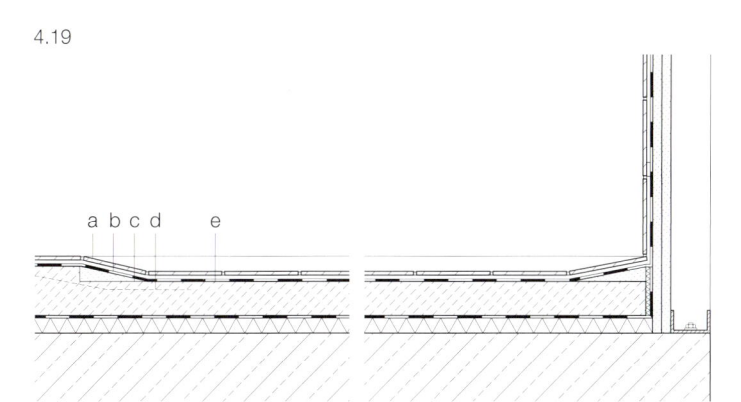

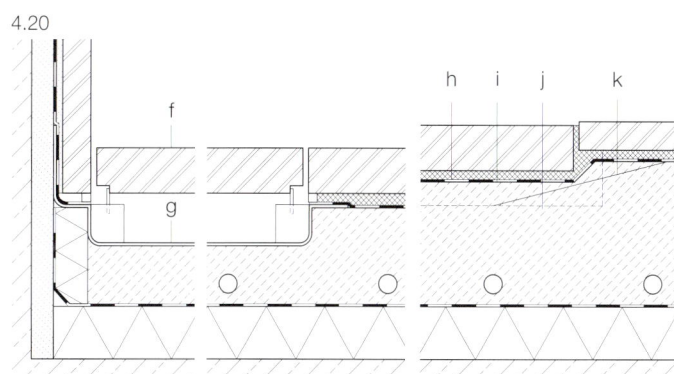

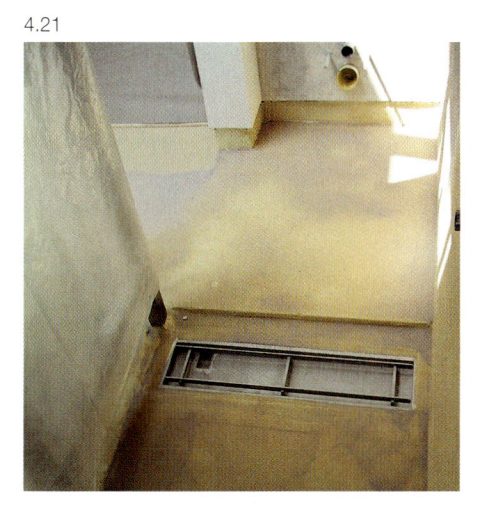

Kitchen and Bathroom as Living Space
by Eckhard Feddersen and Insa Lüdtke

Living a Lifetime Long

A place to live is something you need your whole life long. The need for security and safety is immanent in all phases of life. For our entire life, everyday habits and rituals mark our daily routine, our habits and thus our ways of living: sleeping, bathing, eating. The only thing that changes are the priorities, which depend on one's lifestyle and phase of life. A family needs several rooms, while a single person prefers a large living room with a sleeping alcove. However, the importance of housing and the immediate surroundings increases for the elderly especially, as seniors spend more than 80 percent of their time at home or in the immediate vicinity.

In parallel with the ageing of society, at present the consciousness is growing for a design that simplifies life, and therefore the general level of comfort is growing as well. In future not only the elderly, but also such residents as families with baby carriages, will profit from more barrier-free design in the environment. Shower stalls level with the floor, stairwells and balconies without thresholds are becoming standard – not only in new housing, but also as measures to convert existing dwellings.

Universal Design as a Strategy

"Universal Design", which emerged in the U.S. in the 1970s, is a holistic strategy for approaching design concepts. Although term "design" suggests a special, or perhaps even formal, prescription of shaping and styling, while "universal" implies general forms and standardization, neither of these definitions pertains. "Universal Design" has many faces, which combine to yield a sublime approach to a draft, comparable to the grammar of a language: Thanks to the conventions and rules, even complete strangers can communicate with each other, yet the contents and wording of their conversation is left up to the individuals.

Obviously, "Universal Design" does not concern standardized solutions. In this concept life is conceived as a continuum in which all phases of life flow into each other and merge. The flexible and versatile use of the residential surroundings (e.g. a terraced plaza design that provides seating for seniors and a place for children to play) and of everyday objects (e.g. towel racks in the bathroom that also serve as gripholds for seniors) is one of the significant basic principles. In the conception of an entire residential quarter, the architect consciously forgoes adjustments for "special" groups (e.g. people with disabilities, or children) in order to prevent exclusion and stigmatization and allow diverse options and peculiarities.

"Universal Design" focuses on allowing individuals to live a self-determined life, independent of their age, education or income. It propagates a design of everyday objects and the environment that can be used by everyone, on the small scale, as for the handy door handle, and on the large, such as public buildings, traffic structures and urban space. Although intellectual abilities are not yet well developed in childhood and subject to decline among seniors with dementia, the sensual experience of basic needs like security and orientation, intimacy and community should be possible for everyone: for instance, through a catchy, often repeated canon of materials; by implementing different mood lighting; and through the emphasis of entryways.

This approach places high demands on materials, design and comfort, and integrates objects (such as handles) into the surroundings from the outset. Well designed, such buildings, products and environments unify function, security, comfort and aesthetics.

"Universal Design" also means skilled arrangement, along the lines of the "work triangle" in the kitchen, for instance (see the section "Security and Convenience in the Kitchen" below) or of sanitary installations in the bathroom. Clearance for a wheelchair to fit under the workspace in the kitchen or the sink in the bathroom, a lowered mirror or a bathtub accessible from three sides (to provide room for care-givers) are further elements. A multifunctional object like the Vario Grip serves as a towel rack or shelf for accessories, but also has a second, auxiliary function as a grip hold.

5.1 Residence in Gstadt, view of wheelchair-friendly bathroom on ground floor, 2004; architect Florian Höfer

5.2

Concept of Life, Not of Age – The Kitchen and the Bathroom as Personal Signatures

Even today, it is no longer possible to record a life career in the schematic and linear way it was forty years ago. Thanks to a longer and more active (working) life, in future many people will be able – and forced – to shape their biographies ever more individually. This development requires that suitable housing be available. Increasingly, the kitchen and bathroom will take on the meaning of signatures in the individual home. Here is where a person's demands for security, comfort and quality come together with the desire for prestige, which dictates that the home should serve as a showpiece of the individual personality.
Increasingly, the boundaries between residential rooms are dissolving. The trend is toward flowing transitions between individual rooms. The kitchen, for instance, previously a separate room of its own, is being opened up and shifting to the centre of a communally used living and eating area. One's own four walls constitute the social and communicative centre of life, and this brings with it the tendency toward creating a world oriented toward the needs of the individual. In the quest for an antipole to the rising demands for achievement in public life, and in keeping with our society's marked awareness of the body and health consciousness, the home is increasingly becoming a place to withdraw and relax. In this the bathroom, too, is undergoing a transformation: from the utilitarian shower stall or tub to a location of recovery replete with a wellness function. Its previously limited space is thus expanding and opening up to the sleeping and living areas.

Security and Convenience in the Kitchen

Like the bathroom, the kitchen is a residential element that spans generations. As regards security and comfort, the meeting point for all family members requires painstaking planning. Despite a wide variety of ideas, for all users the various facets of convenience are in the foreground: ergonomics, convenience, security, and savings in energy, space, and ultimately also time.
Today's demographic shift provided occasion for Diana Kraus to dedicate her degree dissertation at Coburg University of Applied Sciences, in collaboration with the manufacturer Miele, to the Küchenkonzept 50 Plus, which is conceived with "Universal Design" in mind: The U-shaped floor plan is supposed to allow an optimum work flow, since all cabinets and drawers can be reached with the simplest of rotating movements. What is designated the "niche wall" between the wall unit and the counter space protrudes at a slant, so that kitchen machines or storage containers can be reached more easily. To prevent objects from sliding, the forward edge of the counter bulges upward slightly. So that full pots of water do not have to be carried from the sink to the stove, an armature that can be slid horizontally takes care of transport, and a long, retractable hand-held shower hose makes it easy to add more water. An integrated tilt control reduces the strength needed to pour out the pot (ill. 5.2). Most of these ideas are still a long way from being implemented in regular households. Yet anyone who wants to cook in a kitchen planned according to ergonomic criteria today can save himself a lot of walking, claims a "path study" issued by kitchen manufacturers. The distance walked can

be reduced from around 190 kilometres per year to just 75. Every kitchen has three work centres, generally referred to as the "work triangle": supply of stocks with refrigerator and cabinets, the stove, and the sink. For a right hander, the optimum workflow is from right to left (fetch on the right, process in the middle, deposit on the left); for a lefty the ideal sequence runs in the opposite direction. To maximize ergonomics, at least two of the work centres should be no more than two arm-lengths apart. This is why double file kitchens and L-shaped or U-shaped kitchens are considered especially efficient.

For right handers, the cabinets and refrigerator are on the right, and on their left comes a preparation counter, ideally 120 cm long, with enough room for all food and cooking utensils and for tasks that require a lot of space, like baking. Planners recommend a location at a window as a source of daylight, since this is the workplace most frequently used. The adjacent cooking zone should have a working area between 90 and 120 cm long. For the sink and draining board 60 cm are sufficient; next to this are the dishwasher and a cupboard. Cooks who prepare large quantities of vegetables and salad can integrate the sink into the larger counter surface.

Even an "old kitchen" can be rearranged. A critical look at the kitchen will reveal optimization potential like shifting pots, pans, wooden spoons and sieves to a location next to the stove, or storing spices near the preparation counter, perhaps in a drawer at the stove. Heavier objects should be kept out of hanging cupboards whenever possible. A location below shoulder-height makes them easier to lift out. The space in corner cabinets can be optimized using carousel units, which also allow convenient access to the required contents. In contrast, the corner sinks and corner counters so popular among designers turn out to be less than ideal, as hanging cupboards often restrict headroom.

To determine the right height for the countertop, the Deutsche Gütegemeinschaft Möbel e.V., recommends that a space of 15 cm be left free between the countertop and the lower arm, stretched forward and held parallel to the countertop (with the elbow at the body). The previous benchmark was a height of 86 cm; today experts recommend at least 92, often even 97 or 102 cm. To prevent back injuries, ideally the sink, oven, dishwasher and microwave should be as high as possible as well – around 90 cm (ill. 5.3).

Yet solutions do not have to be complicated. Simply bringing order into the kitchen creates a high degree of convenience. Drawers viewed from above present an overview of stocks and cooking utensils. With inserts for flatware, spices, foil and plastic wrap, and knives, anyone can organize the best arrangement for his needs. Lighting integrated into the shelves of the wall cupboards with spotlights over the counter, along with a multiple outlet strip, facilitate precise work. Mounting the sink under the counter rather than on top of it saves caulking and thus tiresome dirt traps. A soap dispenser integrated into the sink, which can be filled from above, eliminates the need to constantly wipe away traces of dried-on detergent that a separate container would leave behind.

As far as kitchen appliances are concerned, the professional kitchen can offer the hobby cook some clever ideas. These days manufacturers have applied healthy and energy-saving cooking methods to the home kitchen as well, like the induction stove top, for instance: An induction coil under the ceramic stovetop generates an electromagnetic field. Warmth is generated only in the bottom of the pot, with the cooking area and surroundings remaining practically cold. If a cooking vessel is pushed out of the cooking zone during operation, the coil shuts off. Because it is hardly heated, the stove top is easy to clean. Magnetic switch components provide for even more security; these can be simply removed when the stove is not in use.

Equipping your oven with coarsely textured panels on the roof and the back wall means you will never have to clean it again. Together with the heat, the oxygen that collects in the hollows neutralizes grease and smells during baking. Fully extendable glide racks minimize the risk of burnt fingers. Cooks who would rather spend time visiting with guests than busy in the kitchen alone can take advantage of a low-pressure steam cooker set into the countertop. Heated up to between 30 and 230 degrees Celsius, even reheated dishes can be served up delicious and full of vitamins.

To ensure accurate timing, a heated drawer can be used to keep cooked meals and plates warm, or to precook or simmer them, at around 30 to 38 degrees Celsius. This keeps the oven located above the drawer free for baking, roasting and cooking. For reasons of hygiene, the interior of the drawer should be made of hygienic stainless steel and be big enough to hold dinner plates and soup bowls (30 cm high and 70 cm wide).

5.2 Kitchen concept 50 Plus, Diana Kraus, University of Applied Sciences Coburg
5.3 weelschair-adapted kitchen in Graz (work bench height 72 cm), 2004; monomere architects

5.3

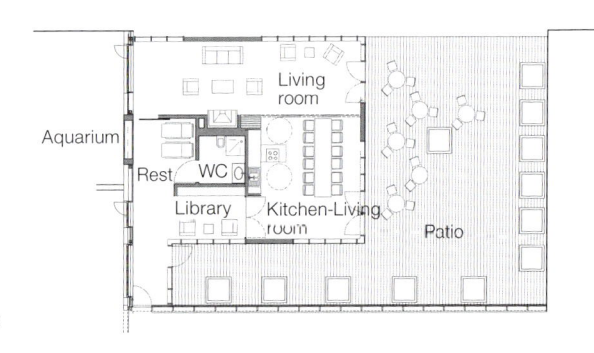

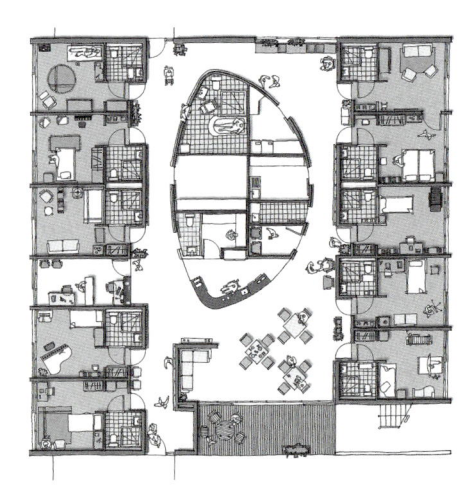

The Kitchen-Living Room as Living Space for the Senile

Dementia sufferers can profit especially from a kitchen-living room as living space; here is where socializing tasks are performed, and the homely aspect counts as well. As society continues to age, an increasing number of ambulant living communities are being created for the growing number of seniors with dementia (currently 1.2 million, 2030 estimated at 2.5 million) in addition to in-patient facilities. Both residential forms are based on the concept of the "house community": Eight to twelve residents spend the day in an open kitchen-living room, cared for by a nurse for the elderly. When their memory begins to fail, it is especially those familiar habits like peeling potatoes or ironing linens that keep people grounded. Biographical experiences and personal rituals require an architectural expression. Just as in the private kitchen, here, too, all demands on security and comfort must be fulfilled. An open counter can be used for multiple functions: as countertop, stove, dining counter, bar and meeting place, and even as a care station.

A spectrum of different activities offered around the functional kitchen should animate the residents to spend time there: a feeling of security in the group, as well as withdrawal into niches. Ideally, the living zones bordering on the open kitchen – like the dining area, a club corner and a library – should be grouped around a fixed core, in which facilities like the bathroom are located. Sliding walls can separate the zones into individual "rooms" when needed.

Based on the house community concept, the Kompetenzzentrum Demenz in Nürnberg offers target-group specific living areas with colour-coded kitchen-living rooms in striking schemes designed to ease orientation. In the "Patio" type a glazed inner courtyard lets a great deal of daylight into the interior, with light colour tones supporting the open character. By contrast, a fixed-core arrangement in the neighbouring "Janus" house provides a feeling of security, with its darker colours reflected in the kitchen cell as well. The corner bench in the third house, "Bauernstube", is supposed to be reminiscent of rural space. By day the residents can wander through the connected buildings and linger wherever they please (ills. 5.4–5.7).

Sensuality and Corporeality in the Bathroom

Like the kitchen, the bathroom is a symbol for self-determination and autonomy. It is the room for the daily rituals of the morning toilet, washing, and bathing. In the bathroom a process of transforming the unclean to the clean takes place – within as without, thus increasing the individual's feeling of self-worth as well. This is particularly important for the elderly, who are confronted with the deterioration of their bodies. These days bathroom outfitters have recognized the general trend toward (medical) wellness and now offer products for the home bath that extend far beyond "hygiene and utilities", instead promoting the bathroom as an oasis of relaxation and restoration, a home spa.

Design and nature meet in the bathroom, the latter in the form of water, which is set in scene as an event of nature. New fittings and "flood showers" simulate waterfalls or tropical rain showers. Designers and manufacturers are oriented toward natural ideals. For instance, washing basins take on the shape of lagoons, or tubs are reminiscent of egg shells, and even towel holders look as if they were carved from a branch. Yet designers also like to juxtapose these rounded shapes with hard, reduced geometries in the form of rectangular tubs and square sinks. Both styles have their entitlement, for in our complex world there is a growing desire for clarity and purism, for calm and serenity, but also for naturalness and security. Design responds with a clear language, yet accommodates the need for harmony with soft, organic images. Another development in bathroom design is a trend toward creating an autonomous artistic space furnished with "sculptures": Freestanding marble tubs and stone sinks rest on pedestals, and even offer comfortable entry steps, further heightening their resemblance to exhibition objects in a gallery.

Regardless of age and/or disability, the bathroom remains an important element of the private dwelling. Except for (where possible) wider doors, barrier-free shower stall and grip holds on the walls (if required, these can be installed later), the bathroom should exude as much "normality" as possible (ill. 5.8).

A shower stall level with the floor, with a floor foundation of between 9 and 12 cm and a one-percent gradient,combines increased comfort for all users while fulfilling the DIN demand for wheelchair accessibility, and presumably soon will become standard equipment for new residential housing and even existing housing. Aspects that should be taken into consideration for installation are the building's tolerability; the sealing of the building, perhaps through liquid sealing components directly below the tiles or floor paving; soundproofing; and ways to minimize accidents like installing anti-skid materials and special fittings to prevent injuries like scalding.

The "pre-build concept" in Berlin's KWA Stift im Hohenzollernpark keeps itself open for all eventualities. Here any resident can relegate the corner bathtub to the cellar when disability makes it impossible to use: The caretaker of the building need only remove an acrylic strip to create a barrier-free shower area within just a few minutes. The entire floor is tiled from the outset, and the fittings are already located at the required height (ill. 5.9).

An alternative to the classic bathroom expansion is the use of pre-assembled bathroom cubicles. For builders they have the advantage that a model bathroom can be viewed with all of its details ahead of time, allowing builders and residents alike an accurate "on-site impression". Installing cubicles also saves money by reducing construction time.

For existing dwellings, in some cases bathroom enlargement or even complete relocation of the bathroom may be worth considering. Such measures depend on the location of the water pipes and the structure of the building's floor plan. With the approval of the tenant, minor and even reversible measures can be carried out at short notice and independent of the residential development as a whole. For modifications like the installation of a grip hold, however, a static test is required by law.

Atmosphere: Light and Colour
In addition to functionality, the ambient is increasingly important in bathroom design. The use of light and colour can further support the desired mood. Bright lighting is a must. The targeted arrangement of lamps, above or right next to the mirror, for instance, creates a warm impression, and this mood lighting can be extended to the ceiling lamps. Over the shower stall, too, a lamp gives the resident a feeling of safety. Above the bathtub indirect lighting should be used to prevent

5.4 Kitchen, Elbschlossresidence in Hamburg, 2006; feddersenarchitekten
5.5 Kitchen, Kompetenzzentrum Demenz in Nürnberg, 2006; feddersenarchitekten
5.6 floor plan, day room, Elbschlossresidence in Hamburg, 2006; feddersenarchitekten
5.7 floor plan, residential unit "Janus", Kompetenzzentrum Demenz in Nürnberg, 2006; feddersenarchitekten
5.8 "Vario Grip" as handrail, shelf and safety rail; Ecke Design
5.9 Removable corner bathtub in the KWA Foundation in Hohenzollernpark, 2002, feddersenarchitekten

glare. Recessed lighting in a suspended ceiling, for instance, offers an attractive effect and is economical to boot.

The Bath as Wellness Oasis
Not only the private bathroom is becoming homelier: a communal "bath house" with sauna and Kneipp basins along with a "care bathtub" for residents requiring assistance can become an attraction across all generations of residents of a housing development. In addition to the wellness effect and the positive experience of one's own corporeality, the focus here is on the communal experience.

Adapting an Existing Dwelling

Despite the demographic shift and the fact that residents are getting older and older, the desire remains for a life in one's own four walls, as self-determined and normal as possible. Especially here – in the everyday environment – the need for safety grows among the elderly as physical and mental limitations increase. Adaptations to their dwellings make it possible for them to stay in their own homes for the remainder of their lives, or at least to significantly postpone relocation to a facility for seniors or "assisted living".

Many members of the group targeted for housing conversion have been living in their dwellings for decades, and thus predominantly in residences built in the 30s, 50s and 60s. Frequently these older buildings still have the original plumbing. What is needed here is not standardized or global solutions, but rather measures tailored to each individual case, so that the residents can continue to live in a pleasant and relaxed situation.

To simplify application, a practice-oriented catalogue of measures (ill. 5.10) is set forth within the DIN norms: Stage A construction – increased safety standard (e.g. grip holds, mirrors lowered over the washing stand, good lamps); Stage B construction – suitable for the disabled (e.g. raised WC), and Stage C construction – wheelchair accessibility (e.g. shower stall level with the floor). According to survey results, the greatest potential danger in the entire dwelling is in the bathroom. With the removal of these barriers the resident experiences a feeling of security, which allows him to feel at home again in his dwelling and surroundings.

5.10 Stage A construction: increased safety standard, Stage B: suitable for the disabled, Stage C: wheelchair-accessible elaborated in "Wohnraumanpassung", feddersenarchitekten
5.11 Bathroom type "Pur", Interboden
5.12 Kitchen, type "Minimal", Yoo

5.10

Living Areas	Stage A Construction	Stage B Construction	Stage C Construction
Cooking area	creation of room to manoeuvre (especially in front of the stove)	reorganization of work area: work space between stove and sink	wheelchair-accessible work area (hob, counter, sink) at seat height with sufficient knee space
	lighting in work area	floor unit with drawers	
	additional electrical outlets in work area	raised elevation of kitchen appliances (e.g. refrigerator, oven, dishwasher)	
	anti-skid flooring	creation of a seated work place (lower than normal counter)	
	elimination of tripping hazards	wall units mounted lower (accessibility; glass shelves for better recognition)	
	standing aids	safe and easily operated fittings	
Washbasins	height-adjustable washbasin	creation of space for washing while seated and for caregivers (e.g. moving the washbasin, changing direction of door opening)	safe and easily operated fittings
	mirror for washing while seated wheelchair	accessibility to washbasin (level waste trap, special washbasin for use while seated)	grip holds on washbasin (sitting down/standing up)
		adjustment of washbasin height (fixed)	
Bathtub	bathtub board	bathtub seat (perhaps swivel-mounted as entry aid)	removable bathtub (floor-level shower)
	grip holds (for various positions)	safe and easily operated fittings	special bathtub
	entry grips (or grip bars, etc.)		bath lift
Shower	grip holds for shower (e.g. offset handle)	shower seat (fixed to wall or as shower stool)	installation of shower level with floor
	easily accessible shower mount	safe and easily operated fittings (e.g. scalding protection, single lever tap)	installation of shower with shallow shower basin
WC	raised toilet seat (if necessary, with cushion)	WC elevation by installing a pedestal	installation of raised WC
	creation of space in front of WC (e.g. by changing direction of door opening)	repositioning of WC (e.g. for lateral manoeuvering space – costly)	support grips (e.g. bracket supports fixed to wall or floor, arm supports integrated in seat, height-adjustable support frame)
Bathroom door	wider doors	removal of threshold	installation of sliding door

Housing Oriented to a Target Group

Today's projects in the luxury sector already show us the direction in which residential housing supply will develop. They are no longer oriented chronologically around phases of life (one-bedroom dwelling for singles, three-bedroom dwelling for families, two-bedroom apartment for seniors), but rather make offers for various "lifestyles"; through striking, characteristic images they can be marketed precisely to the given target groups.

Even today, impressions from the media and from travel influence the style of our dwellings, and this trend will almost certainly continue in the future. As "global players" we can seek inspiration from anywhere in the world that has suddenly become so small: The desire for a Mediterranean ambient at home has prompted many a visitor to Spain to decorate his northern European dwelling with terra cotta tiles, ideally combined with an underfloor heating system suited to our latitudes. The variety of styles will increase further in this age of growing individualization.

The French designer Philippe Starck, in collaboration with the British project developer John Hitchcox, picked up on this development to design four different variants of interior furnishings in different world cities, marketed under the brand name "YOO". They are supposed to cover different preferences: Sensual materials closely bound up with nature are used in the "Nature" type, "Culture" stands for an extravagant lifestyle with trendy colours and a baroque touch, "Minimal" means minimalist furnishings in both shape and colour, and "Classic" is supposed to satisfy the timeless, clear taste (ill. 5.11).

In the intermediate segment of the market, too, there are offers oriented to target groups without any categorization according to age. The future buyer of a residential development by a developer in Ratingen can decide among three different design alternatives for their bathroom before moving in: "Mainstream" in classic white, "Pure" for clear lines, or "Mediterranean" in warm colours (ill. 5.12).

The kitchen, too, is becoming the stage of the resident and can accommodate various life models. An expansion concept that can be modulated allows the individual habits and preferences of a new tenant, or the changed living circumstances of an older tenant, to be addressed in a targeted way. For instance, an eastern German housing association introduces the convertibility of its housing inventory to its (potential) tenants in the form of an exhibition: The "secret cook" cooks in the closed kitchen and prefers to eat in peace in the living room. The "TV cook", in contrast, celebrates his or her culinary skills before friends in the open pantry kitchen. The "social cook" casually uses the kitchenette integrated into the generous loft. All kitchen segments can be converted from one variant to another through minor construction should a tenant move out, enlarge the family, or become disabled.

Even today residential housing is less a question of age than of lifestyle, which has adapted to the market's increasing demands for comfort and convenience, and this trend is certain to increase in the future.

5.11

5.12

Architects – Project details

"Miss Sargfabrik" in Vienna

Client:
Verein für integrative Lebensgestaltung, Vienna
Architects: BKK-3, Vienna
With:
Franz Sumnitsch, Johann Winter, Regina Geschwendtner, Christoph Moerkl
Structural engineering:
Fröhlich & Locher Zt GmbH, Vienna
Date of completion: 2000

mail@bkk-3.com
www.bkk-3.com

Frank Sumnitsch
Born 1961; 1990 degree from the University of Graz, since 1989 member of the Baukünstlerkollektiv.

Johann Winter
Born 1949; studied; office in Vienna.

establishment of BKK-3

Multi-generational House in Stuttgart

Client:
City of Stuttgart, Depts of Social Welfare, Youth and Health
Architects:
Kohlhoff & Kohlhoff, Stuttgart
With:
Johannes Meinke (project leader), Jörg Schust, Christine Caprano, Hsin-Yi Chou
Project management:
Tech. Dept. of Construction, Christine Heizmann-Kerres, Alexander Hofmann
Structural engineering:
Eng. Office W. Lehrle & Partner, Stuttgart
Date of completion: 2001

Sven Kohlhoff
Born 1943; 1965–73 studied architecture at the University of Stuttgart and in Canada; 1974 establishment of Asplan; 1975–85 teaching position at the University of Stuttgart, Institute for Building and Design; 1989–2001 practice with Claudia Kohlhoff.

2002 establishment of Kohlhoff Architects

Multi-generational Housing in Vienna

Client:
Kallco Bauträger GmbH, Vienna
Architects:
Peter Ebner and Franziska Ullmann
With:
Christiane Feuerstein, Silvia Lechner
Structural engineering:
Javurek & Schweiger, Bad Vöslau
Date of completion: 2001

www.ebner-ullmann.com

Peter Ebner
Born in Hallwang; cabinet-making apprenticeship; studied mechanical engineering in Salzburg; studied architecture at the University of Graz and UCLA, Los Angeles; degree from the University of Graz; studied at the University of Economics, Linz; 1995 established office in Salzburg; since 2003 professor for domestic construction and economics at the University of Munich; 2006 guest professor at Harvard Graduate School of Design, Boston.

Franziska Ullmann
Born in Baden near Vienna; studied at the University of Vienna; 1983 established office in Vienna; 1985-94 teaching position at the University of Applied Arts in Vienna; since 1995 professor for spatial design at the University of Stuttgart; 2000 guest professor at Harvard Graduate School of Design, Boston.

1998 establishment of Ebner and Ullmann in Vienna

Apartment Building in Vienna

Client: GESIBA
Architects: PPAG, Vienna
With:
Corinna Toell (project leader), Klaus Moldan, Lilli Pschill, Ali Seghatoleslami
Structural engineering:
Eng. Office V. Stehno + Partner
Date of completion: 2006

ppag@ppag.at
www.ppag.at

Anna Popelka
1980–1987 studied at the University of Graz; 1987 degree from the University of Graz.

Georg Popuschka
1986-94 studied at the University of Graz and School of Architecture Paris-Tolbiac; 1994 degree from the University of Graz; 1997–98 guest professor at the University of Vienna, Institute for Spatial Design.

1995 establishment of PPAG Popelka Popuschka, Vienna

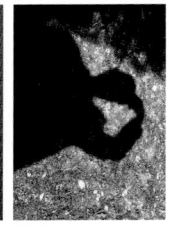

Renovation of a Department Store in Eschweiler

Client:
Anna Maria and Andrea Breuer, Cologne
Architects:
BeL, Anne-Julchen Bernhardt, Jörg Leeser, Cologne
With:
Eveline Jürgens, Thomas Schneider
Structural engineering:
Jürgen Bernhardt, Cologne
Date of completion: 2006

office@BeL.cx
www.BeL.cx

Anne-Julchen Bernhardt
Born 1971 in Cologne; 1997 degree from the RWTH Aachen; 1997 free-lance in Berlin; since 1999 in Cologne; 2001-05 technical assistant at the RWTH Aachen, Dept of Building Construction III.

Jörg Leeser
Born 1967 in Essen; 1997 degree from the RWTH Aachen; 1994-98 Leeser Architecture, New York; 1998 technical assistant at Rensselaer Polytechnic Institute Troy, New York; 1999-2006 technical assistant at the RWTH Aachen in constructional design.

2000 establishment of BeL, Cologne

Community Centre in Stuttgart

Client:
Catholic Community of St. Antonius, Stuttgart-Zuffenhausen
Architects:
Arno Lederer, Jórunn Ragnarsdóttir, Marc Oei Stuttgart/Karlsruhe
With:
Thilo Holzer
Structural engineering:
Eng. Office Andreas Bewer, Neuhausen a.d.F.
Date of completion: 2001

mail@archlro.de
www.lederer-ragnarsdottir-oei.de

Arno Lederer
Born 1947 in Stuttgart; studied architecture in Stuttgart and Vienna; degree 1976; free-lance since 1979; since 1985 in partnership with Jórunn Ragnarsdóttir; since 1992 in partnership with Marc Oei; since 2005 head of the Institute for Public Construction and Design, Stuttgart University.

Jórunn Ragnarsdóttir
Born 1957 in Akureyri, Iceland; degree 1982 from Stuttgart University; various stage sets in theatres in Reykjavik.

Marc Oei
Born 1962 in Stuttgart; 1988 degree from the Institute of Technology in Stuttgart; teaching positions at the Universities of Karlsruhe and Stuttgart.

Seniors' Residence in Zurich

Client:
Spirgarten Foundation, Zurich
Architects: Miller & Maranta, Basle
With:
Petra Baumberger, Katrin Gromann, Nicole Winteler, Sven Waelti, Patrick von Planta, Marc Kloth, Niggi Bruggmann
Structural engineering:
WGG Schnetzer Puskas Ing. AG SIA/USIC, Basle
Date of completion: 2006

info@millermaranta.ch
www.millermaranta.ch

Quintus Miller
Born 1961 in Aarau; 1987 degree from the Federal Institute of Technology Zurich; 2000–01 guest professor at the Federal Polytechnic Lausanne; since 2005 member of the commission for the restoration of historic constructions in Zurich and the commission for fine arts in the municipality of Reihen (near Basle); 2007 guest professor at the Academy of Architecture in Menridisio.

Paola Maranta
Born 1959 in Chur; 1986 degree from the Federal Institute of Technology Zurich; 1990 MBA from IMD Lausanne; 2000-01 guest professor at the Federal Polytechnic Lausanne; 2001–05 member of the commission for city structure of the canton Basle-City; since 2003 member of the commission for city structure in the municipality of Reihen (near Basle); 2007 guest professor at the Academy of Architecture in Menridisio.

1994 est. of Miller & Maranta, Basle

Multengut Seniors' Residence near Bern

Client:
GVB Building Insurance of the Canton of Bern
Architects:
Burkhalter Sumi, Zurich
With:
Yves Schihin, Florian Schoch, Bettina Halbach
Structural engineering:
Dr. Lüchinger + Meyer, Zurich
Date of completion: 2004

www.burkhalter-sumi.ch

Marianne Burkhalter
Born 1947 in Thalwil; apprenticeship in technical drafting; 1973–75 at the University of Princeton; since 1970 architectural employment in various practices; guest professor at the Southern Institute of Architecture in Los Angeles and at the Federal Polytechnic Lausanne.

Christian Sumi
Born 1950 in Biel; 1977 degree from the Federal Institute of Technology Zurich; guest professor at the School of Architecture in Genf, in Harvard and the Federal Polytechnic Lausanne.

Yves Schihin
Born in Bern; apprenticeship in technical drafting; 2000 degree from the Federal Polytechnic Lausanne; since 2004 partner in Burkhalter Sumi Architects.

1984 establishment of Burkhalter Sumi Architects

Housing Development and Aged Care Centre in Alicante

Client:
IWSA Institutao Valenciano de Vivenda S.A.
Architect:
Javier García-Solera Vera, Alicante
With:
Pilar Fructuoso, Marcos Gallud, Javier Mateu
Structural engineering: Domingo Sepulcre, Valencia
Date of completion: 2005

jgsold@arquired.es

Javier García-Solera Vera
Born 1958 in Alicante; 1984 degree from the Escuela Técnica Superior de Arquitectura in Madrid; since 1999 professor of design in Alicante; since 2002 guest professor at various universities and schools of architecture in Spain and Latin America.

High-rise Apartment Building in Rotterdam

Client:
Stichting Ouderenhuisvesting Rotterdam
Architects:
Arons en Gelauff architecten
With:
Jan Bart Bouwhuis, Felix Fassbinder, Hilde Gründemann, Mariska Koster, Jacco van der Linden, Menno Mekes, Irene Siljama, Erik Jan Vermeulen
Structural engineering:
Peter Stout, bouwkundig adviesburo Baas BV
Leendert Kool, Dura Vermeer bouw Rotterdam BV
Date of completion: 2006

mail@aronsengelauff.nl
www.aronsengelauff.nl

Floor Arons
Born 1968 in Haarlem, Netherlands; 1993 Master from the University of Delft; 1997 teaching position at the Amsterdam Academy of Architecture.

Arnoud Gelauff
Born 1963 in The Hague, Netherlands; 1988 degree from the Hogeschool van Amsterdam; 1996 Master from the Amsterdam Academy of Architecture; 1997 teaching position at the Amsterdam Academy of Architecture.

1996 establishment of Arons en Gelauff architecten

Senior Dwellings in Domat/Ems

Client: Jürgen Schwarz
Architect:
Dietrich Schwarz, Domat/Ems
With:
Peter Silber, Sebastian Streck
Structural engineering:
T. Cavelli AG, Domat/Ems
Date of completion: 2004

www.schwarz-architektur.ch

Dietrich Schwarz
Born 1964 in Chur; studied architecture 1985-90 at the Federal Institute of Technology Zurich; 1991 degree from the Federal Institute of Technology Zurich; since 2002 lecturer at the Academy of Architecture in Menridisio; guest professor at the Institute of Liechtenstein; since 2002 director of Glassx AG.

1992 establishment of own practice

Centre for Seniors in Lich

Client:
Oberhessisches Diakoniezentrum Johann-Friedrich Foundation
Architects:
Pfeifer Roser Kuhn, Freiburg
Structural engineering:
Eng. Office L. Fischer, Lich
Date of completion: 2003

architekten@pfeifer-kuhn.de
www.pfeifer-kuhn.de

Günter Pfeifer
Born 1943 in Schopfheim; 1967 degree from the State Werkkunstschule, Kassel;
since 1975 own practice in Lörrach and Freiburg; since 1992 professor at the University of Darmstadt; 2001 establishment of pfeifer roser kuhn architects in Freiburg.

Christoph Kuhn
Born 1966 in Saarbrücken; 1993 degree from the University of Berlin; 1998 establishment of roser I kuhn architects in Freiburg; 2001 establishment of pfeifer roser kuhn architects in Freiburg.

2005 establishment of pfeifer kuhn architects in Freiburg

Long House in Henza Island

Client: Zenichi Miyazato
Architects:
Kawai Architects/
Toshiaki Kawai, Kyoto
With:
Emina Hirota
Structural engineering:
Masaichi Taguchi (TAPS)
Date of completion: 2006

shownen@kawai-architects.com
www.kawai-architects.com

Toshi Kawai
Born 1967; 1991 degree from Kyoto University, Japan; 1993 Master from Kyoto University, Japan; 1994 education at the AA, London; 1995 graduation "Kenchiku Shownen"

1999 establishment of Kawai Architects

Renovation of a Seniors' Centre in Magdeburg

Client: City of Magdeburg
Architects:
Löhle Neubauer Architects BDA, Augsburg
Rainer Löhle Regina Neubauer

1st building stage:
Project leader:
Christian Moosbichler
With:
Joachim Müller, Martin Oppelt, Tobias Handel, Martin Obst, Andreas Paluch, Anita Ivic
Structural engineering:
Furche + Zimmermann, Köngen
Bautra GmbH, Magdeburg
Date of completion: 2003

2nd building stage:
Project leader: Steffen Moik
With; Silvio Hahn, Tobias Handel, Christian Moosbichler, Raimund Bollinger, Andreas Paluch, Annette Gärtner, Anita Ivic, Nico Schmitz
Structural engineering:
Bautra GmbH, Magdeburg
Date of completion: 2004

info@loehle-neuauer.de

Reiner Löhle
Born 1963 in Memmingen; studied and degree from the Institute of Technology, Augsburg; studied and degree from the University of Stuttgart.

Regine Neubauer
Born 1966; studied and degree from the Institute of Technology, Augsburg.

Residence for Seniors in Neumarkt am Wallersee

Client:
Municipality Neumarkt,
City of Neumarkt and Henndorf
Architects: Kada + Wittfeld, Aachen
With:
Stefan Haass (project leader), Patrick Müller-Langguth, Berndt Rickert, Arndt Schüle, Frank Berners, Aldrik Lichtwark
Structural engineering:
Bernd Ferstl & Partner, Salzburg
Date of completion: 2001

www.kadawittfeldarchitektur.de

Klaus Kada
Born 1940 in Leipnitz, Styria; 1971 degree from the Institute of Technology, Graz; 1995–2006 professor at the RWTH Aachen for high-rise design and construction; since 1996 own practice.

Gerhard Wittfeld
Born 1968 in Moers; 1995 degree from the RWTH Aachen; 1997–2004 teaching position at the RWTH Aachen dept. of design and construction; since 2004 professor at the Institute of Technology Bochum, dept. of construction.

1999 establishment of
Kada + Wittfeld, Aachen

Centre for Seniors in Steinfeld

Client:
Social Welfare Assoc. Spittal/Drau
Architect Dietger Wissounig
Structural engineering:
ARGE urban & Pock, Spittal/Drau
Date of completion: 2005

office@wissounig.at
www.wissounig.at

Dietger Wissounig
Born 1969 in Klagenfurt; 1984–89 HTL Villach; 1991–97 studied architecture at Graz University; 1997 employed in Kuala Lumpur; 1992–2002 employed in Graz; since 2004 teaching position at Graz University. 2002 establishment of own practice

Ambulant Care Day Centre in Kamigyo

Client: Nagahara Clinic, Kyoto
Architect: Toshiaki Kawai, Kyoto
With:
Teruko Shinmei
Structural engineering:
T.I.S. & Partners, Kyoto
Date of completion: 2000

shownen@kawai-architects.com
www.kawai-architects.com

Toshi Kawai
Born 1967; 1991 degree from Kyoto University, Japan; 1993 Master from Kyoto University, Japan; 1994 education at the AA, London; 1995 graduation Kenchiku Shownen.

1999 establishment of
Kawai Architects

Residence in Gstadt

Clients:
Veronika and Roman Schnellbach
Architect: Florian Höfer
Structural engineering:
a.k.a. engineers, Munich
Date of completion: 2004

www.florianhoefer.de

Florian Höfer
Born 1971 in Rosenheim; 1992 cabinet-maker; 1996 commenced architecture at the Institute of Technology, Munich, 2001 degree; employed by Hild and K, Munich, Eng. Office Held, Munich and Schelbert-Scholz-Wille Architects. 2002 establishment of own practice.

Multi-generational House in Waldzell

Clients:
Heidi and Rudi Frauscher
Architect: Helga Flotzinger
Structural engineering:
Rudi Frauscher
Date of completion: 2005

office@arch-flotzinger.at

Helga Flotzinger
Born 1972 in Salzburg; 2000 degree from the University of Innsbruck; 1999 establishment of the group "convoi architektinnen"; since 2004 free-lance architect; 2005 teaching position in design at the University of Innsbruck.

Multi-generational House in Darmstadt

Client: private
Architects:
Kränzle + Fischer-Wasels, Karlsruhe
Klotz + Knecht, Darmstadt
Project management:
Jürgen Ludwik, Reinheim
Structural engineering:
ISG, Darmstadt
Date of completion: 2003

info@kraenzle-fischerwasels.de
www.kraenzle-fischerwasels.de
info@klotzundknecht.de
www.klotzundknecht.de

Nikolaus Kränzle
Born 1947 in Walldorf/Hessen; 1975 degree from the Institute of Technology, Karlsruhe; since 1985 own practice in Karlsruhe.

Christian Fischer-Wasels
Born 1961 in Frankfurt am Main; 1991 degree from the Institute of Technology, Karlsruhe.

1991 establishment of
Kränzle + Fischer-Wasels Architects

Iris Braun (née Klotz)
Born 1972 in Darmstadt; 2003 degree from the Institute of Technology in Frankfurt am Main.

Christian Knecht
Born 1971 in Lampertheim; 1999 degree from the Institute of Technology in Frankfurt am Main.

2000 establishment of
Klotz + Knecht Architectural Office

City House in Munich

Client: MGS
Architects: Fink + Jocher, Munich
With:
Stephan Riedel, Christoph Schreyer
Project management:
Peter Helsper,
Architectural Office Wallner
Structural engineering:
Eng. Office Dr. Müller, Munich
Date of completion: 2005

architekten@fink-jocher.de
www.fink-jocher.de

Dietrich Fink
Born 1958 in Burgau; 1984 degree from the University of Technology Munich; 1988 academic adviser for the Institute for City and Regional Planning at the University of Technology Munich; 1998 guest professor at the University of Technology Munich; 1999–2004 professor at the University of Technology Berlin; since 2004 professor at the University of Technology Munich.

Thomas Jocher
Born 1952 in Benediktbeuern; 1980 degree from the University of Technology Munich; 1984–90 academic adviser for the Institute for City and Regional Planning at the University of Technology Munich; 1991 postgraduate diploma; since 1997 professor at the University of Stuttgart; 2004 guest professor at the Tongji University in Shanghai.

1991 establishment of
Fink + Jocher, Munich

Multi-generational Housing Development in Freiburg

Client: Freiburger Stadtbau GmbH
Architects: Pfeifer Roser Kuhn, Freiburg
Date of completion: 2004

architekten@pfeifer-kuhn.de
www.pfeifer-kuhn.de

Günter Pfeifer
Born 1943 in Schopfheim; 1967 degree from the State Werkkunstschule, Kassel;
since 1975 own practice in Lörrach and Freiburg; since 1992 professor at the University of Darmstadt; 2001 establishment of pfeifer roser kuhn architects in Freiburg.

Christoph Kuhn
Born 1966 in Saarbrücken;
1993 degree from the University of Berlin; 1998 establishment of roser I kuhn architects in Freiburg; 2001 establishment of pfeifer roser kuhn architects in Freiburg.

2005 establishment of
pfeifer kuhn architects in Freiburg

Housing Development in Wiesbaden

Client: Gemeinnützige Wohnungsgesellschaft mbH Hessen
Architects: Dietz Joppien Architects, Frankfurt am Main
With: Matthias Schönau, Christine Lüpke
Structural engineering: Eng. Office Rack, Frankfurt am Main
Date of completion: 2000

Albert Hans Dietz
Born 1958 in Saarbrucken; studied architecture at the Institute of Technology, Darmstadt; 1986 Master of Architecture from the University of Oregon; since 2005 teaching position in construction at the University of Wuppertal.

Anett-Maud Joppien
Born 1959 in Frankfurt am Main; studied architecture at the University of Berlin and the Institute of Technology, Darmstadt; 1986 Master of Architecture from the University of California/Berkeley; since 2003 professor at the University of Wuppertal.

1989 establishment of Joppien Dietz Architects in Frankfurt am Main

2004 establishment of Dietz Joppien
Architects AG

Housing Development in Ypenburg

Client: Amvest BV, Amsterdam
Ceres Projecten, The Hague
Ipse Hootolorp
Architects: John Bosch
in collaboration with
van den Oever, Zaaijer & Partners architecten, Amsterdam
With:
Naomi Felder, Urs Primas, Tycho Saariste, Wendy Saunders
with Bouwkunde Office
Structural engineering:
Walter Spangenberg, ABT Delft
Date of completion: 2003

info@oz-p.nl
www.oz-p.nl

John B. W. Bosch
Born 1960; graduated from the HTS Architecture Amsterdam; 1983–89 Technical University Delft; since 1996 teaching position at the University of Delft and the Academy of Architecture Rotterdam, Amsterdam and Arnhem;
since 2000 own practice; since 2006 partner with van den Oever, Zaaijer & Partners architecten.

Authors

Christian Schittich (editor)
born 1956
studied architecture at the Technical University of Munich,
followed by seven years' office experience and work as journalist,
since 1991 editorial board of DETAIL, Review of Architecture,
since 1992 responsible editor, since 1998 editor-in-chief.
Author and editor of numerous textbooks and technical articles.

Peter Ebner
born 1968
studied architecture at the Technical University of Graz and at UCLA, Los Angeles,
studied at the University of Economics Linz, 1995 opened own practice in Salzburg,
since 1998 combined practice with Franziska Ullmann in Vienna,
since 2003 professor at the Technical University of Munich,
Department of Housing and the Economics of Housing,
2006 guest professor at the Harvard School of Design, Boston.
Author of numerous textbooks and technical articles.

Joachim Giessler
born 1944
studied industrial design at the College of Fine Arts, Kassel, 1974 own planning practice,
since 1975 teaching positions at the Technical Colleges of Rosenheim and Coburg,
the Instutute of Wood Sciences and Plastics Rosenheim, the Hadassah College Jerusalem and
the Industrial Design School Tel-Aviv, 2003 establishment of the "Instituts Wohnen im Alter e.V.".
Author of numerous textbooks and technical articles.

Lothar Marx
born 1941
studied architecture at the Technical University of Berlin, since 1988 own architectural office,
since 1988 teaching positions at the Technical University of Munich,
the College for Architecture Weimar and the Institute of Technology Munich,
member of the standards committees NABAU, DIN 18024/18205, DIN 180030 and "Betreutes
Wohnen", partner in the "Institut für Barrierfreies Planen und Bauen" in Dresden, Munich and Ulm.
Author of numerous textbooks and technical articles.

Eckhard Feddersen
born 1946
studied architecture at the Technical University of Karlsruhe and the Technical University of Berlin,
since 1973 own architectural office, 1980–82 teaching position at the Technical University of Berlin,
since 2002 architectural office Feddersen Architects.
Author of numerous textbooks and technical articles.

Insa Lüdtke
born 1972
studied architecture at the Technical University of Darmstadt,
since 2002 worked in public relations for Feddersen Architects.
Author of numerous technical articles on architecture and health.

Bibliography

Books

Ackermann, Kurt; Bartz, Christian; Feller, Gabriele:
Behindertengerechte Verkehrsanlagen. Planungshandbuch für Architekten und Ingenieure,
Dusseldorf 1997

American Institute of Architects:
Design for Aging,
Review Images Publishing,
Victoria 2004

Andritzky, Michael u.a.:
Neues Wohnen im Alter,
Frankfurt am Main 2004

Barsuhn, Astrid:
Mehrgenerationenhäuser,
Wohlfühlen unter einem Dach,
Taunusstein 2006

Bertelsmann Stiftung / Kuratorium Deutsche Altershilfe:
Neue Wohnkonzepte für das Alter und praktische Erfahrungen bei der Umsetzung,
Cologne 2003

Blomensaht, Arlt:
Barrierefreies und kostengünstiges Bauen für alle Bewohner, Analyse ausgeführter Projekte nach DIN 18025-2,
Hanover 1994

Bulter, Martin:
Barrierefreies Bauen, Ausarbeitung des Wissenschaftlichen Dienstes des Bundestages,
Berlin 2000

Dettbarn-Reggentin, Jürgen; Reichenbach, Michael:
Bau- und Wohnkonzepte für alte und pflegebedürftige Menschen,
Esslingen 2006

Divers, Jonas:
Planning and Access for disabled People,
London 2003

Fuchs, Dörte; Orth, Jutta:
Umzug in ein neues Leben. Wohnalternativen für die zweite Lebenshälfte,
Munich 2003

Giessler, Joachim F.:
Planen und Bauen für das Wohnen im Alter
Ratgeber für Neubau, Umbau und Renovierung,
Taunusstein 2005

Görnert-Stuckmann, Sylvia:
Umzug in die dritte Lebensphase,
Freiburg 2005

Großhans, Hartmut:
Wohnumfeld und Quartiersgestaltung
Für das Wohnen im Alter im Generationenverbund, Stuttgart 2001

Held, Christoph; Ermini-Fünfschilling, Doris:
Das demenzgerechte Heim,
Lebensraumgestaltung, Betreuung und Pflege für Menschen mit Alzheimerkrankheit,
Basle 2006

Höfs, Jutta; Loeschcke, Gerhard:
Die rollstuhlgerechte Wohnung. Planungsgrundlagen, Grundrisse, Ausstattung, Gebäudeerschließung, Gebäudetechnik, Planungshilfen im Detail,
Stuttgart 1981

Höpflinger, François:
Traditionelles und neues Wohnen im Alter
Age Report 2004,
Zurich 2004

Holland, Caroline; Peace, Sheila:
Inclusive housing in an ageing society,
Bristol 2001

Imrie, Rob:
Accessible Housing,
Routledge 2005

König, Barbara:
Stadtgemeinschaften
Das Potential der Wohnungsgenossenschaften für die soziale Stadtentwicklung,
Berlin 2004

Kraemer, Karl H.:
Modellprojekt "Integriertes Wohnen",
Munich 1981

Lord, Geoffrey; Wycliffe Noble, C.:
Access for disabled people to art premises,
New York 2003

Marx, Lothar:
Barrierefreies Planen und Bauen für Senioren und behinderte Menschen,
Stuttgart 1994

Marx, Lothar:
Erfassung internationaler Normen über die baulichen und infrastrukturellen Voraussetzungen für Menschen mit Behinderungen und für alte Menschen,
Stuttgart 1989

Marx, Lothar:
Neue Technologien für altersgerechte Wohnungen,
Stuttgart 1992

Narte, Renate; Tischer, Sylvia:
Räume für gemeinschaftliche Wohnprojekte älterer Menschen – Erfahrungen aus den Niederlanden, Band 1: Rahmenbedingungen und Nutzungsanalyse,
Cologne 2001

Philippen, Institut T.L.P.e.V.:
Barrierefreies Bauen – Planungshilfe,
Mainz 2000

Riley, Charles A.:
Barrierefreies Wohnen. Designideen für mehr Lebensqualität,
Stuttgart 1999

Rühm, Bettina:
Unbeschwert wohnen im Alter, neue Lebensformen und Architekturkonzepte,
Munich 2003

Schader Stiftung:
Neue Wohnung auch im Alter,
Darmstadt 1997

Schöffler, Mona:
Wohnformen im Alter,
Lahr 2006

Steffen, Gabriele; Fritz, Antje:
Wohnen mit Assistenz, Bauforschung für die Praxis, 78,
Stuttgart 2006

Stemshorn, Axel:
Barrierefreies Bauen für Behinderte und Betagte,
Stuttgart 1999

Stolarz, H.; Lenz, G.:
Altenwohnungen zum Bau und Umbau von Wohnungen für ältere Menschen und für Menschen aller Altersgruppen mit Behinderungen. Entwurf zur Neufassung,
Stuttgart 1989

Torrington, Judith:
Upgrading Buildings for Older People,
London 2004

Voss, K.:
Entwicklung eines zielgruppenorientierten Wohnmodells für das integrierte Wohnen alleinstehender jüngerer Menschen im innerstädtischen Bereich,
Stuttgart 1978

Weeber, Rotraut; Wölfle, Gunther;
Rösner, Verena:
Gemeinschaftliches Wohnen im Alter,
Bauforschung für die Praxis, 58,
Stuttgart/Berlin 2001

Wüstenrot Stiftung:
Wohnen im Alter,
Stuttgart 2005

Journals

AIT
Gesundheit und Soziales,
Stuttgart, Nov. 2005, pp 88ff.

Architektur + Wettbewerb (197)
Seniorenresidenzen,
Stuttgart, March 2004

barrierefrei
AT-Fachverlag GmbH,
Fellbach

Brandl, Brigitte:
barrierefrei
"Großfamilie liegt im Trend.
Generationenübergreifendes Wohnen",
Fellbach 2001

Deutsches Architektenblatt,
Barriere im Kopf,
Bremen 2000

Deutsches Architektenblatt,
Mobile Generation 50plus – 1. Mio. Niedersachsen wollen Wohnsituation verändern,
Bremen 2007

Die Zeit
Leben, Die Welt der Alten,
Hamburg, 23.March 2006

Finanztest
Seniorenresidenzen im Test,
Berlin, Feb. 2006, pp 55ff.

form Zeitschrift für Gestaltung (204)
Design for the Elderly,
Neu-Isenburg, Nov./Dec. 2005, pp 30ff.

Helbig, Gerda:
Wohnbund-Informationen,
"Ein bundesweites Netzwerk für gemeinschaftliche Wohnprojekte",
Munich 2004, Issue II/2004

Scherzer, Ulrike:
Wohnbund-Information, Integriertes Wohnen.
Eine Analyse von Modellprojekten in der Nutzungsphase,
Munich 2004, Issue II/2004

Stadt und Raum
Bonacker, Margit; Ecks, Bettina; Lohmann, Ulla:
Freiraumplanung und ältere Menschen. Sechs Module für bessere Standards,
Winsen/Aller 2006

Broschures

Barrierefreies Bauen 1: Barrierefreie Wohnungen
Leitfaden für Architekten, Fachingenieure und Bauherren zur DIN 18025, Teil 1 und 2, Vergleichende Betrachtung und Erläuterungen,
Munich 1992

Barrierefreies Bauen 2: Öffentlich zugängige Gebäude und Arbeitsstätten
Leitfaden für Architekten, Fachingenieure, Bauherren zur DIN 18024, Teil 2. Planungsgrundlagen, vergleichende Betrachtung und Erläuterungen,
Munich 1997

Barrierefreies Bauen 3: Straßen, Plätze, Wege, Öffentliche Verkehrs- und Grünanlagen sowie Spielplätze
Leitfaden für Architekten, Fachingenieure und Bauherren zur DIN 18024, Teil 1. Planungsgrundlagen, vergleichende Betrachtung und Erläuterungen,
Munich 2001

Institut für Bauforschung e.V. Hannover:
Planungshilfe zur Umsetzung des barrierefreien Bauens,
Stuttgart 2004

Landesinstitut für Bauwesen des Landes NRW:
Barrierefreies Bauen im staatlichen Hochbau, Dokumentation ausgewählter Beispiele,
Aachen 2001

Landesinstitut für Bauwesen und Angewandte Bauschadensforschung:
Planen und Bauen für Menschen mit und ohne Behinderungen. Einleitung, Grundlagen, Anforderungen, Planungsbeispiele, Checkliste,
Aachen 1992

Ministerium für Arbeit und Soziales des Landes Nordrhein-Westfalen:
Sicher und bequem zu Hause wohnen. Wohnberatung für ältere und behinderte Menschen,
Dusseldorf 2000

Ministerium der Finanzen des Landes Rheinland-Pfalz; Ministerium für Arbeit, Soziales und Gesundheit des Landes Rheinland-Pfalz:
Barrierefrei Bauen, Mainz 2000

Planungsgrundlagen für barrierefreie öffentlich zugängliche Gebäude, andere bauliche Anlagen und Einrichtungen,
Dresden, 2000

Weeber und Partner:
Planen und Bauen für alte und behinderte Menschen, Beispiele und Planungshilfen für das Land Brandenburg,
Potsdam 1992

Advisory Centres (selection)

Kuratorium Deutsche Altershilfe (KDA)
An der Pauluskirche 3
50677 Cologne
tel: +49 (0)221 931847-0
fax: +49 (0)221 931847-6
www.kda.de

Bundesarbeitsgemeinschaft der Senioren-Organisationen (BAGSO) e.V.
Eifelstraße 9
53119 Bonn
tel: +49 (0)228 249993 0
fax: +49 (0)228 249993 20
e-mail: kontakt@bagso.de
www.bagso.de

Bundesinteressenvertretung der Altenheimbewohner e.V. (BIVA)
Vorgebirgsstraße 19
53913 Swisstal
tel: +49 (0)2254 7045
fax: +49 (0)2254 7046
e-mail: info@biva.de
www.biva.de

Schweizerische Fachstelle für Behindertengerechtes Bauen
Kernstr.57
CH–8004 Zurich
tel: +41 (0)44 299 97 97
fax: +41 (0)44 299 97 98
e-mail: info@hindernisfrei-bauen.ch
www.hindernisfrei-bauen.ch

Fachstelle Wohnberatung in Bayern
Korbinianplatz 15a
80807 Munich
Sabine Nowack Dipl.- Soz.päd. (FH)
tel.: +49 (0)89 35 70 43 15
fax: +49 (0)89 35 70 43 29
www.wohnberatung-bayern.de
info@wohnberatung-bayern.de

Bayerische Stiftung für Qualität im Betreuten
Wohnen e.V.
Geschäftsstelle Munich
Barbarossastraße 19
81677 Munich
tel: +49 (0)89 4444 61 541
fax: +49 (0)89 4444 61 741

Bayerische Architektenkammer
Beratungsstelle Barrierefreies Bauen
Frau Marianne Bendl
Postfach 190165
80601 Munich
tel. +49 (0)89 13 98 80 31
fax +49 (0)89 13 98 80 33
e-mail: barrierefrei@byak.de
www.byak.de

Architektenkammer Baden-Württemberg
Danneckerstraße 54
70182 Stuttgart
tel: +49 (0)711 21960
fax: +49 (0)711 2196103
e-mail: info@akbw.de
www.akbw.de

Architekten- und Stadtplanerkammer Hessen
Mainzer Straße 10
65185 Wiesbaden
tel: +49 (0)611 17380
fax: +49 (0)611 173840
e-mail: info@akh.de
www.akh.de

Architektenkammer Nordrhein-Westfalen
Zollhof 1
40221 Düsseldorf
tel: +49 (0)211 49 67 0
fax: +49 (0)211 49 67 99
e-mail: info@aknw.de
www.aknw.de

Architektenkammer Sachsen
Goetheallee 37
01309 Dresden
tel.: +49 (0)351 317460 oder 3105301
fax: +49 (0)351 3111286
e-mail: dresden@AKSachsen.org
www.aksachsen.org

Architektenkammer Sachsen-Anhalt
Fürstenwall 3
39104 Magdeburg
tel.: +49 (0)391 53 611-0
fax: +49 (0)391 56 19 29 6
e-mail: info@ak-lsa.de
www.ak-lsa.de

Internet Addresses (selection)

www.generationendialog.de
Initiative zur Verbesserung des Dialogs zwischen den Generationen

www.nwia.de
Verein Neues Wohnen im Alter, Arbeitsgemeinschaft zur Förderung selbstständiger Wohn- und Hausgemeinschaften mit Älteren

www.schader-stiftung.de/wohn_wandel
Informationsplattform zum Thema Wohnformen im Alter

www.aktiv-leipzig.de
Homepage des Arbeitskreises Integriertes Wohnen

www.wohnbund.de
Netzwerk von wohnungspolitisch engagierten Organisationen, die mit ihrer Arbeit zur Entwicklung und Realisierung zeitgemäßer Wohnformen beitragen

www.fgwa.de
Forum gemeinschaftliches Wohnen

www.neue-wohnformen.de
Informationsseite und Kontaktbörse zum Thema Wohnen im Alter

www.bmfsfj.de
Homepage des Bundesministeriums für Familien, Senioren, Frauen und Jugend

www.mehrgenerationenhaeuser.de
Informationen über Mehrgenerationenhäuser in Deutschland

www.barrierefrei.de
Portal für behindertengerechtes Bauen&Wohnen

www.wohnen-muehle.ch
Wohngemeinschaft Obere Mühle, Gelterkinden

www.stmas.bayern.de/senioren/wohnen/
Bayerisches Staatsministerium
für Arbeit und Sozialordnung, Familie und Frauen

www.hhrc.rca.ac.uk
Research centre of the Royal College of Art for the development of inclusive products appropriate to the eldery

www.independentliving.org
Organisation for people with disabilities

www.jrf.org.uk/housingandcare/lifetimehomes
Joseph Rowntree Foundation, Informationen barrrier-free living

www.housingcare.org
Information on various lifestyle alternatives for the elderly

www.shelteredhousing.org
Information on the topic of sheltered housing

www.bundesregierung.de/Content/DE/EMagazines/ebalance/043/t3-haeuser-fuer-mehrere-generationen.html
Förderung für die Entstehung von Mehrgenerationenhäusern

www.stmi.bayern.de/bauen/wohnungswesen/foerderung
Förderung für Anpassung von Mietwohnungen bzw. Eigenheimen für schwerbehinderte oder schwerkranke Menschen

Illustration credits

The authors and editor wish to extend their sincere thanks to all those who helped to realize this book by making illustrations available. All drawings contained in this volume have been specially prepared in-house. Photos without credits are form the architects' own archives or the archives of "DETAIL, Review of Architecture". Despite intense efforts, it was not possible to identify the copyright owners of certain photos and illustrations. Their rights remain unaffected, however, and we request them to contact us.

from photographers, photo archives and image agencies:
- Altenkirch, Dirk, Karlsruhe: pp. 121–123
- Archiv Feddersen, Berlin: 5.9
- Archiv Ebner, Munich: 2.3
- Becker, Markus, Frankfurt: pp. 134–137
- Braun, Zooey, Stuttgart: pp. 94, 96 middle
- Dempf, Christine, Munich: p. 115
- Erlau AG, Aalen:5.8
- Felix, Alexander, Munich: p. 62 top
- Focke, Andreas J., Munich: pp. 114, 158
- Giessler, Joachim F., Bad Tölz: 3.9–3.11
- Giovanelli, Francesca, Weiningen: pp. 84–89, 3.3b
- González, Brigida, Stuttgart: 3.6
- Grunert-Held, Roland, Veitshöchheim: 5.5
- Halbe, Roland/artur, Essen: p. 150
- Halbe, Roland, Stuttgart: pp. 52–57, 70, 72, 144
- Heinrich, Michael, Munich: pp. 125–129
- Helfenstein, Heinrich, Zurich: pp. 65–69
- Hirai, Hiroyuki, Tokyo: pp. 90–93, 110–113
- Hoekstra, Rob, Kalmthout: pp. 74 top, 76–77
- Holz, Michael, Hamburg: 5.4
- Hurnaus, Hertha, Vienna: pp. 10, 27–31
- Interboden Innovative Lebenswelten GmbH + Co. KG, Ratingen: 5.12
- Janzer, Wolfram/artur, Essen: pp. 32–35
- Kawai, Toshiaki, Kyoto: 2.18
- Keystone, Zurich: p. 167, 2nd from left
- Kramer, Luuk, Amsterdam: pp. 138 top, 139–140, 143
- Kraus, Diana, Geldersheim: 5.2
- Krauss, Roland, Vienna: pp. 42–45
- Landwehr, Veit, Cologne: pp. 46–48, 50–51
- Marx, Lothar, Munich: 4.2, 4.7, 4.10–4.12, 4.17, 4.21–4.23
- Monomere, Vienna: 5.3
- Musch, Jeroen, Amsterdam: pp. 74 bottom, 75
- Ott, Paul, Graz: p. 104
- Roig, Joan, Valencia: p. 71
- Rosenberg, Simone, Munich: 2.10
- Schäffler, Nikolaus, Munich: 2.6, 4.6
- Schinzler, Peter, Munich: p. 8
- Schuster, Oliver, Stuttgart: pp. 96 top, 98, 99 top
- Seidl, Manfred, Vienna: 2.13
- Spiluttini, Margherita, Vienna: pp. 36–39, 41, 100–103
- 't Hart, Rob, Rotterdam: p. 138 bottom
- Theny, Christian, Feldkirchen: pp. 105 – 109
- Tusch, Martin, Vienna: pp. 116–119
- Walti, Ruedi, Basle: 2.5, pp. 58–63, 130–133
- Wicky, Gaston, Zurich: pp. 78–83, 3.3a
- Wutzer, Manuela, Innsbruck: p. 170, 2nd from left
- Yoo Deutschland GmbH, Cologne: 5.11
- Zimmermann, Reinhard, Adliswil: 2.11

Articles and introductory b/w photos:
- p. 8; Community Centre Pasing, Landau + Kindelbacher, Munich
- p. 10; "Sargfabrik" in Vienna, BKK-2, Vienna
- p. 144; Senior's Centre in Stuttgart, Kauffmann Theilig & Partner, Ostfildern
- p. 150; Community Hall in San Sebastian, Rafael Moneo, Madrid
- p. 158; Residence in Gstadt, Florian Höfer, Oberneuching

Dust-jacket photo:
Residence in Gstadt
Architect: Florian Höfer, Oberneuching
Photo: Andreas J. Focke, Munich